Frommer's

Honolulu and Oahu day BY day®

4th Edition

by Martha Cheng

FrommerMedia LLC

Contents

Published by:

FrommerMedia LLC

ISBN: 978-1-628-87372-6 (paper); 978-1-628-87373-3(ebk)

Editorial Director: Pauline Frommer
Development Editor: Elizabeth Heath
Production Editor: Kelly Dobbs Henthorne
Photo Editor: Meghan Lamb
Cartographer: Roberta Stockwell
Indexer: Kelly Dobbs Henthorne

Front cover photos, left to right: ©Sorin Colac, ©Malgorzata Litkowska, ©tomas del amo

Back cover photo: ©Allen.G

For information on our other products and services, please go to Frommers.com.

Frommer's also publishes its books in a variety of electronic formats. Some content that appears in print may not be available in electronic formats.

Manufactured in China

5 4 3 2 1

About This Guide

Organizing your time. That's what this guide is all about.

Other guides give you long lists of things to see and do and then expect you to fit the pieces together. The Day by Day guides are different. These guides tell you the best of everything, and then they show you how to see it in the smartest, most time-efficient way. Our authors have designed detailed itineraries organized by time, neighborhood, or special interest. And each tour comes with a bulleted map that takes you from stop to stop.

Planning to snorkel with sea turtles along the North Shore or take surfing lessons on Waikīkī Beach? Shopping for fresh flower leis or alohawear in Honolulu's Chinatown? Whatever your interest or schedule, the Day by Days give you the smartest routes to follow. Not only do we take you to the top attractions, hotels, and restaurants, but we also help you access those special moments that locals get to experience— those "finds" that turn tourists into travelers.

The Day by Days are also your top choice if you're looking for one complete guide for all your travel needs. The best hotels and restaurants for every budget, the greatest shopping values, the wildest nightlife—it's all here.

Why should you trust our judgment? Because our authors personally visit each place they write about. They're an independent lot who say what they think and would never include places they wouldn't recommend to their best friends. They're also open to suggestions from readers. If you'd like to contact them, please send your comments our way at feedback@frommers.com, and we'll pass them on.

Enjoy your Day by Day guide—the most helpful travel companion you can buy. And have the trip of a lifetime.

About the Author

Martha Cheng came to Hawai'i for a boy and stayed for its food, ocean, and people. She is the former food editor of *Honolulu Magazine* and now writes feature stories for local and national publications on everything from squash farms in Waimea to fly fishing in Maui. Originally from San Francisco, she's a former pastry chef, line cook, food truck owner, Peace Corps volunteer, and Google techie. These days, she surfs, eats, and writes.

An Additional Note

Please be advised that travel information is subject to change at any time—and this is especially true of prices. We therefore suggest that you write or call ahead for confirmation when making your travel plans. The authors, editors, and publisher cannot be held responsible for the experiences of readers while traveling. Your safety is important to us, however, so we encourage you to stay alert and be aware of your surroundings.

Star Ratings, Icons & Abbreviations

Every hotel, restaurant, and attraction listing in this guide has been ranked for quality, value, service, amenities, and special features using a **star-rating system.** Hotels, restaurants, attractions, shopping, and nightlife are rated on a scale of zero stars (recommended) to three stars (exceptional). Within each tour, we recommend cafes, bars, or restaurants where you can take a break. Each of these stops appears in a shaded box marked with a coffee-cup-shaped bullet ☕.

The following **abbreviations** are used for credit cards:

AE	American Express	MC	MasterCard
DC	Diners Club	V	Visa

A Note on Prices

In the "Take a Break" and "Best Bets" sections of this book, we have used a system of dollar signs to show a range of costs for 1 night in a hotel (the price of a double-occupancy room) or the cost of an entree at a restaurant. Use the following table to decipher the dollar signs:

Cost	Hotels	Restaurants
$	under $100	under $10
$$	$100–$200	$10–$20
$$$	$200–$300	$20–$30
$$$$	$300–$400	$30–$40
$$$$$	over $400	over $40

Frommers.com

Now that you have this guidebook to help you plan a great trip, visit our website at www.frommers.com for additional travel information on more than 3,600 destinations. We update features regularly to give you instant access to the most current trip-planning information available. At Frommers.com, you'll find scoops on the best airfares, lodging rates, and car rental bargains. You can even book your travel online through our reliable travel booking partners. Other popular features include:

- Online updates of our most popular guidebooks
- Vacation sweepstakes and contest giveaways
- Newsletters highlighting the hottest travel trends
- Online travel message boards with featured travel discussions

An Invitation to the Reader

In researching this book, we discovered many wonderful places—hotels, restaurants, shops, and more. We're sure you'll find others. Please tell us about them, so we can share the information with your fellow travelers in upcoming editions. If you were disappointed with a recommendation, we'd love to know that, too. Please write to: Support@FrommerMedia.com.

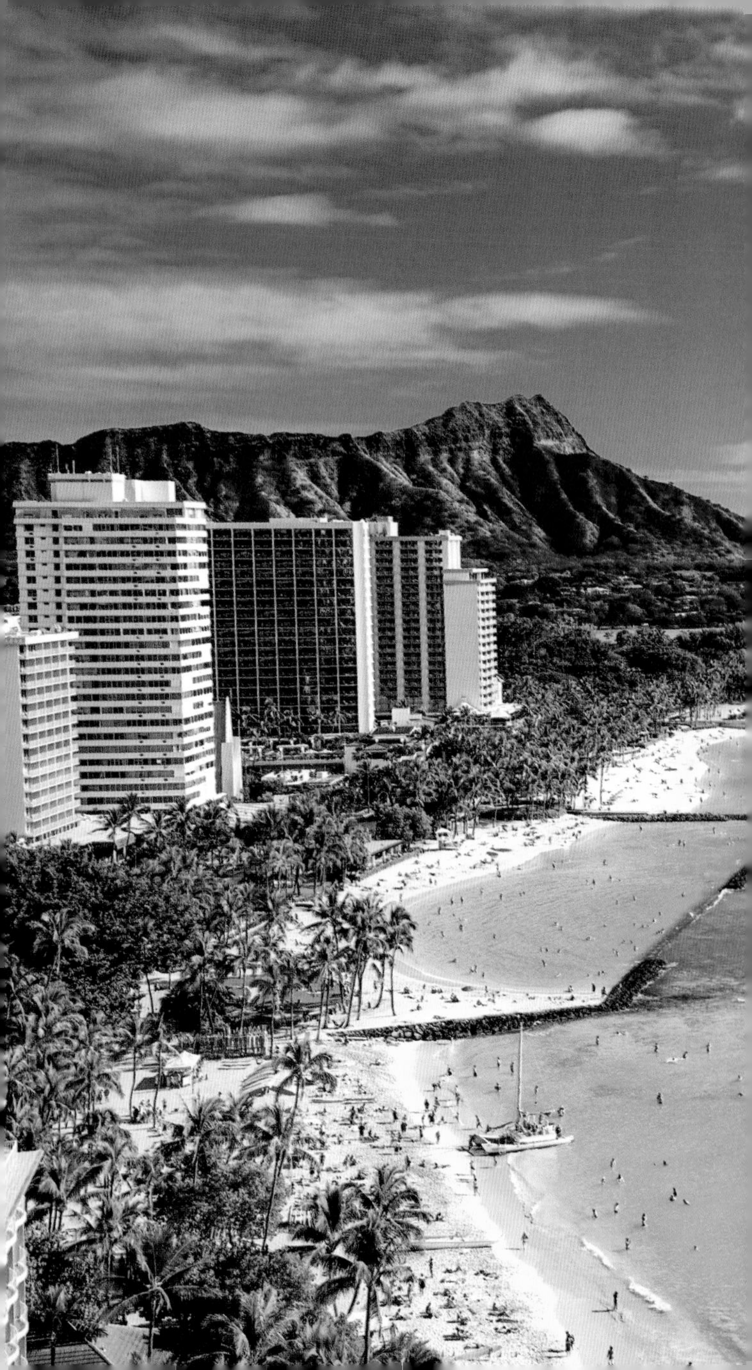

16 Favorite Moments

16 Favorite **Moments**

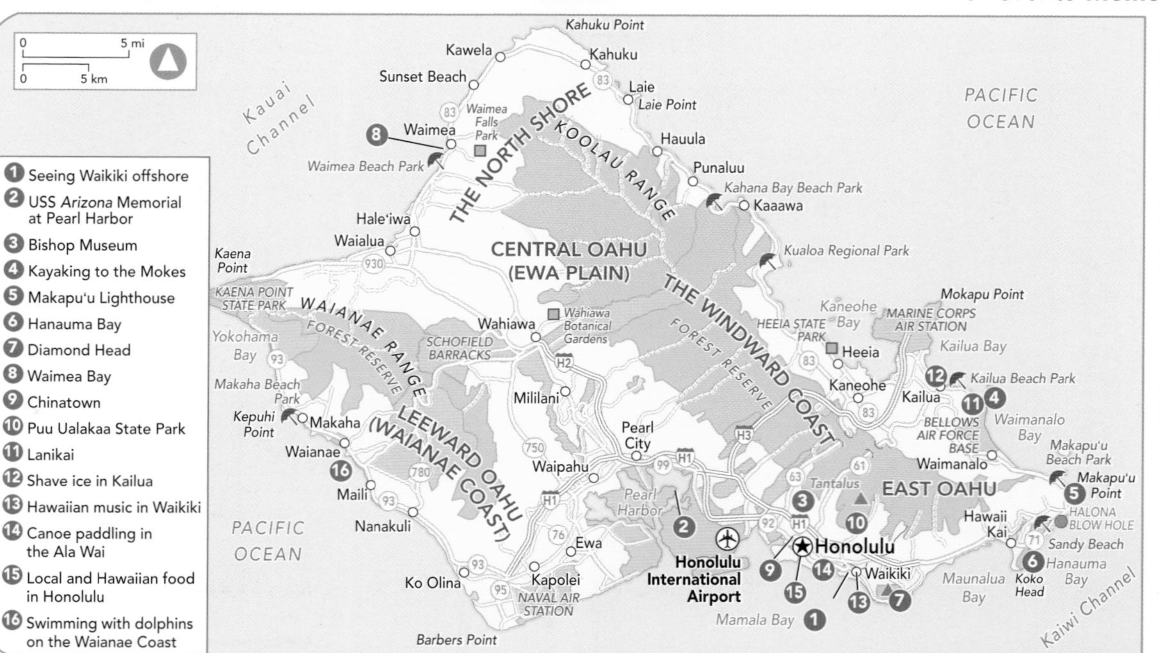

Previous page: Waikīkī Beach, with the Diamond Head crater in the background

Honolulu is filled with so many magical moments: the orange glow as the sun rises behind the outline of Diamond Head, the silvery reflection of the moon on the inky black waters of Waikīkī at night, the intoxicating smell of plumeria flowers in the air, the quiet whisper of bamboo dancing in the breeze. I hope this chapter helps you find a few favorite moments of your own.

❶ **Seeing Waikīkī offshore.** If you think Waikīkī is beautiful, wait until you see it from a boat. I strongly urge you either to take a boat cruise during the day, when it seems as if you can look through the deep, aquamarine waters all the way down to the ocean floor, or for the more romantically inclined, take a sunset cruise and watch the sun go down and the lights of Waikīkī and Honolulu come up. *See p 13.*

❷ **Experiencing a turning point in America's history: the bombing of Pearl Harbor.** I guarantee that you will never forget your reaction when you step on the deck of the USS *Arizona* Memorial at Pearl Harbor and look down from the deck into the water at the dark oil oozing like blood from the ship underneath. The horror of December 7, 1941, the day when the 608-foot (185m) *Arizona* sank in just 9 minutes after being bombed during the Japanese air raid, no longer seems like something from a book—it's very real. The 1,177 men on board plunged to a fiery death—and the United States went to war. ***My tip:*** Absolutely reserve a spot online to avoid a wait. You must wear closed-toe shoes. *See p 14.*

❸ **Walking back in history at the Bishop Museum.** To get a sense of what Hawai'i was like before the Europeans landed, head to the Bishop Museum. Don't think dreary rooms with stuff crowded into cases—think living history: You'll hear a booming voice break into Hawaiian chant when you enter the Hawaiian Hall and see live performances of traditional hula. Created by a Hawaiian princess in 1899, the Bishop Museum not only is the foremost repository for Hawaiian cultural artifacts but also has a new Science Center, where you can step into the interior of an erupting volcano. *See p 21.*

The USS Arizona Memorial at Pearl Harbor

Calm, shallow Hanauma Bay is a favorite snorkeling spot.

④ **Kayaking to the Mokes from Kailua Beach.** The Windward side is full of gorgeous, white sand beaches, but only Kailua has the Mokulua islands, or the Mokes, as locals call them. I love skimming across the turquoise waters to the twin islands, and then turning back to see the Koolau mountains behind me. And if I'm feeling particularly adventurous, I'll walk around to the rugged back side of Moku Nui and jump into the deep waters behind. *See p 181.*

⑤ **Whale watching from Makapu'u Point Lighthouse.** The short, paved hike to this working lighthouse gives you a clear view of the Windward coast. But even better, during the winter, you'll see humpback whales cavorting offshore, sending up spouts of water, flipping their tails and fins as if waving hello, and sometimes breaching out of the water, sending up great big geysers when they land. No matter how many times I drive along this coast and see them, I always have to stop and take a look. *See p 166.*

⑥ **Snorkeling among the rainbow-colored fish in the warm waters of Hanauma Bay.** I love this underwater park, once a volcanic crater, because it's teeming with tropical fish and bordered by a 2,000-foot (610m) gold-sand beach. Plus, the bay's shallow water (10 ft/3m in places) is perfect for neophyte snorkelers. Arrive early to beat the crowds—and be aware that the bay is closed Tuesdays, when the fish have the day off. *See p 177.*

⑦ **Hiking to the top of Diamond Head for the perfect view of the island.** See Waikīkī and Honolulu from the top of Hawai'i's most famous landmark. Nearly everyone can handle this 1.4-mile (2.3km) round-trip hike, which goes up to the top of the 750-foot (229m) volcanic cone, where you have a 360-degree view of O'ahu. Allow an hour for the trip up and back, bring $1 for the entry fee, and don't forget your camera. *See p 165.*

⑧ **Watching the North Shore's big waves.** When monstrous waves—some 30 feet (9.1m) tall—steamroll into Waimea Bay (Nov–Mar), I head out to the North Shore. You can watch the best surfers in the world paddle out to challenge these freight trains—it's shocking to see how small they appear in the lip of the giant waves. My favorite part is feeling those waves when they break on the shore—the ground actually shakes, and everyone on the beach is covered with salt-spray mist. And this unforgettable experience doesn't cost you a dime. *See p 178.*

❾ **Buying a lei in Chinatown.** I love the cultural sights to see and exotic experiences to be had in Honolulu's Chinatown. Wander through this several-square-block area with its jumble of Asian shops offering herbs, Chinese groceries, and acupuncture services, where you'll hear conversations in Tagalog, Vietnamese, and Cantonese tumbling over each other. Be sure to check out the lei sellers on Maunakea Street (near N. Hotel St.)—you'll be intoxicated by the fragrant perfumes of the puakenikeni, pikake and tuberose flowers, and ginger leis. Even the most simple plumeria lei is a beautiful, perfumed delight, and costs just $5. *See p 120.*

❿ **Basking in the best sunset you'll ever see.** Anyone can stand on the beach and watch the sun set, but my favorite viewing point for saying *aloha 'oe* to the sun is on top of a 1,048-foot (320m) hill named after a sweet potato. Actually, it's more romantic than it sounds. Puu Ualakaa State Park, at the end of Round Hill Drive, translates into "rolling sweet potato hill" (the name describes how early Hawaiians harvested the crop). This majestic view of the sunset is not to be missed. *See p 21.*

Exotic perfumes permeate the air in Chinatown's lei shops.

⓫ **Watching the full moon rise over the ocean.** You've seen the sunset—now look for the full moon rise. I like to head to the Lanikai Pillboxes around dusk on a full moon night. If the skies are clear, you'll see the moon begin to peek out over the horizon and start its ascent, sending a glimmering beam along the water. *See p 29.*

⓬ **Ordering a shave ice in a tropical flavor you can hardly pronounce.** I think you can actually taste the islands by slurping shave ice. It's not quite a snow cone, but similar: Ice is shaved so that it's soft and fluffy, and then drenched in a fruit syrup. My favorite spot is the Local Hawai'i, where the syrups are made with local fruit, such as liliko'i (passionfruit) and lychee. *See p 95.*

⓭ **Listening to the soothing sounds of Hawaiian music.** Just before sunset, I head for the huge banyan tree at the Moana Surfrider's Banyan Veranda in Waikīkī, order a libation, and sway to live Hawaiian music. Another quintessential sunset oasis is the Halekulani's House Without a Key, a sophisticated oceanfront lounge with wonderful hula and steel guitar music, a great view of Diamond Head, and the best mai tais on the island. *See p 131.*

⓮ **Discovering the ancient Hawaiian sport of canoe paddling.** For something uniquely Hawaiian, find a comfortable spot at Ala Wai Park, next to the canal, and watch hundreds of canoe paddlers recreate this centuries-old sport of taking traditional Hawaiian canoes out to sea. Or try it yourself off Waikīkī Beach. *See p 161.*

Sweet, fruity shave ice is an O'ahu tradition.

⑮ **Local and Hawaiian food.** Poke, raw fish glistening with soy sauce and sesame oil; laulau, pork wrapped in taro leaves and then swaddled in ti leaves and steamed; malasadas, deep-fried dough dusted in sugar: these are some of the only-in-Hawai'i favorite foods. They tell the story of Hawai'i's history, from the native Hawaiians to the plantation laborers brought to work the sugar and pineapple fields. Hawai'i is a mishmash of cultures, and there's no better way to experience it than through its food. *See p 95.*

⑯ **Swimming with dolphins.** There are few things more magical than jumping into the ocean and seeing dolphins around you, their sleek bodies gracefully sliding through the water in unison, their high-pitched voices carrying through the water. You might see them right below you, beside you, in front of you, when you jump on one of the Wild Side Tours heading out from the Wai'anae Coast. *See p 182.* ●

Finding Your Way Around, O'ahu-Style

Mainlanders sometimes find the directions given by locals a bit confusing. You seldom hear the terms east, west, north, and south; instead, islanders refer to directions as either ***makai*** (ma-*kae*), meaning toward the sea, or ***mauka*** (*mow*-kah), toward the mountains. In Honolulu, people use **Diamond Head** as a direction meaning to the east (in the direction of the world-famous crater called Diamond Head), and **Ewa** as a direction meaning to the west (toward the town called Ewa, on the other side of Pearl Harbor).

So, if you ask a local for directions, this is what you're likely to hear: "Drive 2 blocks *makai* (toward the sea), then turn Diamond Head (east) at the stoplight. Go 1 block, and turn *mauka* (toward the mountains). It's on the Ewa (western) side of the street."

1 Strategies for Seeing O‘ahu

Strategies for Seeing O'ahu

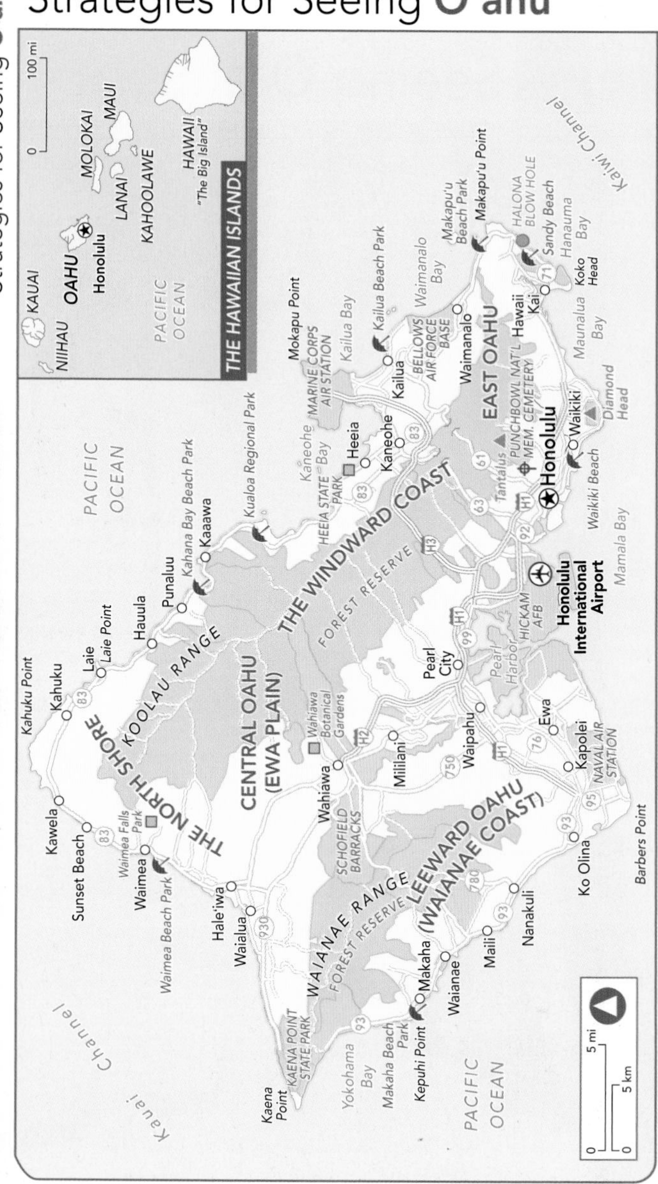

Previous page: Surfboards lined up in the rack on Waikīkī Beach

O'ahu may be an island, but it's a good-sized island, and your vacation time is precious. There really is just one cardinal rule: Relax. Don't run yourself ragged trying to see absolutely everything—take the time to experience the magic of the island. In this chapter, I offer several suggestions for making the most of your visit.

Rule #1. Go in the off-season. Not only will you save a bundle, but there will be fewer people, the beaches will be less crowded, and it'll be easier to get into your favorite restaurants. The "off season," September to November and March to May, is also when the weather is at its best (not too hot, not too rainy).

Rule #2. Think about how you want to spend your vacation. Is this a lie-on-the-beach vacation or a get-up-early-and-go-on-an-adventure-every-day vacation? Or a combination of the two? Whether you are traveling with your sweetie or you're bringing your family, make sure that everyone gets in on the planning—it makes for a vacation that everyone can enjoy.

Rule #3. Don't overschedule. Don't make your days jam-packed from the time you get up until you drop off to sleep at night. This is Hawai'i: Stop and smell the plumeria. Allow time to just relax. And don't forget that you will most likely arrive jet-lagged, so ease into your vacation. Exposure to sunlight can help reset your internal clock, so hit the beach on your first day (and bring your sunscreen).

Take time to stop and smell the plumeria!

Rule #4. Allow plenty of time to get around the island. If you glance at a map, O'ahu looks deceptively small—as though you could just zip from one side of the island to the other. But you have to take traffic into consideration; from 6 to 9am and 3 to 6pm, the main roads will be bumper-to-bumper with rush-hour traffic. Plan accordingly: Sleep late and get on the road after the traffic has cleared

A drive along the North Shore rewards with stunning beaches and numerous historic sites.

Poke, seasoned cubes of raw fish, is an island staple.

out. I highly recommend that you rent a car, but don't just "view" the island from the car window. Plan to get out as much as possible to breathe in the tropical aroma, fill up on those views, and listen to the sounds of the tropics.

Rule #5. If your visit is short, stay in one place.
Most places on O'ahu are within easy driving distance of each other, and checking in and out of several hotels can get old fast. There's the schlepping of the luggage, the waiting in line to check in, the unpacking, and more . . . only to repeat the entire process a few days later. Your vacation time is too dear.

Rule #6. Pick the key activity of the day and plan accordingly.
To maximize your time, decide what you really want to do that day, and then plan all other activities in the same geographical area. That way you won't have to track back and forth across the island.

Rule #7. Remember that you are on the island of aloha.
Honolulu is not the U.S. mainland. Slow down. Smile and say "aloha"; it's what the local residents do. Ask them: "Howzit?" (the local expression for "How are you?"). When they ask you, tell 'em, "Couldn't be better—I'm in Hawai'i!" Wave at everyone. Laugh a lot, even if things aren't going as planned.

Rule #8. Use this book as a reference, not a concrete plan.
You will not hurt my feelings if you don't follow every single tour and do absolutely everything I suggest in the itinerary. Pick and choose according to your interests—don't feel like you have to follow my suggestions to the letter.

Rule #9. Eat as the locals do.
The local cuisine tells the history of a place. In Hawai'i's case, its food is the story of waves of immigration: the original Polynesian voyagers; the missionaries; the laborers from Japan, China, the Philippines, and Portugal, who came to work the plantations in the 20th century; the military. So skip the chain restaurants and head to down-home joints where you can eat popular dishes invented in Hawai'i, like poke (cubes of seasoned raw fish), laulau (pork wrapped in taro leaves), and loco moco (rice topped with a hamburger patty, gravy, and fried egg). (See p 95, "Going Local.") ●

2 The Best Full-Day Tours

The Best of O'ahu in Three Days

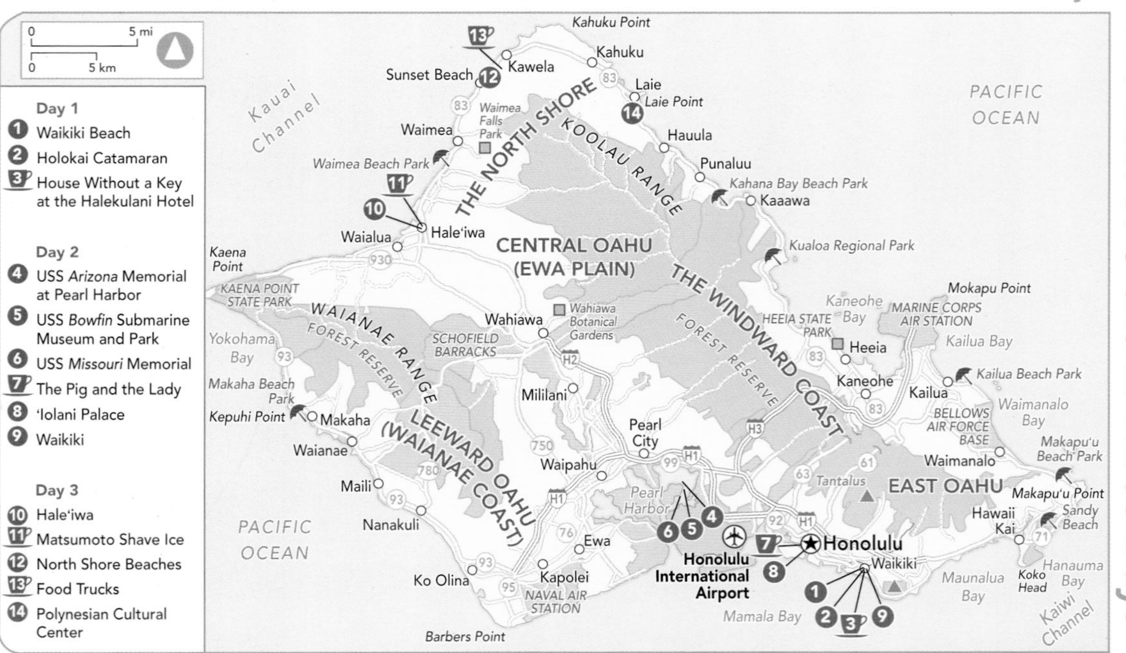

Previous page: A sunset sail from Waikīkī Beach

You could spend weeks on O'ahu without running out of things to do, but it's possible to see the highlights of this romantic isle in just 3 days. Following this tour will let you see the best of O'ahu, from Waikīkī to the North Shore. You'll definitely need to rent a car, so remember to plan for that cost. Each day begins and ends in Waikīkī, which, like most urban cities, has traffic congestion, so allow plenty of travel time, especially during rush hour.

Day 1

1 ★★★ Waikīkī Beach. You'll never forget your first steps onto the powdery sands of this world-famous beach. If you're just off the plane, plan to spread your towel on the beach, take in the smell of the salt air, feel the warm breeze on your skin, and relax; you're in Hawaii. *See p 76.*

Walk down Waikīkī Beach toward the Halekulani.

2 ★★ Holokai Catamaran. One of the most fun and effortless ways to get on the water is a sail off Waikīkī. Many catamarans launch from Waikīkī, but this is our favorite of the "booze cruises." It's the least crowded and rowdy, and the drink selection is the best, with multiple Maui Brewing Co. brews and a decent island cocktail. If you're feeling more active, you can sign up for the Turtle Canyon Adventure Sail, which takes you snorkeling with turtles and bright, tropical fish. *1½–2 hr. Gray's Beach in front of the Halekulani. www.sailholokai.com. ☎ 808/922-2210. Tradewind Sail $35. Turtle Canyon Adventure Sail $60.*

3 ★★★ House Without a Key at the Halekulani Hotel. As the sun sinks toward the horizon, take a break with a mai tai at one of the most beautiful hotels on Waikīkī Beach. You can watch a former Miss Hawai'i dance hula to the riffs of Hawaiian steel guitar. With the sunset and ocean glowing behind her, and Diamond Head visible in the distance, the scene is straight out of a storybook—romantic, evocative, nostalgic. *2199 Kalia Rd. (Diamond Head side of Lewers St.) www.halekulani.com. ☎ 808/923-2311. $$$.*

First order of business after touch-down in Honolulu? Hit the beach!

Day 2

Get an early start to beat the crowds at Pearl Harbor. Drive west on H-1 past the airport to the USS *Arizona* Memorial exit and then follow the green-and-white signs; there's ample free parking. Bus: 20, then transfer to 52.

❹ ★★★ **USS *Arizona* Memorial at Pearl Harbor.** The top attraction on O'ahu is this unforgettable memorial. On December 7, 1941, the Japanese launched an air raid on Pearl Harbor that plunged the U.S. into World War II. This 608-foot (185m) battleship sank in 9 minutes without firing a shot, taking 1,177 sailors and Marines to their deaths. The deck of the *Arizona* lies 6 feet (1.8m) below the surface of the sea, with oil still slowly oozing up from the engine room and staining the harbor's calm, blue water. Some say the ship still weeps for its lost crew. The excellent, 2½-hour ★★★ **audio tour** makes the trip even more meaningful—it's like having your own personal park ranger as a guide. The fee is $7.50 and worth every nickel (reserve the audio tour in advance at ☎ 877-444-6777 or www.recreation.gov). ***Note:*** Boat rides to the *Arizona* are sometimes suspended because of high winds. Check the World War II **Valor in the Pacific** Facebook page (www.facebook.com/valorNPS) for updated information on boat ride suspensions. Due to increased security measures, visitors cannot carry purses, handbags, fanny packs, backpacks, camera bags, diaper bags, or other items that offer concealment on the boat. Storage is available for a fee. ⏲ *3 hr.; book online to be assured a spot, or go first thing in the morning to avoid the huge crowds; waits of 1–3 hr. are common. Pearl Harbor.* ☎ *808/422-3300. www.nps.gov/usar. Free admission. Daily 7am–5pm (programs run 7:30am–3pm). Shirts and closed-toe shoes required; no swimsuits or flip-flops allowed. Wheelchairs gladly accommodated.*

Explore life on a WWII submarine at the USS Bowfin Museum and Park.

If you're a real nautical history buff, stop in at the next few museums, which are described in the "Wartime Honolulu" tour starting on p 46. Otherwise, head directly to Chinatown.

❺ ★ **USS *Bowfin* Submarine Museum & Park.** *See p 47,* ❷.

❻ ★ **USS *Missouri* Memorial.** *See p 47,* ❸.

From Arizona Memorial Dr., turn right on Kamehameha Hwy. (Hwy. 99). Take the ramp onto H-1 East toward Honolulu. Take Exit 18A toward HI-92 East/Nimitz Hwy. Take the exit toward Iwilei Rd., turn right onto Iwilei, turn right onto N. King St. Bus 40, 42.

❼ ★★★ **The Pig and the Lady.** This is one of the liveliest dining rooms in Honolulu's Chinatown, with brick walls, benches upholstered with burlap rice bags, and a rotating gallery of fun, bright prints by local, young artists. The Pig and

It's Not New York City

Unfortunately, Honolulu does not have convenient public transportation, which is why I strongly recommend that you rent a car. In case that's not possible, I've added information on how to get around using O'ahu's public bus system (called TheBus), which costs $2.50 per ride, $1.25 for ages 6 to 17, and free for children 5 and under. But TheBus is set up for Hawai'i residents, not tourists carrying coolers, beach toys, or suitcases (all carry-ons must fit under the bus seat). Some trips may require several transfers, or TheBus may not stop right in front of your destination. Before you set out, always call **TheBus** (☎ **808/848-5555,** or 808/296-1818 for recorded information) or check out www.thebus.org.

the Lady introduces you to a world of Vietnamese noodle soups beyond pho—such as one with oxtail, another with crab and tomato. But chef Andrew Le also applies creative twists to Southeast Asian food for unique eats like a pho French dip banh mi—an absolute must with its melting slices of braised brisket, smeared with a bright Thai basil chimichurri and served with a side of pho broth for dipping. *83 N. King St. ☎ 808/383-2152. www.thepigandthelady.com. $$*

Continue down King St. by foot or car to 'Iolani Palace.

❽ ★★ **'Iolani Palace.** Once the site of a *heiau* (temple), 'Iolani Palace took 3 years and $350,000 to complete in 1882, with all the modern conveniences of its time (electric lights were installed here 4 years before they were in the White House). Royals lived here for 11 years, until Queen Lili'uokalani was deposed and the Hawaiian monarchy fell forever in a palace coup led by U.S. Marines on January 17, 1893, at the

'Iolani Palace, the last home of the Hawaiian monarchy

Surfing at Waikīkī Beach

demand of sugar planters and missionary descendants. The territorial and then the state government used the palace until 1968. At that point, the palace was in shambles, so it has since undergone a $7-million overhaul to restore it to its former glory. *1–2 hr. 364 S. King St. (at Richards St.). www.iolanipalace.org. ☎ 808/538-1471. Guided tour $22 adults, $6 children 5–12; not available Mon; reservations recommended. Audio tour $15 adults, $6 children 5–12. Gallery tour $7 adults, $3 children 5–12. Mon–Sat 9:30am–4pm; closed Sun.*

Continue down King St., turn slightly right onto Kapi'olani Blvd. Turn right onto Kalākaua Ave. and follow it into Waikīkī. Bus: 19 or 20.

9 Surf lesson in Waikīkī. End the day with a sunset surf session, when the sun is less hot. Waikīkī has great waves for learning, and a surf lesson with Hans Hedemann Surf School will have you riding the waves in no time. *2 hr. At the Park Shore Waikīkī. www.hhsurf.com. ☎ 808/924-7778. $75 for 2-hour group lesson.*

Day 3

Spend your third day on O'ahu on the North Shore. Take H-1 west out of Waikīkī and then take the H-2 north exit (Exit 8A) toward Mililani/ Wahiawā. After 7 miles (11km), H-2 becomes Kamehameha Hwy. (Hwy. 80). Look for the turnoff to Hale'iwa town. Bus: 20, then transfer to 55.

10 ★★★ Hale'iwa. Start your day exploring this famous North Shore surfing town, full of boutiques, art galleries, food trucks, and plenty of surf shops. *See p 137, 2.*

11 ★ Matsumoto Shave Ice. For a tropical taste of the islands, stop at this 50-plus-year-old shop where Hawai'i's rendition of a snow cone is served: Instead of crushed ice, the ice is actually shaved and is soft and fluffy. Favorites of the rainbow of flavors available include lychee, liliko'i (passionfruit) and li hing mui (pronounced lee hing moo-ee), which is a salty-sweet-tart preserved plum powder. *66–111 Kamehameha Hwy. Suite #605, Hale'iwa. ☎ 808/ 637-4827. www.matsumotoshaveice.com. $.*

Continue down Kamehameha Hwy. Bus: 52.

A famous surfing town, Hale'iwa is also known for its food trucks.

⑫ ★★★ **North Shore beaches.** Choose any one of the North Shore beaches to spend the afternoon. If it's winter time and the surf's up, you'll want to head to Pipeline or Sunset to watch the surfers on some of the best waves in the world. If it's summer, head to Waimea to swim in the calm, beautiful bay or to Shark's Cove for snorkeling. *See p 159.*

13 **Food trucks.** You'll notice lots of food trucks lining Kam Highway, all the way from Hale'iwa to Sunset Beach to Kahuku, where the shrimp trucks are famous (p 27). My favorite of the ones near Sunset Beach is The Elephant Truck, particularly in the evening, when the strands of light strung up around the picnic tables makes for particularly charming alfresco dining. The specialty here is simple and fresh Thai food: try the fish tossed in a tangy chili and lime vinaigrette. The vegan options are terrific, too. *59-712 Kamehameha Hwy. ☎ 808/638-1854. www.808elephant.com. $.*

Drive down Kamehameha Hwy. to the town of Lā'ie. Bus: 55.

⑭ ★★ **Ha: Breath of Life at the Polynesian Cultural Center.** Catch the evening show at the Polynesian Cultural Center, the "living museum" of Polynesia. Native students from Polynesia who attend Hawai'i's Brigham Young University play roles in **Ha: Breath of Life,** a coming-of-age story told through the different Polynesian dances of Pacific islands or archipelagos—Fiji, New Zealand, Samoa, Tahiti, Tonga, and Hawai'i. Some of the dances are full of grace, some are fierce, and all thrilling. This is one of O'ahu's best shows. ⏱ *1½ hr. 55–370 Kamehameha Hwy., Lā'ie. ☎ 800/367-7060, 808/293-3333. www.polynesia.com. Admission: $45 adults, $35 children 5–11. Mon–Sat 7:30pm*

A performance at the Polynesian Cultural Center

To get back to Waikīkī, just continue along Kamehameha Hwy. (Hwy. 83), which follows the windward coastline for about 22 miles (35km). Look for the sign for the Likelike Hwy. (Hwy. 63). From Likelike Hwy. take the Kalihi St./H-1 exit. Take H-1 to Waikīkī. Bus: 55, then transfer to 19 or 20.

Waimea Bay Beach Park offers calm waters for summertime swimming.

The Best of O'ahu in One Week

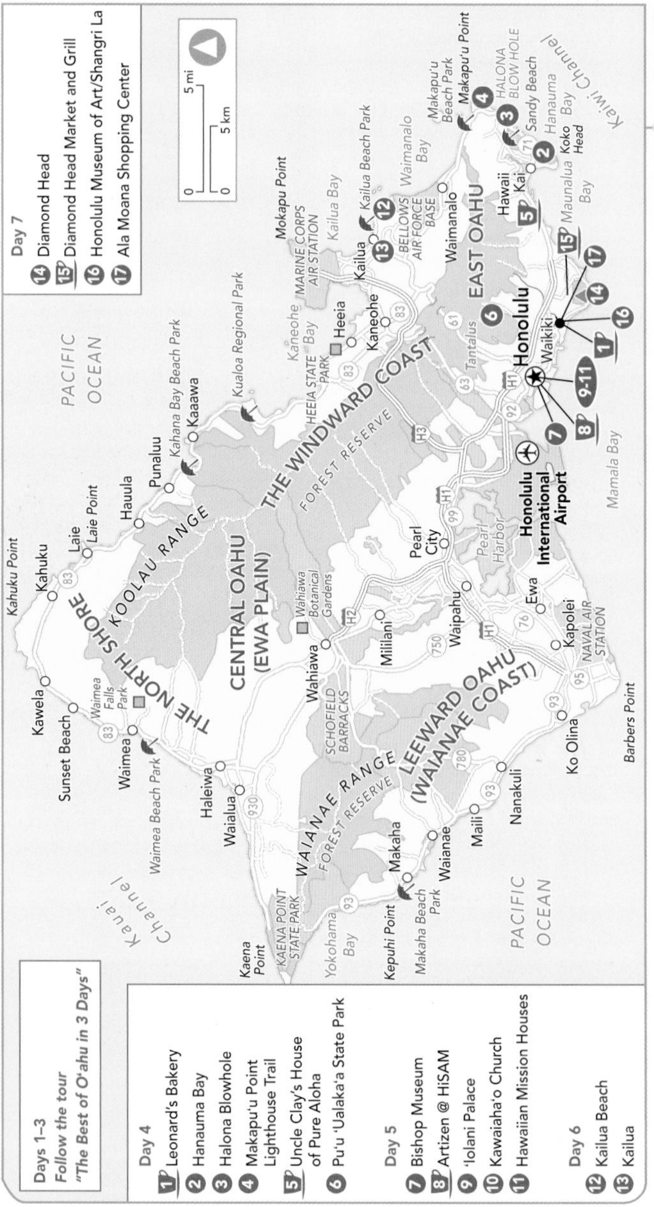

Days 1–3
Follow the tour
"The Best of O'ahu in 3 Days"
Day 4
1 Leonard's Bakery
2 Hanauma Bay
3 Halona Blowhole
4 Makapu'u Point Lighthouse Trail
5 Uncle Clay's House of Pure Aloha
6 Pu'u 'Ualaka'a State Park
Day 5
7 Bishop Museum
8 Artizen @ HiSAM
9 'Iolani Palace
10 Kawaiaha'o Church
11 Hawaiian Mission Houses
Day 6
12 Kailua Beach
13 Kailua
Day 7
14 Diamond Head
15 Diamond Head Market and Grill
16 Honolulu Museum of Art/Shangri La
17 Ala Moana Shopping Center
PACIFIC OCEAN
Kauai Channel
Kaiwi Channel
THE NORTH SHORE
KOOLAU RANGE
CENTRAL OAHU (EWA PLAIN)
THE WINDWARD COAST
FOREST RESERVE
WAIANAE RANGE
LEEWARD OAHU (WAIANAE COAST)
EAST OAHU
Honolulu
Waikiki
Honolulu International Airport
Kahuku Point
Kahuku
Laie
Laie Point
Hauula
Punaluu
Kahana Bay Beach Park
Kaaawa
Kualoa Regional Park
Kaneohe Bay
HEEIA STATE PARK
Heeia
Kaneohe
Mokapu Point
MARINE CORPS AIR STATION
Kailua Bay
Kailua
Kailua Beach Park
BELLOWS AIR FORCE BASE
Waimanalo
Waimanalo Bay
Makapu'u Beach Park
Makapu'u Point
HALONA BLOW HOLE
Sandy Beach
Hanauma Bay
Koko Head
Hawaii Kai
Maunalua Bay
Tantalus
Kawela
Sunset Beach
Waimea Falls Park
Waimea
Waimea Beach Park
Haleiwa
Waialua
Wahiawa Botanical Gardens
Wahiawa
SCHOFIELD BARRACKS
Mililani
Pearl City
Pearl Harbor
Waipahu
Ewa
Kapolei
NAVAL AIR STATION
Barbers Point
Ko Olina
Nanakuli
Maili
Waianae
Makaha
Makaha Beach Park
Kepuhi Point
Yokohama Bay
KAENA POINT STATE PARK
Kaena Point
Mamala Bay
0 5 mi
0 5 km

If possible, stay on O'ahu for at least 1 week so that you can take in the sights at a leisurely, island-style pace. You'll have time to see all the sights I recommended in the 3-day tour, plus explore the enchanting underwater world at Hanauma Bay, delve into Hawaiian history and culture, visit the art world, do some shopping, and spend more time at the beach.

Days 1–3

For your first 3 days on O'ahu, follow the itinerary for "The Best of O'ahu in Three Days," starting on p 12, with one exception: On day 2, instead of visiting 'Iolani Palace (don't worry—you'll see it later on this tour), spend the afternoon exploring Chinatown (see my tour of this neighborhood on p 72) or just relax and wander through Waikīkī for shops, sun, and surf.

Day 4

From Waikīkī, head down Kalākaua Ave. and turn left on Kapahulu Ave. Bus 13.

Malasadas (holeless doughnuts) from Leonard's Bakery

1 ★★★ Malasadas at Leonard's Bakery Join the locals and tourists at Leonard's Bakery, which was started in 1952 by Portuguese immigrants. Grab a malasada (a hole-less doughnut), hot and fresh out of the fryer and dipped in sugar and cinnamon. *933 Kapahulu Ave. ☎ 808/737-5571. www.leonardshawaii.com. $.*

Take H-1 East, which becomes the Kalaniana'ole Hwy. Look for the Koko Head Regional Park on the left; the beach is on the right (ocean side). Avoid the crowds by going early, about 8am, on a weekday; once the parking lot's full, you're out of luck. Take the 18 or 24 to The Hanauma Bay Shuttle Bus (Bus: 22), which runs from Waikīkī to Hanauma Bay every half-hour from 8:45am to 1pm. You can catch it at any city bus stop in Waikīkī. It returns every hour from noon to 4pm.

2 ★★★ Hanauma Bay. Spend the morning at O'ahu's best snorkeling beach. ***Note:*** The beach is closed on Tuesdays. *See p 155.*

Continue to drive east on Kalaniana'ole Hwy. Stop at mile marker 11. Bus 22.

3 Halona Blowhole. *See p 143, 3.*

Continue to drive east on Kalaniana'ole Hwy. Look for the Makapu'u Point sign and turn right into the parking lot. Bus 22.

4 ★★ Makapu'u Point Lighthouse Trail. You've seen this famous old lighthouse on episodes of *Magnum, P.I.* and *Hawaii Five-O.*

Tranquil Hanauma Bay is a great place for novice snorkelers.

No longer staffed by the Coast Guard (it's fully automated now), the lighthouse sits at the end of a precipitous cliff trail on an airy perch looking over the Windward Coast, Manana (Rabbit) Island, and the azure Pacific. The view of the ocean all the way to Moloka'i and Lāna'i is often so clear that, from November to March, if you're lucky, you'll see migrating humpback whales. ⏱ *1 hr. Makapu'u Lighthouse Rd.*

Turn left onto Kalaniana'ole Hwy. Turn right onto W. Hind Dr. Bus: 23.

5 Uncle Clay's House of Pure Aloha. Here's a rare shave ice spot that uses syrups made with local fruit. Unlike other places that rely on artificially colored and flavored syrups, at Uncle Clay's, the pineapple and mango are the real deal. Top it off with a scoop of ice cream. *820 W. Hind Dr. Unit 116* ☎ *808/373-5111. www.uncleclays.com. $.*

Turn right onto Kalaniana'ole Hwy., and continue onto H-1 West. Take exit 24A Wilder Ave.

Tour Honolulu from a Trolley Car

Hop on a 34-seat, open-air, motorized Waikīkī Trolley for a fun way to get around the island. The Honolulu City Line loops around Waikīkī and downtown Honolulu, stopping every 40 minutes at 12 key places (such as 'Iolani Palace, Chinatown, the State Capitol, the Aloha Tower, and Restaurant Row). The driver provides commentary along the way. Stops on the new 3-hour, fully narrated Ocean Coast Line on the southeast side of O'ahu include Sea Life Park, Diamond Head, and Waikīkī Beach. Book online for the best rates: A 1-day trolley pass—which costs $45—allows you to jump on and off all day long (8:30am–11:35pm). Four-day passes cost $65. Call ☎ **800/824-8804** or 808/593-2822 for more information, or go to www.waikikitrolley.com.

Continue onto Wilder Ave. Turn right onto Punahou St. Turn left onto Nehoa St. Take the second right onto Makīkī St. Take the second left onto Round Top Dr. Continue onto Pu'uali'i Pl. Make a slight left onto Round Top Dr. No bus service.

6 ★ Pu'u 'Ualaka'a State Park. My favorite sunset view of Honolulu is from a 1,048-foot-high (319m) hill named for sweet potatoes. The poetic Hawaiian name means "rolling sweet potato hill," which describes how early planters used gravity to harvest their crop. On a clear day (which is almost always), the majestic, sweeping views stretch from Diamond Head to the Wai'anae Range—almost the length of O'ahu. At night, several scenic overlooks provide romantic spots for young lovers to smooch under the stars with the city lights at their feet. It's a top-of-the-world experience—the view, that is. *15–20 min. At the end of Round Top Dr. Daily 7am–6:45pm (to 7:45pm in summer). No bus service.*

Day 5

Take Ala Wai Blvd. out of Waikīkī. Turn right at Kalākaua Ave., left on S. Beretania St., and right at Piikoi St. Make a left onto Lunalilo St. and bear left onto H-1 West. Take Exit 20B, which puts you on Haloma St. Turn right at Houghtailing St. and then left on Bernice St. Bus: 2.

7 ★★★ Bishop Museum. If you are the least bit curious about what ancient Hawai'i was like, this museum is a must-see. This multi-building museum has the world's greatest collection of natural and cultural artifacts from Hawai'i and the Pacific. Another highlight is the terrific new 16,500-square-foot (1,533-sq.-m) Science Adventure Center, specializing in volcanology and oceanography. In the Hawaiian Hall, you can venture back in history and see what Hawaiian culture was like before Westerners arrived. Don't miss my favorites: the **hula performances ★** at 2pm, and the shows in the planetarium, where you explore the night sky. Stop by the café, by local favorite restaurant **Highway Inn,** for a classic Hawaiian plate lunch. *3–4 hr. 1525 Bernice St., just off Kalihi St. (aka Likelike Hwy.). ☎ 808/847-3511. www.bishopmuseum.org. Admission $23 adults, $20 seniors, $15 children 4–12, free for children 3 & younger. Daily 9am–5pm.*

The Waikīkī Trolley on Kalakaua avenue in Waikīkī

The Bishop Museum presents a vast collection of cultural and natural Hawaiian artifacts.

Turn right out of the parking lot onto Bernice St., right on Houghtailing St., and left on Olomea St. Continue on to N. Vineyard St. Turn right on Punchbowl St. and right again on S. Beretania St. Take the first left on Richards St. Bus: 2.

8 **Artizen @ HiSAM.** Take a break to sip a cool pineapple and mango iced tea, and order any one of the almost-too-pretty-to-eat desserts in the display case, which range from chocolate cake to liliko'i mousse. HiSAM at 250 S. Hotel St. ☎ *808/586-0300. www.artizenbymw.com. $.*

Walk across the street.

9 ★★ **'Iolani Palace.** Visit what was once the official residence of Hawai'i's monarchy. *See p 15,* 8.

Continue to walk toward Diamond Head on S. King St. to Punchbowl St.

10 ★ **Kawaiaha'o Church.** When the missionaries came to Hawai'i, the first thing they did was build churches. Four thatched grass churches had been built on this site before Rev. Hiram Bingham began building what he considered a "real" church—a New England–style congregational structure with Gothic influences. Between 1837 and 1842, the building of the church required some 14,000 giant coral slabs (some weighing more than 1,000 lb.). Hawaiian divers raped the reefs, digging out huge chunks of coral and causing irreparable environmental damage. Kawaiaha'o, Hawai'i's oldest church, has been the site of numerous historical events, such as a speech made by King Kamehameha III in 1843, an excerpt of which became Hawaii's state motto (*"Ua mau ke ea o ka 'āina i ka pono,"* which translates to "The life of the land is preserved in righteousness"). The clock tower in the church, which was donated by King Kamehameha III and installed in 1850, continues to tick today. Don't sit in the pews in the back, marked with kahili feathers and velvet cushions; they are still reserved for the descendants of royalty. *957 Punchbowl St. (at King St.).* ☎ *808/469-3000. www.kawaiahao.org. Free admission (donations appreciated). Mon–Fri 8am–4:30pm; Sun services 9am.*

The mausoleum of King Lunalilo at Kawaiaha'o Church

Kailua Beach Park

Continue in the Diamond Head direction on S. King St.

⓫ **Hawaiian Mission Houses.** The original buildings of the Sandwich Islands Mission Headquarters still stand, and tours are often led by descendants of the original missionaries to Hawaii. The missionaries brought their own prefab houses along with them when they came around Cape Horn from Boston in 1819. Finished in 1821, the Frame House is Hawai'i's oldest wooden structure. Designed for New England winters, it had small windows and must have been stiflingly hot inside. The missionaries believed that the best way to spread the Lord's message to the Hawaiians was to learn their language and then to print literature for them to read. So it was the missionaries who gave the Hawaiians a written language. ⏲ *1 hr. 553 S. King St. (at Kawaiaha'o St.). ☎ 808/447-3910. www.missionhouses.org. $10 adults, $8 seniors, $6 students and children ages 6 and over. Tues–Sat 10am–4pm. Guided tours on the hour 11am–3pm.*

To get back to Waikīkī, continue toward Diamond Head on S. King St. Make a slight right on Kapi'olani Blvd. Go right again on Pi'ikoi St. and left on Ala Moana Blvd. into Waikīkī. TheBus: 19.

Day 6

Take H-1 west to Exit 21B (Pali Hwy. north) and continue along the Pali Hwy./Hwy. 61. Continue on Kailua Rd. and then turn right on Kalaheo Ave. to the beach. TheBus: 20, then transfer to TheBus 56.

⓬ ★★★ **Kailua Beach.** Spend the entire day on the windward side of O'ahu at one of the island's most fabulous beaches. *See p 156.*

⓭ ★ **Kailua.** This residential town is seeing more and more tourists who are savvy to the beauty of Kailua Beach. The center is bustling with hamburger joints, antique and vintage shops, and boutiques selling beachy clothes and modern aloha shirts. Kailua is also famous for its pancake and breakfast spots, of which Moke's Bread and Breakfast (p 150) is my favorite.

Day 7

In Waikīkī, drive to the intersection of Diamond Head Rd. and 18th

A trek to the top of Diamond Head is rewarded with spectacular views.

Ave. Follow the road through the tunnel (which is closed 6pm–6am) and park in the lot. Bus: 23.

⑭ ★ **Diamond Head.** Get a bird's-eye view of the island from atop this 760-foot (232m) extinct volcano. *See p 165.*

Head left on Diamond Head Road. Continue down Monsarrat Ave.

15 ★ **Diamond Head Market and Grill.** Take a break at this casual takeout spot for a local plate lunch with 'ahi (tuna) steaks or kalbi (Korean-marinated short ribs). Don't miss dessert: the lemon crunch cake is a perfect capper to a Diamond Head hike. *3158 Monsarrat Ave. www.diamondheadmarket.com. ☎ 808/732-0077. $.*

Head left onto Campbell Ave. Turn right onto Castle St. Turn left onto 6th Ave. Turn left onto Harding Ave. and left to merge onto H-1 West. Take exit 23 to merge onto Lunalilo St. Turn left onto Pensacola St. Turn right onto S. Beretania St. Bus 2.

⑯ ★★★ **Shangri La.** Take a shuttle from the Honolulu Museum of Art to tobacco heiress Doris Duke's private palace on a 5-acre sanctuary in Black Point. It's absolutely stunning, packed with Islamic art and intricate tilework from Iran, Turkey, and Syria; textiles from Egypt and India; and custom-painted ceilings by Moroccan artisans. Outside's not so bad either, with ocean views all the way to Diamond Head. 🕓 *2½ hrs. Shuttles from the Honolulu Museum of Art, 900 S. Beretania St., www.honolulumuseum.org. ☎ 808/532-3853 for*

Hawai'i's Early History

Paddling outrigger sailing canoes, the first ancestors of today's Hawaiians followed the stars, waves, and birds across the sea to Hawai'i, which they called "the land of raging fire." Those first settlers were part of the great Polynesian migration that settled the vast triangle of islands stretching among New Zealand, Easter Island, and Hawai'i. No one is sure when they arrived in Hawai'i from Tahiti and the Marquesas Islands, some 2,500 miles to the south, but recent archaeological digs at the Malu'uluolele Park in Lāhainā date back to A.D. 700 to 900.

All we have today are some archaeological finds, some scientific data, and ancient chants to tell the story of Hawai'i's past. The chants, especially the *Kumulipo,* which is the chant of creation and the litany of genealogy of the *ali'i* (high-ranking chiefs) who ruled the islands, discuss the comings and goings between Hawai'i and the islands of the south, presumed to be Tahiti. In fact, the channel between Maui, Kaho'olawe, and Lanai is called *Kealaikahiki,* or "the pathway to Tahiti."

Around 1300, the transoceanic voyages stopped for some reason, and Hawai'i began to develop its own culture in earnest. The settlers built temples, fishponds, and aqueducts to irrigate taro plantations. Each island was a separate kingdom, and the *ali'i* created a caste system and established taboos. Violators were strangled, and high priests asked the gods Lono and Ku for divine guidance. Ritual human sacrifices were common.

Ala Moana Shopping Center

Shangri La reservations. $25. Wed–Sat.

Turn left, heading toward the ocean, on Ward Ave. and then make a left on Ala Moana Blvd. Bus: 17.

⓱ ★★ **Ala Moana Shopping Center.** Spend some time wandering through Hawai'i's largest shopping center. It's the perfect place to find souvenirs and gifts for your friends and relatives back home. The food options are also worth exploring. In Hawai'i, you'll find some of the best Japanese food outside of Japan. Sample some of it at the **Shirokiya Japan Village Walk**. *See p 124.*

The Best of O'ahu in Ten Days

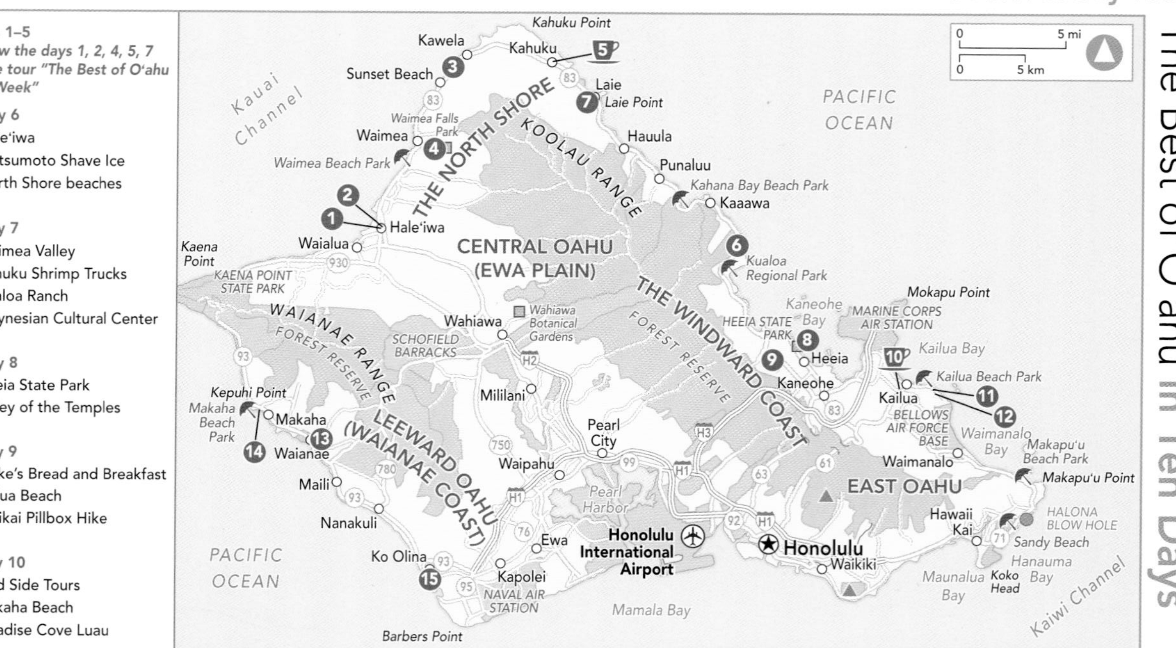

A week and a half on O'ahu is perfect: It gives you enough time to see all the sites and experience the true flavor of Hawai'i with plenty of time left to relax and really enjoy some down time. You'll spend two nights on the North Shore, giving you more time to soak in the surfer vibe, and then a night in Kailua to marvel at the rugged Windward side. Plus, you'll explore more incredible beaches, swim with dolphins, and attend a lū'au.

Days 1–5

For your first 5 days on O'ahu, follow the itinerary for "The Best of O'ahu in One Week," starting on p 18, but skip day 3 on the North Shore and day 6 in Kailua: you'll explore those areas more fully later in this tour.

Day 6

Spend your sixth day on O'ahu on the North Shore. Take H-1 west out of Waikīkī and then take the H-2 north exit (Exit 8A) toward Mililani/Wahiawā. After 7 miles (11km), H-2 becomes Kamehameha Hwy. (Hwy. 80). Look for the turnoff to Hale'iwa town. Bus: 20, then transfer to 55.

❶ ★★★ **Hale'iwa.** It's time to take a break from Honolulu and head up to the North Shore. Start your day exploring this famous North Shore surfing town. *See p 137,* ❷.

2 ★ **Matsumoto Shave Ice.** A rainbow of exotic flavors awaits at this venerated shave ice vendor. See p 16.

Continue down Kamehameha Hwy. Bus: 52.

❸ ★★★ **North Shore beaches.** Choose any one of the North Shore beaches to spend the afternoon. If it's winter time and the surf's up, you'll want to head to Pipeline or Sunset to watch the surfers on some of the best waves in the world. If it's summer, head to Waimea to swim in the calm, beautiful bay or to Shark's Cove for snorkeling. *See p 159.*

Spend the night on the North Shore. The next morning, drive on Kamehameha Hwy. toward Waimea Bay and turn onto Waimea Valley Rd.

Day 7

❹ ★ **Waimea Valley.** A visit here offers a lush walk into the past. The valley is packed with archaeological sites, including the 600-year-old Hale O Lono, a heiau dedicated to the Hawaiian god Lono, the god of peace, fertility, and agriculture. Walk through the gardens, which contain more than 5,000 species of tropical plants and wind up at 45-foot-high Waimea Falls—bring your bathing suit and you can dive into the cold, murky water. ⏲ *2 hr. 59-864 Kamehameha Hwy. waimeavalley.net* ☎ *808/638-7766. Admission $16 adults, $12 seniors, $8 children 4–12. Daily 9am–5pm.*

Turn right onto Kamehameha Hwy. and head toward Kahuku. Bus: 55.

5 **Kahuku Shrimp Trucks.** Shrimp farming took hold in in the '90s and, before long, the first shrimp truck set up, serving fresh shrimp from a lunch wagon window. Now you can smell the garlic cooking before you see all the trucks and shrimp shacks—at least five, by last count. Giovanni's Original White Shrimp Truck, is the most popular—so much so that a makeshift food court with picnic tables, shade, and a handful of other businesses has sprung up around

ATV tours at Kualoa Ranch, setting for several famous Hollywood films

the beat-up old white truck scrawled with tourists' signatures. Even though the shrimp are now imported and previously frozen, Giovanni's knows how to cook them perfectly. Scampi style is my favorite—shell-on shrimp coated in lots of butter and garlic. 56-505 Kamehameha Hwy. ☎ *808/293-1839. www.giovannis shrimptruck.com. $.*

Continue south on Kamehameha Hwy. toward Kualoa Ranch. Bus: 55.

6 ★★ Kualoa Ranch. The setting here is stunning, a 4,000 acre private nature reserve and working cattle ranch backed up against the fluted Ko'olau mountain range. Sign up for one of the adventure packages: Options include horseback riding and ATV rides that take you through the locations where movies like *Jurassic Park* and *Godzilla* were filmed. Get your adrenaline going on the new zipline course, which allows you to fly through the treetops at the ranch. *1–21/2 hr. 49-560 Kamehameha Hwy., Ka'a'awa. www.kualoa.com.* ☎ *800/231-7321 or 808/237-7321. Single activities $46–$120. Daily 8am–3:30pm.*

Head north on Kamehameha Hwy. toward Lā'ie. Bus: 55.

7 ★★ Ha: Breath of Life at the Polynesian Cultural Center. Catch the evening show at the Polynesian Cultural Center. *See p 17,* 14.

Return to the North Shore for the night.

Day 8

From the North Shore, head south on Kamehameha Hwy. Turn left onto HI-830 South until you reach He'eia State Park. Bus 55.

8 ★ Kayak or Stand-up Paddle in Kāne'ohe Bay. Since you saw the Ko'olau mountains up close yesterday, see them from the water today. Revel in amazing views both above and below the water on the Windward Coast with **Holokai Kayak and Snorkel Adventures.** Spend the day beaching. Sign up for a 4-hour guided tour and you'll see the majestic Ko'olau Range from your kayak. Then, as you head to Coconut Island (aka Gilligan's Island), you'll stop to snorkel and admire the fish and turtles in the almost-always calm Kāne'ohe Bay. Or, you can go at your own pace with the self-guided kayak or stand-up paddleboard option—they'll point you in the direction of the disappearing sandbar Ahu o Laka, as well as the good snorkel spots. What's even better? Proceeds go to Kama'aina Kids (which runs environmental education programs for children) and improving He'eia State Park. *46-465 Kamehameha Hwy., Kāne'ohe, at He'eia State Park. www.holokaiadventures.com;* ☎ *808/781-4773. $55-$129.*

Head north on HI-830 North. Turn left onto HI-83 East, or Kahekili Hwy. Bus 55.

9 ★ Valley of the Temples. This famous cemetery in a cleft of the pali is stalked by wild peacocks and about 700 curious people a day, who pay to see the 9-foot meditation Buddha, acres of ponds full of more than 10,000 Japanese koi carp, and a replica of Japan's 900-year-old Byodo-In Temple of Equality. The original, made of wood, stands in Uji, on the outskirts of Kyoto; the Hawai'i version, made of concrete, was erected in 1968 to commemorate the 100th anniversary of the arrival of the first Japanese immigrants to Hawai'i. *1 hr. 47–200 Kahekili Hwy. (across the street from Temple Valley Shopping Center). 808/239-8811. www.byodo-in.com. Admission $3 adults, $2 seniors 65 & over & children 11 & under. Daily 9am–5pm.*

Spend the night on the Windward side, around Kailua or Kāne'ohe.

Day 9

10 ★ **Moke's Bread and Breakfast.** One of the advantages of staying in Kailua is getting to hit its famous breakfast spots before the crowds. Of all the pancake joints in Kailua, Moke's is my pick, for their tender, fluffy pancakes topped with a light passionfruit cream sauce. For something savory, try the stuffed hash browns: think omelet fixin's sandwiched by crispy potatoes. *27 Ho'olai St., Kailua. www.mokeskailua.com. 808/261-5565. $.*

Stand-up paddleboard (SUP) rentals are readily available on many island beaches.

11 ★ **Kailua Beach.** Be as active or relaxed as you want. Lay in the sand or play in the water, rent a kayak and head to Flat Island or the Mokulua Islands. You'll see why Kailua Beach is one of the island's best. *See p 177.*

From the beach, walk on Kawailoa Rd., away from the canal. Turn left onto Mokulua Dr. Stay on Mokulua Dr. and turn right onto Aalapapa Dr. Turn right onto Kaelepulu Dr.

12 ★ **Lanikai Pillbox Hike.** Start this short hike up to the Ka Iwi ridge around dusk to appreciate the sunset. It's only about 30 minutes each way up the steep, dirt trail, but the payoff is great: picture-perfect views of Kailua, the Ko'olau mountains, and the Mokulua islands. It makes you realize why the pillboxes were built up here in the first place (they were constructed around WWII as

The Buddhist temple and gardens at Valley of the Temples

Lanikai Beach viewed from the Pillbox Hike

observation posts and later abandoned). 🕓 *1 hr. Kaelepulu Dr.*

Retrace your steps back to Kailua Beach. Either stay in Kailua or the Windward side for the night or head back to Honolulu.

Day 10

Head to the Leeward side via H-1 West. Continue onto HI-93 West, or Farrington Hwy. to the Wai'anae boat harbor.

⓭ ★ **Wild Side Tours.** Spend the morning swimming with dolphins off the Wai'anae coast with this intimate catamaran tour. *See p 182.*

Continue north on Farrington Hwy.

⓮ ★ **Mākaha Beach.** Bliss out at this uncrowded, expansive white sand beach. *See p 158, 178.*

Head south on Farrington Hwy. Take the exit toward Ko Olina. Continue onto Ali'inui Dr.

⓯ **Paradise Cove Lū'au.** For your last night, and while you're out in Ko Olina, experience a lū'au. Don't expect an intimate affair—Paradise Cove generally has some 600 to 800 guests a night. In fact, the small thatched village feels a bit like a Hawaiian theme park. But you're getting more than just a lū'au: Paradise Cove provides an entire cultural experience, with Hawaiian games, craft demonstrations, Tahitian and hula dancing, and a beautiful shoreline looking out over what is usually a storybook sunset. You'll find typical lū'au cuisine (Hawaiian kalua pig, lomi salmon, poi, and coconut pudding and cake) and basic American fare (salads, rice, pineapple, chicken, and so on). 🕓 *3½ hr. Ali'inui Dr., Ko Olina.* ☎ *808/842-5911. www.paradisecovehawaii.com. $92 adults, $81 children 13–20, $70 children 12 & under. Daily 5–9pm.* ●

The luau at Paradise Cove is an immersive cultural experience.

3 The Best Special-Interest Tours

Honolulu & O'ahu **with Kids**

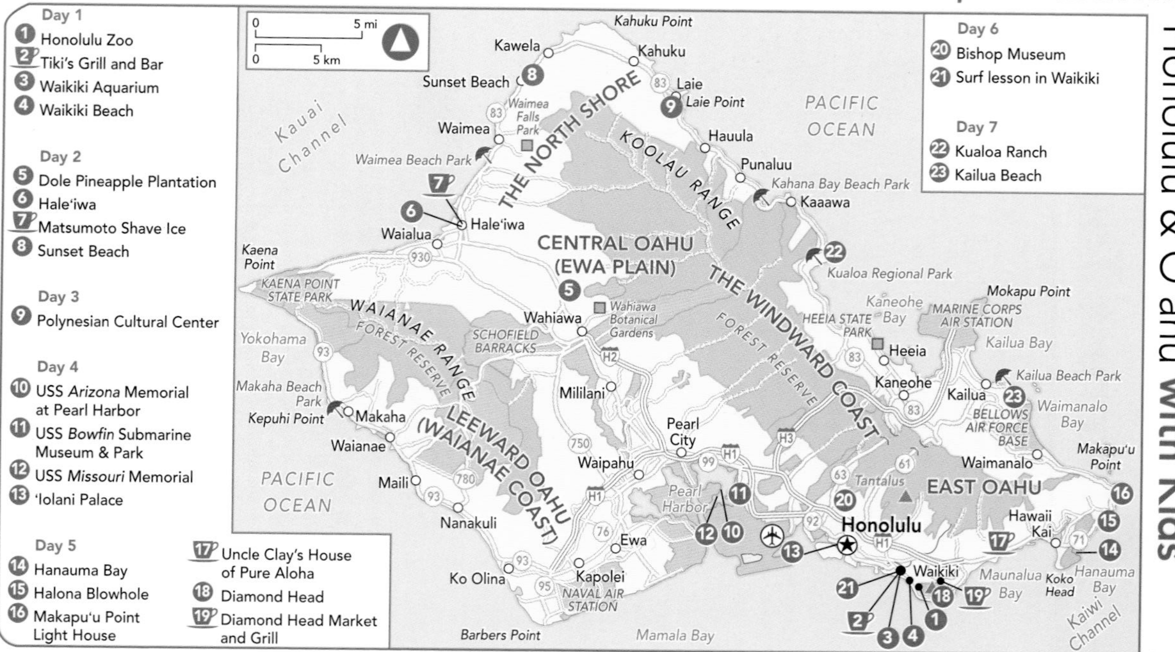
Day 1
1 Honolulu Zoo
2 Tiki's Grill and Bar
3 Waikiki Aquarium
4 Waikiki Beach
Day 2
5 Dole Pineapple Plantation
6 Hale'iwa
7 Matsumoto Shave Ice
8 Sunset Beach
Day 3
9 Polynesian Cultural Center
Day 4
10 USS *Arizona* Memorial at Pearl Harbor
11 USS *Bowfin* Submarine Museum & Park
12 USS *Missouri* Memorial
13 'Iolani Palace
Day 5
14 Hanauma Bay
15 Halona Blowhole
16 Makapu'u Point Light House
17 Uncle Clay's House of Pure Aloha
18 Diamond Head
19 Diamond Head Market and Grill
Day 6
20 Bishop Museum
21 Surf lesson in Waikiki
Day 7
22 Kualoa Ranch
23 Kailua Beach
0 5 mi
0 5 km
Kauai Channel
Kahuku Point
Kawela
Kahuku
Sunset Beach
Laie
Laie Point
Waimea
Waimea Falls Park
Waimea Beach Park
THE NORTH SHORE
KOOLAU RANGE
Hauula
Punaluu
Kahana Bay Beach Park
Kaaawa
PACIFIC OCEAN
Hale'iwa
Waialua
Kaena Point
KAENA POINT STATE PARK
CENTRAL OAHU (EWA PLAIN)
Kualoa Regional Park
THE WINDWARD COAST
FOREST RESERVE
Wahiawa
Wahiawa Botanical Gardens
WAIANAE RANGE
FOREST RESERVE
SCHOFIELD BARRACKS
Yokohama Bay
Makaha Beach Park
Kepuhi Point
Makaha
Waianae
LEEWARD OAHU (WAIANAE COAST)
Mililani
Pearl City
Waipahu
Maili
Nanakuli
PACIFIC OCEAN
Pearl Harbor
Ewa
Kapolei
NAVAL AIR STATION
Ko Olina
Barbers Point
Mamala Bay
Kaneohe Bay
HEEIA STATE PARK
Heeia
Kaneohe
Mokapu Point
MARINE CORPS AIR STATION
Kailua Bay
Kailua Beach Park
Kailua
BELLOWS AIR FORCE BASE
Waimanalo Bay
Waimanalo
Makapu'u Point
Tantalus
EAST OAHU
Honolulu
Hawaii Kai
Waikiki
Maunalua Bay
Koko Head
Hanauma Bay
Kaiwi Channel

Previous page: A commemorative ceremony at the USS Arizona Memorial, Pearl Harbor

Families flock to O'ahu not only for the island's breathtaking beauty but also for the abundance of activities. Waikīkī is famous for every type of ocean activity you can think of, plus there's the Honolulu Zoo, the Waikīkī Aquarium, and fun-filled Kapi'olani Park. Dotted around the rest of the island are great family outings like the Polynesian Cultural Center and Kualoa Ranch. This tour gives families a fun-filled week with something for everyone.

Day 1

1 ★ Honolulu Zoo. If the kids aren't too tired from the flight, head for this 43-acre (17-ha) municipal zoo. My favorite section is the 10-acre (4-ha) African Savannah, with more than 40 critters roaming around in the open. *Best time to go is when the gates open; the animals are more active in the morning.* *2–3 hr. 151 Kapahulu Ave. (between Paki & Kalākaua aves.), at entrance to Kapi'olani Park. ☎ 808/971-7171. www.honoluluzoo.org. $14 adults, $6 kids 3–12, free for children 2 & under. Daily 9am–4:30pm.*

The Honolulu Zoo provides a nice break from the sand and surf.

Walk along Kapahulu Ave. toward Kalākaua Ave. and then turn right on Kalākaua.

2 ★Tiki's Grill and Bar. If it is close to lunch and the kids are getting cranky, pop in to Tiki's. Burgers and sandwiches are moderately priced ($11–$16) and the kids get their own menu (all options are $10, which for Waikīkī is cheap) of grilled cheese sandwiches, mini-burgers, chicken strips, even a Hawaiian plate. *Aston Waikīkī Beach Hotel, 2570 Kalākaua Ave. (at Paoakalani St.). ☎ 808/923-8454. www.tikisgrill.com.*

Backtrack on Kalākaua Ave. and walk toward Diamond Head.

3 ★ Waikīkī Aquarium. Explore Hawai'i's underwater world without getting wet. This small but fabulous aquarium houses some 2,500 animals representing more than 420 species. You'll find everything from translucent jellyfish to lumbering turtles to endangered Hawaiian monk seals—and even sharks. My favorite things to see are the chambered nautilus (nature's submarine and inspiration for Jules Verne's *20,000 Leagues Under the Sea*), the Edge of the Reef exhibit (where you see reef fish up close and personal), and the Mahimahi Hatchery (where these delicious fish are raised from egg to adult). *2 hr.; get there early on weekends, before the crowds. 2777 Kalākaua Ave. (across from Kapi'olani Park). ☎ 808/923-9741. www.waquarium.org. $12 adults; $8 active military; $5 seniors and children 4–12. Daily 9am–5pm (last tickets sold at 4:30pm).*

More than 420 species are on display at the Waikīkī Aquarium.

Walk 'Ewa (west) along the beach until you find a spot you like.

❹ ★★★ **Waikīkī Beach.** Finish off your day with some fun in the sun. *See p 161.*

Day 2

Spend your second day on O'ahu on the North Shore. Take H-1 west out of Waikīkī and then take the H-2 north exit (Exit 8A) toward Mililani/Wahiawā. After 7 miles (11km), H-2 becomes Kamehameha Hwy. (Hwy. 99). Continue on Kamehameha Hwy. for about 3 miles (4.8km). Bus 19 or 20, then transfer to bus 52.

❺ ★**Dole Pineapple Plantation.** This is a great place to stop to let the kids stretch out their legs. There are lots of activities for kids: a single-engine diesel locomotive that takes a 22-minute tour around the plantation's grounds, and the Pineapple Garden Maze for the kids to get lost in. Cool down with a Dole Whip, the famously delicious pineapple soft serve. 🕓 *1–2 hr. 64–1550 Kamehameha Hwy.* ☎ *808/621-8408. www.doleplantation.com. Gardens $7 adults, $6.25 kids 4–12; train tickets $10.50 adults, $8.50 kids; pineapple maze $8 adults, $6 kids. Daily 9am–5:30pm.*

Continue on Kamehameha Hwy. Look for the turnoff to Hale'iwa town. Bus: 19, then transfer to 52.

❻ ★★★ **Hale'iwa.** Start your day exploring this famous North Shore surfing town. *See p 137,* ❷.

7 ★ **Matsumoto Shave Ice.** Take time out for a cool, sweet treat at Matsumoto's. *See p 16,* 11.

Calm waters and ample services make Waikīkī Beach a great family beach.

The Pineapple Express train at Dole Pineapple Plantation

Continue down Kamehameha Hwy. for about 6½ miles (10km). Bus: 52.

8 ★★★ Sunset Beach. Spend the rest of the day playing on Sunset Beach. During the summer months, this is a safe beach for swimming. During the winter, it's best to just sit and watch the big wave surfers. *See p 161.*

Head back to Waikīkī or consider spending the night on the North Shore.

Day 3

If you're coming from Waikīkī, get on the H-1 West. Take exit 20A to merge onto Likelike Hwy. Take the HI-83/Kahekili Hwy. ramp and continue on Kahekili Hwy., until you reach Lā'ie. Bus 55.

9 ★★ Polynesian Cultural Center. Spend the day here—it's great for families, informative and fun. Here you can see the lifestyles, songs, dance, costumes, and

Rainy Days

If it's a rainy day, or your little darlings are lobster red from being in the sun (even after you told them to put on more sunscreen), take them directly to the **Hawai'i Children's Discovery Center,** 111 Ohe St. (across from Kakaako Waterfront Park), Honolulu (☎ **808/524-5437;** www.discoverycenterhawaii.org). Perfect for ages 2 to 13, hands-on exhibits, interactive stations, and classes will keep them occupied for hours. Admission is $10, $6 for seniors, and free for kids under 1. Open Tuesday through Friday from 9am to 1pm, Saturday and Sunday from 10am to 3pm. From Waikīkī, take TheBus no. 42; from Ala Moana Center, take no. 42.

Another great rainy day retreat is the **Bishop Museum** (1525 Bernice St., just off the Likelike Hwy.), Honolulu (☎ **808/847-3511;** www.bishopmuseum.org). Admission is $23 adults, $20 seniors, $15 kids ages 4 to 12, and free for kids 3 and under. Head straight for the new Science Adventure Center, where the kids can virtually walk inside an erupting volcano, see the stars in the planetarium, or experience ancient chants in the Hawaiian Hall. Open daily 9am to 5pm. Take TheBus no. 2.

architecture of six Pacific islands or archipelagos—Fiji, New Zealand, Samoa, Tahiti, Tonga, and Hawai'i—in the recreated villages scattered throughout the 42-acre lagoon park.

Native students from Polynesia who attend Hawai'i's Brigham Young University are the "inhabitants" of each village. They engage the audience with spear-throwing competitions, coconut tree–climbing presentations, and invitations to pound Tongan drums. One of my favorite shows is the canoe pageant, daily at 2:30pm; each island puts on a representation of their dance, music, and costume atop canoes in the lagoon. Stay for the evening show, ***Ha: Breath of Life,*** a coming-of-age story told through the different Polynesian dances, some full of grace, some fierce, and all thrilling. It's one of O'ahu's better shows. *55-370 Kamehameha Hwy., Lā'ie. www.polynesia.com. ☎ 800/367-7060, 808/293-3333. $60–$220 adults, $48–$176 children 3–11. Mon–Sat noon–9pm.*

Head back to Waikīkī or consider spending the night on the North Shore.

Shave ice makes for a cooling treat on a hot day.

Day 4

Get an early start to beat the crowds at Pearl Harbor. Drive west on H-1 past the airport to the USS *Arizona* Memorial exit, then follow the green-and-white signs; there's ample free parking. Bus: 20.

⑩ ★★★ USS *Arizona* Memorial at Pearl Harbor. This unforgettable memorial is O'ahu's top attraction. Parents should note that strollers and diaper bags are not allowed at the memorial (you can store them at the visitor center). Also, there are no restrooms at the memorial, so be sure everyone uses the ones at the visitor center. *See p 14,* ④.

Interactive learning at the Polynesian Cultural Center

Family-Friendly Events

Your trip may be a little more enjoyable with the added attraction of attending a celebration, festival, or party in Honolulu, Waikīkī, or other parts of the island. Check out the following events.

- **Chinese New Year,** Chinatown (☎ 808/533-3181). Late January or early February (depending on the lunar calendar). Chinatown rolls out the red carpet for this important event with a traditional lion dance, firecrackers, food booths, and a host of activities.
- **Punahou School Carnival,** Punahou School, Honolulu (☎ 808/944-5753). February. This private school fundraiser is one of O'ahu's biggest events of the year. It has everything you can imagine in a school carnival, from high-speed rides to homemade jellies. The malasadas and mango chutney are legendary. All proceeds go to scholarship funds.
- **Duke Kahanamoku Beach Challenge,** Hilton Hawaiian Village, Waikīkī (☎ 808/923-1802). March. This event features ancient Hawaiian games, such as *ulu maika* (bowling a round stone through pegs), *huki kaula* (tug of war), and an outrigger canoe race. It's also a great place to hear Hawaiian music.
- **Outrigger Canoe Season,** Ala Wai Canal (www.ohcra.com). Weekends May to September. Canoe paddlers across the state participate in outrigger canoe races.
- **World Fire-Knife Competition and Samoan Festival,** Polynesian Cultural Center, Lā'ie (☎ 808/293-3333). Mid-May. Fire-knife dancers from around the world gather for one of the most amazing performances you'll ever see. Authentic Samoan food and cultural festivities round out the fun.
- **'Ukulele Festival,** Kapi'olani Park Bandstand, Waikīkī (☎ 808/971-2510; www.ukelelefestivalhawaii.org). Last Sunday in July. This free concert features some 800 kids (ages 4–92) strumming the 'ukulele. Hawai'i's top musicians all pitch in.
- **Triple Crown of Surfing,** North Shore (☎ 808/638-7266). Mid-November to late December. The North Shore is on "wave watch" during this period, and when the big, monster waves roll in, the world's top professional surfers compete in events for more than $1 million in prize money.

⓫ ★ **USS *Bowfin* Submarine Museum & Park.** *See p 47,* ❷.

⓬ ★ **USS *Missouri* Memorial.** *See p 47,* ❸.

From Arizona Memorial Dr., turn right on Kamehameha Hwy. (Hwy. 99). Take the ramp onto H-1 East toward Honolulu. Take Exit 18A toward HI-92 East/Nimitz Hwy. Take the exit toward Iwilei Rd., turn right onto Iwilei, turn right onto N. King St. Bus 40, 42.

⓭ ★★ **'Iolani Palace.** Once the site of a *heiau* (temple), 'Iolani Palace took 3 years and $350,000 to complete in 1882, with all the modern conveniences for its time (electric lights were installed here 4 years before they were in the White House). It was also in this palace that Queen Lili'uokalani was overthrown and placed under house arrest for 9 months. *See p 15,* **8**.

Continue down King St., turn slightly right onto Kapi'olani Blvd. Turn right onto Kalākaua Ave. and follow it into Waikīkī. Bus: 19 or 20.

Day 5

From Waikīkī, take H-1 East, which becomes the Kalaniana'ole Hwy. Look for the Koko Head Regional Park on the left; the beach is on the right (ocean side). Avoid the crowds by going early, about 8am, on a weekday morning; once the parking lot is full, you're out of luck. The Hanauma Bay Shuttle Bus (TheBus: 22) runs from Waikīkī to Hanauma Bay every half-hour from 8:45am to 1pm. You can catch it at any city bus stop in Waikīkī. It returns every hour from noon to 4pm.

14 ★★★ Hanauma Bay. Spend the morning at O'ahu's best snorkeling beach (note that the beach is closed on Tues). *See p 155.*

Continue to drive east on Kalaniana'ole Hwy. Look for mile marker 11.

15 Halona Blowhole. *See p 143,* **3**.

Continue to drive east on Kalaniana'ole Hwy. Look for the sign for Makapu'u Point.

16 ★★ Makapu'u Point Light House. Hike out to this 647-foot-high (197m) cliff and functioning lighthouse, where, on winter days, you can often spot whales cavorting in the ocean. *See p 144,* **6**.

Turn left onto Kalaniana'ole Hwy. Turn right onto W. Hind Dr. Bus: 23.

17 ★ Uncle Clay's House of Pure Aloha. Here's a rare shave ice spot that uses syrups made with local fruit. Unlike other places that rely on artificially colored and flavored syrups, at Uncle Clay's, the pineapple and mango are the real deal. Top it off with a scoop of ice cream. *820 W. Hind Dr. Unit 116* ☎ *808/373-5111. $.*

Turn right onto Kalaniana'ole Hwy. Continue onto HI-72. Take exit 26 and merge onto Wai'alae Ave. Turn left onto 16th Ave. Turn left onto Harding Ave. Turn right onto 18th Ave. Turn right onto Diamond Head Rd. and into Diamond Head Crater Parking. Bus: 23.

18 ★ Diamond Head. Get a bird's-eye view of the island from atop this 760-foot (232m) extinct volcano. *See p 165.*

Head left on Diamond Head Road. Continue down Monsarrat Ave.

19 ★ Diamond Head Market and Grill. Grab dinner at this casual takeout spot—try a local plate like 'ahi (tuna) steaks or kalbi (Korean-marinated short ribs). Don't miss dessert: the lemon crunch cake is a perfect capper to a Diamond Head hike. *3158 Monsarrat Ave., www.diamondheadmarket.com.* ☎ *808/732-0077. $.*

Head back into Waikīkī via Ala Wai Blvd. Bus: 19 or 20.

Day 6

Take Ala Wai Blvd. out of Waikīkī. Turn right at Kalākaua Ave., left on S. Beretania St., and then right at Pi'ikoi St. Make a left on Lunalilo St. and bear left onto H-1 West. Take Exit 20B, which puts you on Haloma St. Turn right at

The molten lava demonstration at the Bishop Museum

Houghtailing St. and then left on Bernice St. Bus: 2.

⑳ ★★★ **Bishop Museum.** Spend most of the day in this entrancing museum. It covers everything you've always wanted to know about Hawai'i, from grass shacks to how a volcano works. The Science Center, with a molten lava demonstration, and the Planetarium, with shows on how to read the night sky, will delight the young ones. *See p 21.*

Turn right out of the parking lot onto Bernice St. Go right on Houghtailing St. and left on Olomea St. Continue on to N. Vineyard St. Merge onto H-1 east. Take exist 25B for 6th Ave. Turn right onto 6th Ave. Turn right onto Ho'olulu St. Turn left onto Kapahulu Ave. Bus: 2.

Kids' surf lessons on Waikīkī Beach

㉑ **Surf lesson in Waikīkī.** End the day with a late afternoon surf session, when the sun is less hot. Waikīkī has great waves for learning, and a surf lesson with Hans Hedemann Surf School will have your kids riding the waves in no time. ⏲ *2 hr. At the Park Shore Waikīkī. www.hhsurf.com.* ☎ *808/924-7778. $75 for 2-hour group lesson.*

Day 7

Take H-1 west out of Waikiki. Take exit 20A to merge onto HI-63 north/Kalihi St. toward Likelike Hwy. After 7 miles (11km) take the right exit to the HI-83 west/Kahekili Hwy. ramp. Continue onto Kahekili Hwy for 10 miles (16km). Bus 40, 53, or 55.

㉒ ★★ **Kualoa Ranch.** Kids will love any one of the adventure packages offered, which include horseback riding and ATV rides that take you through the locations where movies like *Jurassic Park* and *Godzilla* were filmed. *See p 28.*

Head south on HI-83 for about 10 miles (16km). Merge onto HI-63 north. Continue onto Kāne'ohe Bay Dr. Continue onto Mokapu Saddle Rd. Turn right on Oneawa. Turn left onto Kainui Dr. Turn right onto N. Kalaheo Ave. Continue onto Lihiwai Rd.

㉓ ★★★ **Kailua Beach.** Spend the rest of the day on the windward side of O'ahu at one of the island's most fabulous beaches. *See p 156.*

A Week of O'ahu History & Culture

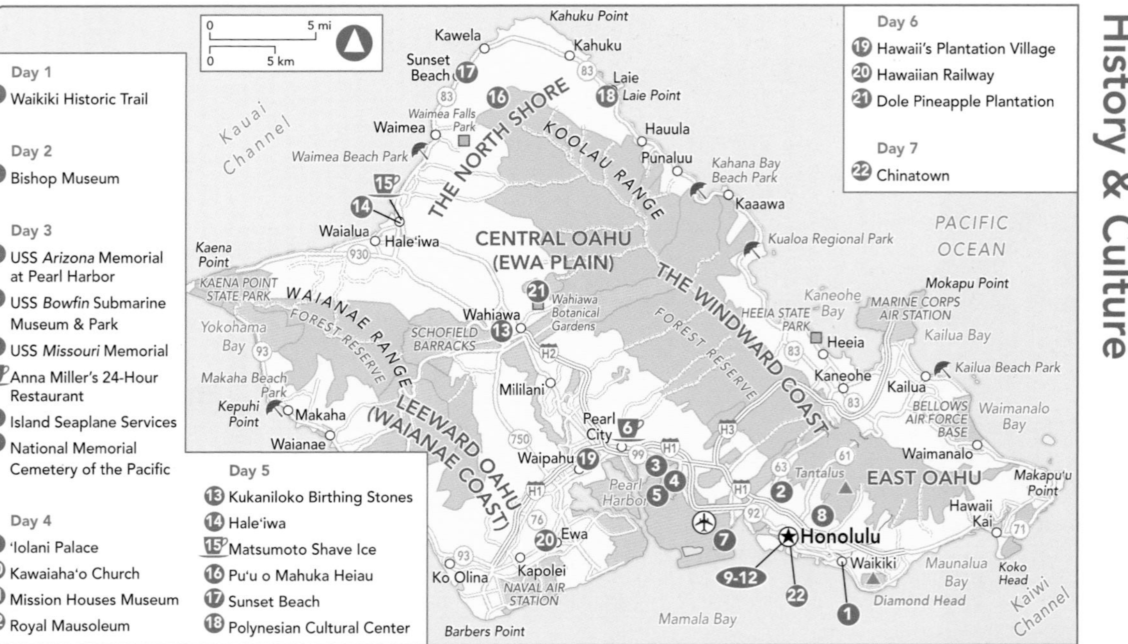

This tour covers O'ahu's most sacred and historically important spots. You'll see ancient sites, visit the birthplaces of Hawaiian royalty, learn about the days of the missionaries and plantations, and reflect on the attack on Pearl Harbor. You'll visit Waikīkī, downtown Honolulu, Chinatown, Central O'ahu, and Pearl Harbor.

Day 1

❶ ★★ **Waikīkī Historic Trail.** To get an overview of Waikīkī's history, take this 4.5-mile (7.2km) walk, with stops marked by 6-foot-tall (1.8m) surfboards explaining the history of today's favorite resort area. For a full description of the trail, see my Historic Waikīkī tour starting on p 50.

Day 2

Take Ala Wai Blvd. out of Waikīkī. Turn right at Kalākaua Ave., left on S. Beretania St., and then right at Pi'ikoi St. Make a left on Lunalilo St. and bear left on H-1 West. Take Exit 20B, which puts you on Haloma St. Turn right at Houghtailing St. and then left on Bernice St. Bus: 2.

❷ ★★★ **Bishop Museum.** Take the entire day to see this entrancing museum, which could be the highlight of your trip. *See p 21,* ❼.

Day 3

Get an early start to beat the crowds at Pearl Harbor. Drive west on H-1 past the airport to the USS *Arizona* Memorial exit and then follow the green-and-white signs; there's ample free parking. Bus: 20, then transfer to 52.

❸ ★★★ **USS *Arizona* Memorial at Pearl Harbor.** Start off your day of viewing wartime Honolulu by seeing these three important reminders of World War II. *See p 14,* ❹.

❹ ★ **USS *Bowfin* Submarine Museum & Park.** *See p 47,* ❷.

❺ ★ **USS *Missouri* Memorial.** *See p 47,* ❸.

From the ethnographic collections of the Bishop Museum

Turn right on Arizona Rd. and then left on Kamehameha Hwy. (Hwy. 99). Turn right on Kaonohi St. No bus service.

6 ★ **Anna Miller's 24-Hour Restaurant.** This always-busy casual dining restaurant is just a couple of miles away, in Pearlridge. Treat yourself to the best fresh strawberry pie on the island (with a generous helping of fluffy whipped cream). *Pearlridge Centre, 98–115 Kaonohi St. (Kamehameha Hwy.). ☎ 808/487-2421. $.*

Turn left on Kamehameha Hwy. (Hwy. 99) and merge onto Hwy. 78 East. Take Exit 3 toward the airport (Puuloa Rd., which becomes Lagoon Dr.). No bus service.

❼ ★★ **Island Seaplane Service.** See the box "World War II History from the Air" on p 48 for details.

From Lagoon Dr., turn right on Nimitz Hwy. and take H-1 East to Exit 21A (Pali Hwy.). Turn right on Kuakini St. and then left on Lusitana St. Go right again on Concordia St., left on Puowaina Dr., and then stay on Puowaina Dr. to the end of the road. Bus: 62, transfer to 6.

8 National Memorial Cemetery of the Pacific. End the day seeing the final outcome of war. The National Cemetery of the Pacific (also known as "the Punchbowl") is an ash-and-lava tuff cone that exploded about 150,000 years ago—like Diamond Head, only smaller. Early Hawaiians called it *Puowaina,* or "hill of sacrifice." The old crater is a burial ground for 35,000 victims of three American wars in Asia and the Pacific: World War II, Korea, and Vietnam. Among the graves, you'll find many unmarked ones with the date December 7, 1941, carved in the headstone. *1 hr. Punchbowl Crater, 2177 Puowaina Dr. (at the end of the road). ☎ 808/532-3720. Free. Daily 8am–5:30pm (Mar–Sept to 6:30pm).*

Day 4

If the kids are old enough to appreciate Hawaiian history (and it won't be a boring day), then start with a drive in the 'Ewa direction (west). Head out of Waikīkī on Ala Moana Blvd. Turn right (toward the mountains) on Ward Ave. and then left ('Ewa) on S. Beretania Blvd. Turn left on Richards St. The best place to park for our first stop at the 'Iolani Palace is the parking garage, Ali'i Place (1099 Alakea St.). The cost of parking is $3 per hour for the first 2 hours and $1.50 for each additional half-hour. There is limited metered street parking. After you park your car, continue up Alakea St., make a right on Hotel St. and another right on Richards St. TheBus: 2 or 13.

9 ★★ 'Iolani Palace. To understand Hawai'i, come to this royal palace, built by King David Kalākaua in 1882. *See p 15,* 8.

Continue to walk toward Diamond Head on S. King St. to Punchbowl St.

10 ★ Kawaiaha'o Church. Don't miss the crowning achievement of the first missionaries in Hawai'i—the first permanent stone church, complete with bell tower and colonial colonnade. *See p 22,* 10.

Continue in the Diamond Head direction on S. King St.

11 Mission Houses Museum. Step into life in 1820 among 19th-century American Protestant missionaries. *See p 23,* 11.

The National Memorial Cemetery of the Pacific at the Punchbowl crater

Built between 1837 and 1842, Kawaiaha'o Church is Hawaii's oldest.

Retrace your steps to your car at the parking garage. Continue in the Diamond Head direction on King St. and make a left on Alapai St. Turn left again on S. Beretania St. Take the third right onto Punchbowl St. Then go left on S. Vineyard Blvd. and right on Nu'uanu Ave. The Royal Mausoleum is located between Wyllie and Judd sts. Bus: 4.

⓬ ★ **Royal Mausoleum.** In the cool uplands of Nu'uanu, on a 3.7-acre (1.5-ha) patch of sacred land dedicated in 1865, is the final resting place of King Kalākaua, Queen Kapi'olani, and 16 other Hawaiian royals. Only the Hawaiian flag (instead of both the Hawaiian and the American) flies over this gravesite, a remnant of the kingdom. ⏲ *1 hr. 2261 Nu'uanu Ave. (between Wyllie and Judd sts.).* ☎ *808/536-7602. Free. Mon–Fri 8am–4:30pm.*

To return to Waikīkī, take Nuuanu Ave. down to Nimitz Hwy. Turn left toward Diamond Head on Nimitz Hwy., which becomes Ala Moana Blvd., and follow it into Waikīkī. Bus: 4.

Day 5

Take H-1 West out of Waikīkī. Take the H-2 North exit (Exit 8A) toward Mililani/Wahiawā. After 7 miles (11km), H-2 becomes Kamehameha Hwy. (Hwy. 80). Look for the sign between Wahiawā and Haleiwa, on Plantation Rd., opposite the road to Whitmore Village. No bus service.

⓭ **Kukaniloko Birthing Stones.** The most sacred site in central O'ahu, this is where women of ancient Hawai'i gave birth to potential *ali'i* (royalty). *See p 137,* ❶.

Retrace your route back to Kamehameha Hwy. (Hwy. 80) and turn left. At the fork in the road, remain right on Kamehameha Hwy. (which now becomes Hwy. 99). Follow the signs into Hale'iwa.

⓮ ★★★ **Hale'iwa.** Start your day exploring this famous North Shore surfing town. *See p 137,* ❷.

15 ★ **Matsumoto Shave Ice.** Take time out for a cool, sweet treat at Matsumoto's. *See p 16,* 11.

Continue down Kamehameha Hwy. for about 6½ miles (10km). Turn right (or *mauka*) on Pūpūkea Rd.,

Ancient, sacred Kukaniloko Birthstones, where royal women gave birth to future sovereigns

off Kamehameha Hwy. at Foodland, and drive .7 mile (1.1km) up a switchback road. Bus: 55, then walk up Pūpūkea Rd.

⑯ ★ **Pu'u o Mahuka Heiau.** This is the place to feel the *mana* (sacred spirit) of this 18th-century *heiau* (temple), known as the "hill of escape." Sitting on a 5-acre (2-ha), 300-foot (91m) bluff overlooking Waimea Bay and 25 miles (40km) of O'ahu's wave-lashed North Coast, this sacrificial temple (the largest on O'ahu) appears as a huge rectangle of rocks twice as big as a football field, with an altar often covered by the flower and fruit offerings left by native Hawaiians. ***Warning:*** Never walk on, climb, or even touch the rocks at a *heiau.* ⏲ *30 min. Pūpūkea Rd.*

Retrace your route back to Kamehameha Hwy. and turn right. A couple of miles down Kamehameha Hwy., you see Sunset Beach Park on your left.

⑰ ★★★ **Sunset Beach.** Spend the rest of the morning playing on Sunset Beach. During the summer months, this is a safe beach for swimming. During the winter, it's best to just sit and watch the big wave surfers. *See p 161.*

Drive another 12 miles (19km) down Kamehameha Hwy. to the town of Lā'ie. Bus: 52 to Turtle Bay Resort, then 55.

⑱ ★★ **Ha: Breath of Life at the Polynesian Cultural Center.** Catch the evening show at the Polynesian Cultural Center, the "living museum" of Polynesia. *See p 17,* ⑭.

Retrace your route back toward Hale'iwa.

Day 6

Take H-1 west to the Waikele-Waipahu exit (Exit 7); get in the left lane on the exit and turn left on Paiwa St. At the 5th light, turn right on Waipahu St.; after the 2nd light, turn left. Bus: 19 or 20 to Ala Moana Shopping Center, transfer to 42 to the Waipahu Transit Center, a 10-minute walk; if you don't want to walk, then transfer to 43 or 432.

⑲ ★ **Hawai'i's Plantation Village.** The tour of this restored 50-acre (20-ha) village offers a glimpse back in time to when sugar planters shaped the land, economy, and culture of Hawai'i. From 1852, when the first contract laborers arrived here from China, to 1947, when the plantation era ended, more than 400,000 men, women, and children from China, Japan, Portugal, Puerto Rico, Korea, and the Philippines came to work the

Fruit and flower offerings are still left at the remains of Pu'u o Mahuka Heiau temple.

Surfing on Sunset Beach

sugar cane fields. ⏲ *1½ hr. Waipahu Cultural Garden Park, 94–695 Waipahu St. (at Waipahu Depot Rd.), Waipahu. ☎ 808/677-0110. www.hawaiiplantationvillage.com. $15 adults, $12 seniors, $8 military personnel, $6 children 4–11 (includes escorted tour). Mon–Sat 10am–2pm (tours on the hour).*

Head south (Diamond Head direction) on Waipahu St. Take the 2nd left on Waikele Rd. and then continue on Pupupuhi St. Turn right on Farrington Hwy. (Hwy. 90) and turn left to merge onto Fort Weaver Rd. (Hwy. 76) toward 'Ewa Beach. Turn right on Renton Rd. TheBus: Walk to the Waipio Transit Center for E and transfer to 44.

20 ★ **Hawaiian Railway.** All aboard! This is a train ride back into history. Between 1890 and 1947, the chief mode of transportation for O'ahu's sugar mills was the O'ahu Railway and Land Co.'s narrow-gauge trains. The line carried not only equipment, raw sugar, and supplies but also passengers from one side of the island to the other. You can relive those days every Saturday and Sunday during a narrated ride from 'Ewa and ending along the coast at Kahe Point. Don't expect ocean views all the way—you're passing through the heart of suburban Honolulu, but the ride is still entertaining. On the second Sunday of the month, you can ride on the nearly 100-year-old, custom-built, parlor-observation car (no kids 12 and under on this ride). ⏲ *1½ hr. 91–1001 Renton Rd., 'Ewa Beach. ☎ 808/681-5461. www.hawaiianrailway.com. Standard ride $12 adults, $8 seniors & children 2–12, free for children 1 & under (they must be held during ride). Special Sun trip fare $25. Departures Sat 3pm and Sun 1 and 3pm.*

Retrace your route to Fort Weaver Rd. and take the H-1 East (Honolulu direction). Take Exit 8B on the left and merge onto H-2 North (Miilani/Wahiawā). Take Exit 8 onto Kamehameha Hwy. TheBus: 44, then transfer to 42, then transfer to 62, and then transfer to 52.

21 ★ **Dole Pineapple Plantation.** Conclude your day of plantation Hawai'i at this agricultural exhibit/retail area, a modern pineapple plantation with a few adventures for kids. *See p 34,* **6**.

Retrace your route back on Kamehameha Hwy. to H-1 and then take the H-1 to Waikīkī.

Day 7

22 ★★ **Chinatown.** Plan to spend the entire day in this exotic part of Honolulu. Colorful open markets, Buddhist temples, a waterside walkway, and plenty of tempting restaurants will keep you occupied for hours. For complete descriptions, see my Chinatown tour beginning on p 72.

Wartime Honolulu

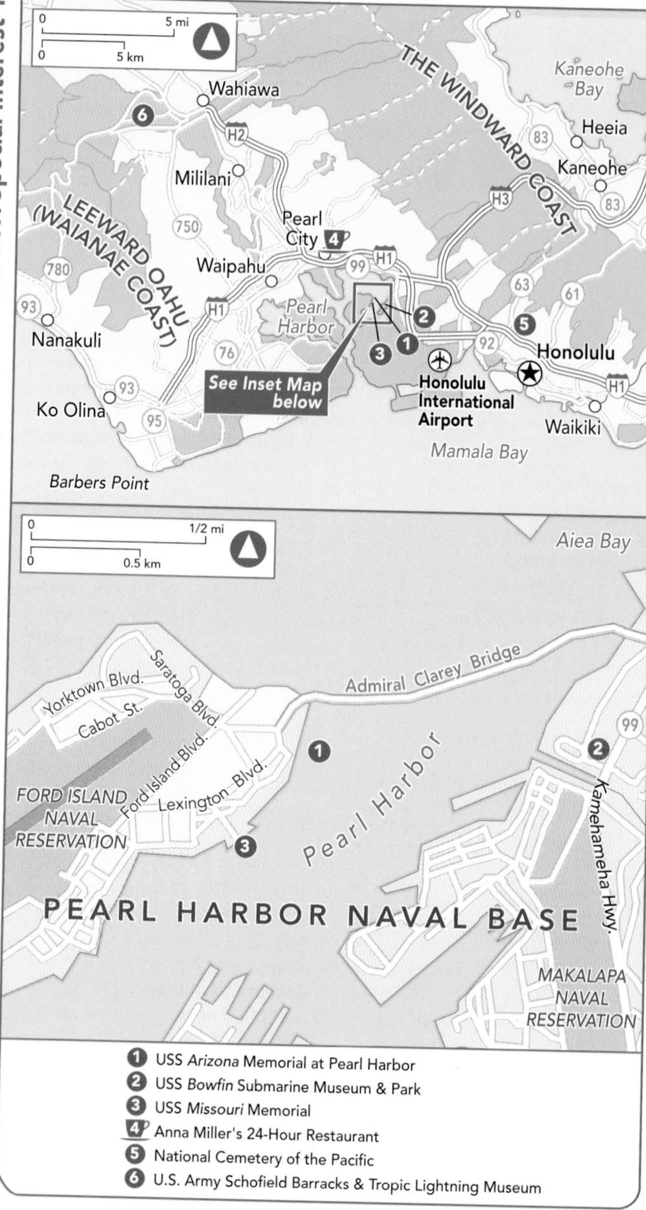

1 USS *Arizona* Memorial at Pearl Harbor
2 USS *Bowfin* Submarine Museum & Park
3 USS *Missouri* Memorial
4 Anna Miller's 24-Hour Restaurant
5 National Cemetery of the Pacific
6 U.S. Army Schofield Barracks & Tropic Lightning Museum

On December 7, 1941, Hawai'i's historic "day of infamy," Pearl Harbor was bombed by the Japanese, and the United States entered World War II. Honolulu has a rich history from the war years, and this 1-day tour covers the highlights.

Drive west on H-1 past the airport to the USS *Arizona* Memorial exit, then follow the green-and-white signs; there's ample free parking. Bus: 20, then transfer to 52.

❶ ★★★ USS *Arizona* Memorial at Pearl Harbor. No trip to Honolulu would be complete without a visit to this memorial at Pearl Harbor. *See p 14,* ❹.

❷ ★ USS *Bowfin* Submarine Museum & Park. This is a great opportunity to see what life was like on a submarine. You can go below deck of this famous vessel—nicknamed the "Pearl Harbor Avenger" for its successful attacks on the Japanese—and see how the 80-man crew lived during wartime. The *Bowfin* Museum has an impressive collection of submarine-related artifacts. The Waterfront Memorial honors submariners lost during World War II. *1 hr. 11 Arizona Memorial Dr. (next to the USS Arizona Memorial Visitor Center). ☎ 808/423-1341. www.bowfin.org. $12 adults, $8 active-duty military & seniors, $5 children 4–12; children 3 & under not permitted for safety reasons. Daily 7am–5pm.*

❸ ★ USS *Missouri* Memorial. On the deck of this 58,000-ton battleship (the last one the navy built), World War II came to an end with the signing of the Japanese surrender on September 2, 1945. I recommend taking the tour, which begins at the visitor center. Guests are shuttled to Ford Island on military-style buses while listening to a 1940s-style radio program. Once on the ship, guests watch an informational film and are then free to explore on their own or take a guided tour. Highlights of this massive battleship include the forecastle (or *fo'c's'le,* in Navy talk), where the 30,000-pound anchors are dropped on 1,080 feet (329m) of anchor chain; the 16-inch (41cm) guns, which can fire a 2,700-pound (1,225kg) shell some 23 miles (37km) in 50 seconds; and the spot where the Instrument of Surrender was signed as Douglas MacArthur, Chester Nimitz, and "Bull" Halsey looked on. *1½ hr. 11 Arizona Memorial Rd. ☎ 877/MIGHTY-MO (644-4896). www.ussmissouri.com. $27 adults, $13 children 4–12; includes 1 of 4 tours ranging from a guided tour to an audiovisual tour.*

A Pearl Harbor veteran in the Shrine Room of the USS Arizona Memorial

See World War II History from the Air

For a unique perspective on O'ahu's historical sites, I highly recommend the **Island Seaplane Service's** (☎ **808/836-6273;** www.islandseaplane.com) 1-hour tour of the island. The tour gives you aerial views of Waikīkī Beach, Diamond Head Crater, Kāhala's luxury estates, and the sparkling waters of Hanauma and Kāne'ohe bays and continues on to Chinaman's Hat, the Polynesian Cultural Center, and the rolling surf of the North Shore. The flight returns across the island, over Hawaii's historic wartime sites. The 1-hour tours costs $299 per person.

The Heart of the Missouri Tour (90 min.) is an additional $25 for adults and $12 for children. Daily 8am–4pm Sept–May, daily 8am–5pm June–Aug. Check in at the USS Bowfin Submarine Museum, next to the USS Arizona Memorial Visitor Center.

Turn right on Arizona Rd. and then left on Kamehameha Hwy. (Hwy. 99). Turn right on Honomanu St., left on Moanalua Rd., and finally right on Kaonohi St. Bus: 42, then transfer to 71.

4 ★ **Anna Miller's 24-Hour Restaurant.** My favorite casual dining treat near Pearl Harbor. See p 41 6.

Go right on Kaonohi St. and right again on Moanalua Rd. Turn right to merge onto HI-78 East, which merges onto H-1 East. Take Exit 21A (Pali Hwy.). Keep left at the fork and follow signs for HI-1. Turn left onto Pali Hwy. (Hwy. 61 N.). Take the first right onto S. School St. Turn left on Lusitana St. Take the second right onto Puowaina Dr. TheBus: 71, then transfer to Bus 62 and Bus 15.

5 ★ **National Memorial Cemetery of the Pacific.** You may know this national cemetery by its nickname, Punchbowl. The Hawaiians called this area "Pūowaina," or "hill of sacrifice." Not only is the cemetery a memorial to 35,000

The USS Bowfin Submarine Museum & Park

The 16-inch guns of the USS Missouri, site of the Japanese surrender in 1945

veterans of wars, but it is also a geological wonder—a former volcanic cone that exploded lava some 150,000 years ago. ⏲ *1 hr. Punchbowl Crater, 2177 Puowaina Dr. (at the end of the road).* ☎ *808/541-1434. www.cem.va.gov. Free. Daily 8am–5:30pm Sept 30–Mar 1, 8am–6:30pm Mar 2–Sept 29.*

Retrace your route on Puowaina Dr., then go left on Lusitana St., and right on School St. Take H-1 West to H-2 North, which becomes Hwy. 99. Turn left on Kunia Rd., then right on Lyman Rd. (through the gate). Turn right on Flagler Rd., then left on Waianae Ave. Museum is in Bldg. 361. Bus: 6, then transfer to 83 and then to 72.

6 ★ U.S. Army Schofield Barracks & Tropic Lightning Museum. With its broad, palm-lined boulevards and Art Deco buildings, this old army cavalry post is the largest of its kind still operating outside the continental U.S. today. You can no longer visit the barracks themselves, but the history of Schofield Barracks and the 25th Infantry Division is told in the small Tropic Lightning Museum. Displays range from a 1917 bunker exhibit to a replica of Vietnam's infamous Cu Chi tunnels. To get on the base, adults will need a photo I.D. Have your rental car agreement for your vehicle ready at the gate to get a free visitor pass. ⏲ *1 hr. Schofield Barracks, Bldg. 361, Wai'anae Ave.* ☎ *808/655-0438. www.garrison.hawaii.army.mil/tlm/index.html. Free. Tues–Sat 10am–4pm.*

Retrace your route back to H-2 and then take H-1 back to Waikīkī.

Historic Waikīkī

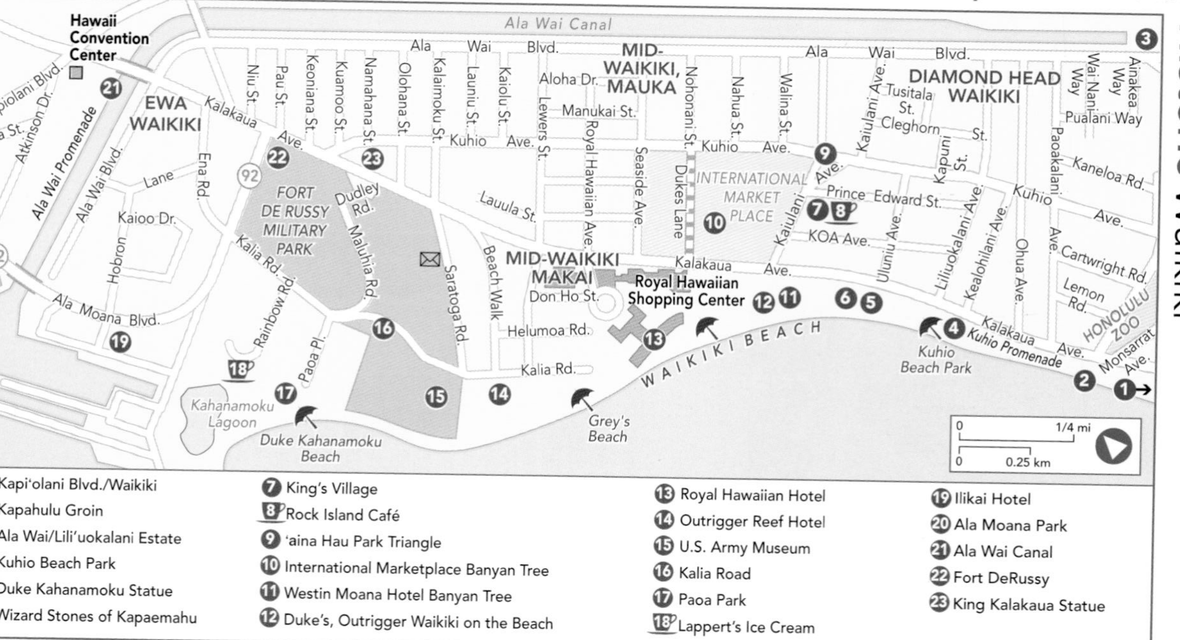

Spend a morning strolling through history. Each of the 21 Waikīkī Historic Trail Markers, 6-foot-tall (1.8m) surfboards, explains the history of Hawai'i's favorite resort area, focusing on the time before Westerners came to its shores (I've thrown in a few extra stops along the way). You could probably speed-walk the entire route in a couple of hours, but I recommend taking all morning, stopping at each one and appreciating this culturally rich area.

❶ ★ Kapi'olani Blvd./Waikīkī. In ancient times, there were two *heiau* (temples) in this area. One was *Kupalaha,* located on the shoreline at Queen's Beach and thought to be part of the *Papa'ena'ena* Heiau, where Kamehameha I made the last human sacrifice in Waikīkī. The other, *Makahuna,* near Diamond Head, encompassed all of Kapi'olani Park and was dedicated to *Kanaloa,* the god of the underworld. *Kalākaua Ave. (near the Natatorium, close to Monsarrat Ave.).*

Walk away from Diamond Head to the Groin at Kapahulu Ave.

❷ ★ Kapahulu Groin. Waikīkī has always been a popular surfing site. Near here, on the slopes of Diamond Head, a *heiau* was dedicated to *he'e nalu,* or surfing, and the priests there were responsible for announcing the surfing conditions to the village below by flying a kite. *Kalākaua & Kapahulu aves.*

Turn *mauka* up Kapahulu Ave. to Ala Wai Blvd.

❸ ★ Ala Wai/Lili'uokalani Estate. This was the site of the estate of Queen Lili'uokalani, who was overthrown by the U.S. government in 1893. She had two homes here: *Paoakalani* (royal perfume), located where the canal now stands, and *Kealohilani* (the brightness of heaven), located opposite Kūhiō Beach. *Kapahulu Ave. & Ala Wai Blvd.*

Continue in the 'Ewa direction on Ala Wai Blvd. and turn left on Paoakalani Ave. Walk down to the beach.

The Queen Lili'uokalani statue greets guests of the Hawaii State Capitol Building in Honolulu.

❹ ★ Kūhiō Beach Park. This beach park is named in honor of Prince Jonah Kalaniana'ole, Hawaii's delegate to the U.S. Congress, 1902–22. Kalaniana'ole successfully got the passage of the Homes Commission Act, giving native Hawaiians some 200,000 acres (80,937 ha) of land. His home, *Pualeilani* (flower from the wreath of heaven), was located on the beach here and was given to the city when he died. It is no longer there, but you can read about its history. *2453 Kalākaua Ave. (btw. Kealohilani & Lili'uokalani sts.).*

Continue walking in the 'Ewa direction down Kalākaua Ave.

❺ ★ Duke Kahanamoku Statue. Olympic swimming champion, internationally known surfer,

An offshore breakwater at Kūhiō Beach creates a calm, shallow swimming area.

movie actor, and Hawai'i's ambassador of Aloha, Duke Paoa Kahanamoku won three gold medals, two silvers, and a bronze in four Olympics. He introduced surfing to Europe, Australia, and the East Coast of the U.S. and appeared in movies from 1925 to 1933. There's no surfboard marker here, just the statue of Duke. *Kalākaua Ave. (btw. Lili'uokalani & Uluniu sts.).*

Continue walking in the 'Ewa direction down Kalākaua Ave.

6 ★ Wizard Stones of Kapaemahu. According to legend, four healers from Tahiti (Kapaemahu, Kahaloa, Kapuni, and Kinohi) came to Hawai'i in perhaps the 15th century. Before they left, they transferred their healing powers into these stones, which were located in Kaimukī, 2 miles (3.2km) away. No one knows how the stones, which weigh approximately 8 tons (7 metric tons), got to Waikīkī. *Diamond Head side of the Waikīkī Police Sub-Station, 2405 Kalākaua Ave.*

The legendary Wizard Stones of Kapaemahu are said to contain healing powers.

At Kaiulani Ave., turn toward the mountain to Koa Ave.

7 ★ King's Village. The home of King David Kalākaua (1836–91) once stood here, surrounded by towering coconut trees. The king loved dancing and revived the hula tradition, which the missionaries had just about succeeded in stamping out. He also loved to give parties and earned the nickname "The Merrie Monarch." The official name for the block-long shopping center that stands here today is King's Village, but everyone calls it King's Alley. *131 Ka'iulani Ave. (btw. Koa Ave. & Prince Edward St.).*

Go inside King's Village.

8 ★ Rock Island Café. Order a Cherry Coke at this nostalgic soda fountain filled with memorabilia from when "Elvis was King, Marilyn was Queen, and they both drank Coca-Cola." *King's Village, 131 Ka'iulani Ave. (btw. Koa Ave. & Prince Edward St.). ☎ 808/923-8033. $.*

Continue *mauka* on Kaiulani Ave. to Prince Edward St.

9 ★ 'āina Hau Park Triangle. This tiny park was once part of the palm tree–lined grand entrance to the 10-acre (4-ha) estate of Governor Archibald Scott Cleghorn and his wife, Hawaiian Chiefess Miriam Kapili Likelike. The chiefess (like her sister, Lili'uokalani, and her brother, Kalākaua) was a composer and wrote the song "'*āinahau*" (land of the hau tree), describing the estate lily ponds, coconut trees, hibiscus, mangos, and a giant banyan tree. The huge, two-story Victorian home stood between what are now Cleghorn and Tusitala streets. *Kaiulani & Kūhiō aves.*

Turn left on Kūhiō and enter the International Marketplace.

10 ★ International Marketplace Banyan Tree. This area once fronted the Apuakehau Stream and was the summer home of King William Kanaina Lunalilo (1835–74), the first elected king of Hawaii. The Hawaiians called him *ke alii lokomaikai,* or "the kind chief." His reign was only 1 year and 25 days—he died due to poor health. *Duke's Lane (btw. Kūhiō & Kalākaua aves.).*

Walk through the International Marketplace toward the ocean. At Kalākaua Ave., cross the street.

11 ★ Westin Moana Surfrider Hotel Banyan Tree. The first hotels in Waikīkī were just bathhouses that offered rooms for overnight stays. Then the Moana Surfrider Hotel opened its doors on March 11, 1901, with four stories (the tallest structure in Hawaii) and 75 rooms (with a bathroom and a telephone in each room). Harry Owens and Webley Edwards's radio show *Hawaii Calls,* which started in 1935, was broadcast live from the hotel. At the peak of the show's popularity, in 1952, it reached 750 stations around the globe. *2365 Kalākaua Ave. (near Kaiulani St.).*

Go next door on the 'Ewa side.

12 ★ Duke's, Outrigger Waikīkī on the Beach. The outside lanai of Duke's Canoe Club was once where the Apuakehau ("basket of dew") Stream, which flowed through the middle of Waikīkī, emptied into the ocean. In the 19th century, *Paradise of the Pacific* magazine described the river as flowing through "taro patches, rice and banana fields . . .

1950s nostalgia is on order at Rock Island Café.

[with] canoes gliding along the shining surface . . . [and] women and children catching shrimp in long narrow baskets, often stopping to eat a few." *3553 Kalākaua Ave. (across the street from Duke's Lane & Kaiulani St.).*

Continue down Kalākaua Ave. in the 'Ewa direction and turn toward the ocean at Royal Hawaiian Ave.

⑬ ★★ Royal Hawaiian Hotel. At one time, this area, known then as Helumoa, was a royal coconut grove filled with 10,000 coconut trees, first planted in the 16th century by Chief Kakuhihewa. Later, Kamehameha I camped here before his conquest of O'ahu. After winning battles in Nu'uanu, he made Waikīkī the capital of the Hawaiian Islands. In 1927, the Royal Hawai'i Hotel opened with 400 rooms. It cost $5 million to build. See p 109. *2365 Kalākaua Ave. (Royal Hawaiian Ave.). ☎ 808/922-3111.*

Retrace your steps back to Kalākaua Ave. and turn left. Turn left (toward the ocean) at Lewers St., then turn right at Kalia Rd.

⑭ ★ Outrigger Reef Hotel. Waikīkī is known today for its incredible beauty, but in the olden days, it was known by the Hawaiians as a powerful place of healing. Very successful *kahuna la'au lapa'au* (medical physicians) lived in this area, and the royal families often came here to convalesce. The beach, stretching from where the Halekulani Hotel is today to the Outrigger Reef, was called *Kawehewehe* (removal), because if you bathed in the waters, your illness would be removed. *2169 Kalia Rd. (Lewers St.). ☎ 808/923-3111.*

⑮ ★ U.S. Army Museum. The grounds where the museum stands today were once the 3-acre (1.2-ha) estate and villa of Chung Afong, Hawaii's first Chinese millionaire and member of King David Kalākaua's privy council. Afong arrived in Honolulu in 1849 and in just 6 years made a fortune in retail, real estate, sugar, rice, and opium (he had the only government license to sell it). In 1904, the U.S. Army Corp of Engineers bought the property for $28,000 to defend Honolulu Harbor. On December 7, 1976, it became a museum. *Ft. DeRussy, near Saratoga & Kalia roads. ☎ 808/955-9552. www.hiarmymuseumsoc.org. Free. Tues–Sat 9am–5pm.*

The coconut grove at the Royal Hawaiian Hotel

Fans of iconic swimmer, surfer and aloha ambassador Duke Paoa Kahanamoku still drape his statue with leis.

Continue in the 'Ewa direction on Kalia Rd.

⑯ ★ **Kalia Road.** In 1897, Fort DeRussy, from Kalia Road *mauka* some 13 acres (5.3 ha), was the largest fish pond in Waikīkī. Called *Ka'ihikapu,* this pond, like hundreds of others in Waikīkī, functioned as "royal iceboxes" where *'ama'ama* (mullet) and *awa* (milkfish) were raised in brackish water. Hawaiians have lots of legends about fishponds, which they believed were protected by *mo'o* (lizards) that could grow to some 12 to 30 feet (4–9m). In 1908, it took the U.S. military more than 250,000 cubic yards of landfill and 1 year to cover Ka'ihikapu. *Kalia Rd. (btw. Saratoga Rd. & Ala Moana Blvd.); mauka to Kalākaua Ave.*

Continue in the 'Ewa direction on Kalia Rd.

⑰ ★ **Paoa Park.** The 20 acres (8 ha) where the Hilton Hawaiian Village stands today was home to Olympic champion Duke Kahanamoku's mother's family, the Paoas. Duke's grandfather, Ho'olae Paoa, was a descendant of royal chiefs and got the land from King Kamehameha III in the Great Mahele of 1848, which allowed the king, chiefs, and commoners to claim private titles to land and for the first time allowed foreigners to own land in Hawai'i. *Kalia Rd. (bordered by Paoa Rd. & Ala Moana Ave.).*

Walk inside the Hilton Hawaiian Village to the Rainbow Bazaar.

18 ★ **Lappert's Ice Cream.** Before you leave the Hilton Hawaiian Village, take an ice-cream break at this yummy local shop, which has some 33 flavors. (My favorite is the Kona coffee.) *Rainbow Bazaar, Hilton Hawaiian Village, 2005 Kalia Rd. (Ala Moana Blvd.).* ☎ *808/943-0256.* www.lappertshawaii.com. *$.*

Make a left on Ala Moana Blvd.

⑲ ★ **Ilikai Hotel.** Waikīkī's third stream, Pi'inaio, once originated here, where the hotel's lanai is today. However, unlike the other two streams (Kuekkaunahi and Apuakehau), Pi'inaio was a muddy delta area with several smaller streams pouring in. It also was a very productive fishing area filled with reef fish, crabs, shrimp,

Waikīkī: It Ain't What It Used to Be

Before Westerners showed up on O'ahu, Waikīkī was a 2,000-acre (809-ha) swamp (compared to the 500 acres/202 ha it occupies today). Waikīkī (which means spouting water) was a very important area because it held the drainage basin for the 5 million gallons (18,927 cubic m) of daily rainfall from the Ko'olau Mountains. When Hawaiians settled in Waikīkī (which historians estimate was around A.D. 600), they slowly turned the swamp into a Hawaiian version of a breadbasket: taro fields, fishponds, and gardens for fruits and vegetables. When Western boats began calling at Honolulu Harbor, they brought the pesky mosquito, which loved the swamps of Waikīkī. In 1927, the just-completed Ala Wai Canal not only drained the swamps but opened up lands that eventually became the resort area of today.

lobster, octopus, eels, and *limu* (seaweed). However, today, Waikīkī is nearly fished out. *1777 Ala Moana Blvd. (at Hobron Lane).*

Continue in the 'Ewa direction down Ala Moana Blvd. After you cross the bridge, look for the marker on the corner of Atkinson Dr. at the entrance to the park.

⑳ ★★ **Ala Moana Park.** In the late 1800s, Chinese farmers moved into Waikīkī and converted the area now occupied by the park and shopping center into duck ponds. In 1931, the city and county of Honolulu wanted to clean up the waterfront and built a park here. In 1959, the 50 acres (20 hectares) across the street opened as one of the largest shopping centers in the U.S. *Diamond Head corner of the entrance to the park, Ala Moana Blvd. (at Atkinson Dr.).*

Turn right toward the mountains on Atkinson Dr. Bear right on Kapi'olani Blvd. The Convention Center is on the corner of Kapi'olani Blvd. and Kalākaua Ave. Go around the back of the center by the Ala Wai Canal to find the marker.

㉑ ★ **Ala Wai Canal.** At the turn of the 20th century, people on

A protected beach and shady lawns make Ala Moana Park a favorite island playground.

Fort DeRussy Beach Park

O'ahu were not very happy with Waikīkī, with its smelly duck farms, coupled with the zillions of mosquitoes from the stagnant swamp lands. Work began on the Ala Wai (fresh water) Canal in 1922 and was completed in 1928. Once the canal had drained the wetlands, the taro and rice fields dried up, and the duck farms and fish ponds disappeared. *Ala Wai Canal Side of the Convention Center, 1801 Kalākaua Ave. (Ala Wai Canal). ☎ 808/943-3500.*

Continue in the Diamond Head direction down Kalākaua to the park on the corner of Ala Moana Blvd.

㉒ ★ **Fort DeRussy.** This green recreation area was named after Brigadier General Rene E. DeRussy, Corps of Engineers, who served in the American-British War of 1812. All of Fort DeRussy and all the land from here to the foothills of Mānoa Valley were planted with taro. By 1870, the demand for taro had diminished, and the Chinese farmers began planting rice in the former taro fields. *Near the corner of Ala Moana Blvd. & Kalākaua Ave.*

Continue toward Diamond Head on Kalākaua Ave. to the intersection of Kūhiō Ave.

㉓ ★ **King Kalākaua Statue.** Next to Kamehameha I, King David Kalākaua is Hawai'i's best-known king and certainly lived up to his nickname, "the Merrie Monarch." He was born to royal parents in 1836, raised in the court of King Kamehameha IV, and elected to the position of king in 1874, after King William Lunalilo died. During his 17-year reign, he restored Hawai'i's rapidly fading culture of chanting, music, and hula (which had been banned by the missionaries for years). He was also forced to sign what has been termed the "Bayonet Constitution," which restricted his royal powers, in 1887. In 1890, he sailed to California for medical treatment and died in San Francisco due to a mild stroke, kidney failure, and cirrhosis. *Kūhiō & Kalākaua aves. intersection.*

King David Kalākaua, affectionately remembered as the "Merrie Monarch"

O'ahu's Best **Gardens**

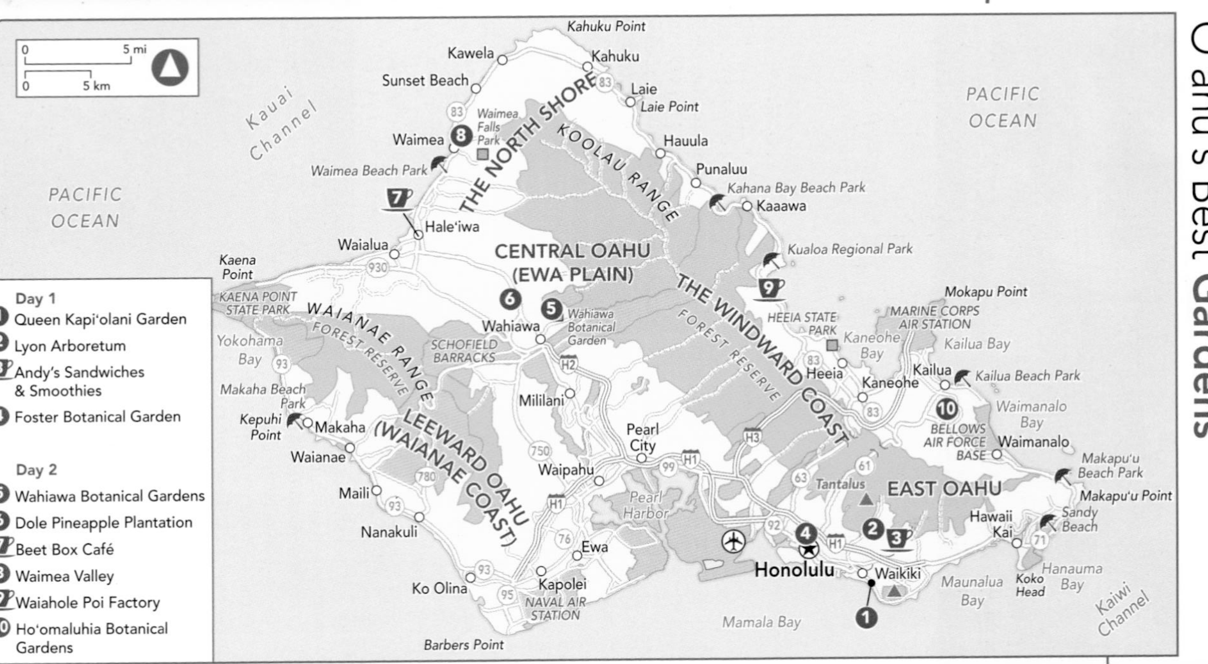

Day 1
1. Queen Kapi'olani Garden
2. Lyon Arboretum
3. Andy's Sandwiches & Smoothies
4. Foster Botanical Garden

Day 2
5. Wahiawa Botanical Gardens
6. Dole Pineapple Plantation
7. Beet Box Café
8. Waimea Valley
9. Waiahole Poi Factory
10. Ho'omaluhia Botanical Gardens

Stop and smell the tuberoses. Or the plumeria. Spend a couple of days exploring the various gardens of Hawai'i, from native Hawaiian plants to orchids, palms, aroids, tree ferns, heliconias, calatheas, and myriad trees.

Located in Waikīkī next door to Kapi'olani Park, on Monsarrat Ave. (between Paki and Leahi aves.). The parking entrance is on Leahi Ave. Bus: 19 or 20.

Day 1

❶ ★ Queen Kapi'olani Garden. Wander into this tiny garden and smell the tropical ornamentals, hibiscus cultivars, and a small collection of native Hawaiian plants. 🕓 *30 min. Kapi'olani Park, on Monsarrat Ave. (btw. Paki & Leahi aves.). Free. Daily 24 hr.*

Head in the Diamond Head direction out of Waikīkī by taking Ala Wai Blvd. Turn right on McCully St., then right on Kapi'olani Blvd., left at University Ave., and right on O'ahu. Look for the slight right at Mānoa Rd. Bus: 8, then transfer to 5.

❷ ★ Lyon Arboretum. Six-story-tall breadfruit trees. Yellow orchids no bigger than a coin. Ferns with fuzzy buds as big as a human head. Lyon Arboretum is 194 budding acres (79 ha) of botanical wonders. Take the self-guided 20-minute hike through this cultivated rainforest to Inspiration Point, and you'll pass more than 5,000 exotic tropical plants full of bird song. 🕓 *2–3 hr. 3860 Mānoa Rd. (near the top of the road). ☎ 808/988-0456. www.hawaii.edu/lyonarboretum. Suggested donation $5 each. Mon–Fri 9am–4pm, Sat 9am–3pm.*

Retrace your route back down E. Mānoa Rd. Bus: 6.

A lotus flower at Lyon Arboretum

❸ ★ Andy's Sandwiches & Smoothies. On the way down the hill, stop at this friendly neighborhood eatery. The tuna or roasted turkey sammies are my favorites. *2904 E. Mānoa Rd., opposite Mānoa Marketplace. ☎ 808/988-6161. www.andyssandwiches.com. $.*

Take E. Mānoa Rd. and make a slight left on Mānoa Rd. Continue to Punahou Rd. Turn right on the H-1 West (Lunalilo Hwy.) ramp to Exit 22, Vineyard Blvd. Bus: 6, then transfer to A.

❹ ★★ Foster Botanical Garden. The giant trees that tower over the main terrace of this leafy oasis were planted in the 1850s by William Hillebrand, a German physician and botanist. Today, this 14-acre (5.7-ha) public garden, on the north side of Chinatown, is a living museum of plants, some rare and endangered, collected from the tropical regions of the world. Of special interest are 26 "Exceptional Trees" protected by state law, a large palm collection, a primitive cycad garden, and a hybrid orchid collection. 🕓 *2–3 hr. 50 N. Vineyard Blvd. (at Nuuanu Ave.). ☎ 808/522-7066. www1.honolulu.*

A cannonball tree at Foster Botanical Garden

gov/parks/hbg/fbg.htm. $5 adults, $1 children 6–12, free for children 5 & under. Daily 9am–4pm; guided tours Mon–Fri 1pm (reservations recommended).

To get back to Waikīkī, drive toward Diamond Head on Vineyard Blvd. Merge onto H-1 East into Waikīkī. Bus: 2.

Day 2

Take H-1 from Waikīkī to H-2, which becomes Kamehameha Hwy. (Hwy. 99). Turn right at California Ave. TheBus: 19 or 20 then transfer to TheBus 40 or 52.

5 ★ Wahiawā Botanical Garden. Originally begun as an experimental arboretum by sugar planters in the 1920s, this 27-acre (11-ha) tropical rainforest garden provides a cool, moist environment for native Hawaiian plants, palms, aroids, tree ferns, heliconias, calatheas, and epiphytic plants. Guided tours can be arranged (call in advance), but there's probably no need for it unless you're an avid gardener. Bring mosquito repellant. *1½–2 hr. 1396 California Ave. (at Iliwa Dr.), Wahiawā. ☎ 808/621-7321. www.honolulu.gov/parks/hbg/wbg.htm. Free. Daily 9am–4pm.*

Go back to Kamehameha Hwy. Turn right and head to the Dole Plantation, 3 miles (5km) past Wahiawā. Bus: 52.

6 ★ Dole Pineapple Plantation. This rest stop/retail outlet/exhibit area also has an interesting self-guided tour through eight minigardens totaling about 1½ acres (.6 ha). The Pineapple Garden Maze, which covers more than 2 acres (.8 ha) with a 1.7-mile (2.7km) hibiscus-lined path. See p 34, 5.

Continue north on Kamehameha Hwy. At the traffic circle, make a left into Hale'iwa. Bus: 52.

7 ★ Beet Box Café. Flavors pack a punch at this vegetarian restaurant, in the form of satisfying sandwiches with portobello and feta or avocado and local greens. The breakfast burritos and smoothies are popular, too. *66-437 Kamehameha Hwy., www.thebeetboxcafe.com. ☎ 808/637-3000. Breakfast and lunch daily. $*

Continue north on Kamehameha Hwy. Turn right onto Waimea Valley Rd. Bus: 52.

8 ★ Waimea Valley. This 1,875-acre (759-ha) park (home to 36 botanical gardens, with about 6,000 rare species of plants and numerous Hawaiian archaeological sites) emphasizes perpetuating and sharing the "living Hawaiian culture." The public is invited to hike the trails and spend a day in this quiet oasis. The botanical collection has 35

Moku Mo'o (Lizard Islet), a freshwater lake at Ho'omaluhia Botanical Garden

Tropical rainforest plants thrive at Wahiawa Botanical Garden

different gardens, including super-rare Hawaiian species such as the endangered *Kokia cookei* hibiscus, and the largest public collection of *kalo*, or taro, varieties. Cultural activities include lei-making, kapa demonstrations, hula lessons, Hawaiian games and crafts, and music and storytelling. ⏲ *2–3 hr. 59–864 Kamehameha Hwy. (Waimea Valley Rd.).* ☎ *808/638-7766.* ***www.waimeavalley.net.*** *$16 adults, $12 seniors, $8 children 4–12. Daily 9am–5pm.*

Continue on Kamehameha Hwy. for 30 miles (48km) and then turn right on Waiahole Valley Rd. Bus: 55.

9 ★ Waiāhole Poi Factory. After seeing all the different kalo varieties at Waimea Valley, it's time to eat it as the locals do. Pair poi, the mashed root of kalo, with laulau (pork wrapped with the kalo leaves and then swaddled in ti leaves and steamed). Get a side of hō'io salad, made with tender fiddlehead ferns that grow wild on the island. For dessert, try the kulolo, a sticky, steamed concoction of grated taro and coconut. And to finish off your edible botanical exploration, wash it all down with mamaki tea, which native Hawaiians believed had beneficial health and medicinal properties. *48-140 Kamehameha Hwy. www.waiaholepoifactory.com.* ☎ *808/239-2222. Daily 11am–5pm. $.*

Continue on Kamehameha Hwy. Merge onto HI-63 north. Turn right onto Anoi Rd. Turn right onto Luluku Rd. Bus: 55.

10 ★ Ho'omaluhia Botanical Gardens. This 400-acre (162-ha) botanical garden at the foot of the steepled Ko'olau Mountains is the perfect place for a picnic. Its name means "a peaceful refuge," and that's exactly what the Army Corps of Engineers created when they installed a flood-control project here, which resulted in a 32-acre (13-ha) freshwater lake (no swimming allowed) and garden. The gardens feature geographical groupings of plantings from the major tropical regions around the world, with a special emphasis on native Hawaiian plants. ⏲ *2–3 hr. 45–680 Luluku Rd. (Visitor Center), Kāne'ohe.* ☎ *808/233-7323.* ***https://www.honolulu.gov/parks/hbg.html.*** *Free. Daily 9am–4pm; guided nature hikes Sat 10am & Sun 1pm (register via phone in advance).*

Continue on Luluku Rd. and then turn right on Kamehameha Hwy. (Hwy. 83). Turn right on Pali Hwy. and then take H-1 East back to Waikīkī. Bus: 55 then transfer to 19 or 20.

Honolulu for **Art Lovers**

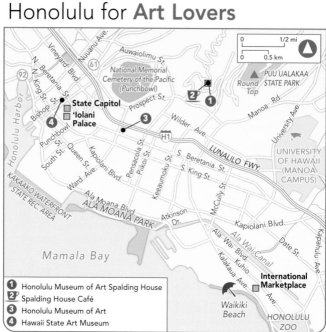

1 Honolulu Museum of Art Spalding House
2 Spalding House Café
3 Honolulu Museum of Art
4 Hawaii State Art Museum

Even if you're not a die-hard art lover, you won't regret giving up a day for this tour. Hawai'i's top three cultural galleries aren't just depositories of artwork—each is an incredible edifice in its own right. It's a part of Hawaii you won't want to miss.

Head in the 'Ewa direction out of Waikīkī by taking Ala Wai Blvd. Turn right on McCully St., left on Beretania St., and then right on Punahou St. Turn left on Nehoa St., then right on Makiki St. When the road forks, take the left onto Makiki Heights Dr. and follow the road about a mile. You will see the sign on the right, just before a hairpin turn. After the turn, the museum entrance is on your right. Bus: 15.

1 ★★ Honolulu Museum of Art Spalding House. Honolulu's best contemporary art gallery is nestled up on the slopes of Tantalus, one of Honolulu's upscale residential communities, and is renowned for its Asian gardens (with reflecting pools, sun-drenched terraces, and

An environmental sculpture at Honolulu Museum of Art Spalding House.

Shangri La in Hawai'i

In the late 1930s, heiress Doris Duke developed her dream property and dubbed it "Shangri La." It reflects Duke's love of both Hawai'i and the Middle East by featuring Islamic art and architecture blended with Hawai'i's sweeping ocean views, exotic gardens, and water features. Tours (2.5 hr.) originate at the Honolulu Museum of Arts, 900 S. Beretania St. (at Ward Ave.), and cost $25. Reservations are required (book at least a week in advance; this tour is popular). For more information, visit www.shangrilahawaii.org or call ☎ **808/532-DUKE** (3853).

views of Diamond Head). Exploring the grounds alone is worth the trip. ⏲ *1½–2 hr. 2411 Makiki Heights Dr. (near Mott-Smith Dr.). ☎ 808/526-1322. honolulumuseum.org/11981-spalding_house. $10 adults, free for children 17 & under. Free garden & gallery tour 1:30pm Tues–Sun. Tues–Sat 10am–4pm, Sun noon–4pm.*

2 ★ Spalding House Café. Treat yourself to the sinfully delicious flourless chocolate cake and a just-brewed latte at this intimate cafe. Call ahead and reserve a Lauhala and Lunch picnic for the lawn. The spread for costs $40 and includes sandwiches or salad, cookies, and drinks packed into a picnic basket. *2411 Makiki Heights Dr. (near Mott-Smith Dr.). ☎ 808/237-5225. http://honolulumuseum.org/12001-contemporary_cafe. $$.*

Turn left and drive down Makiki Height St. Turn left at Mott-Smith Dr., right on Piikoi St., left on Pensacola St., and right on Beretania St. Bus: 15.

3 ★★★ Honolulu Museum of Art. This museum features one of the top Asian art collections in the country. Also on exhibit are American and European masters and prehistoric works of Mayan, Greek, and Hawaiian art. The museum's award-winning architecture is a paragon of graciousness, featuring magnificent courtyards, lily ponds, and tasteful galleries. ⏲ *2–3 hr. 900 S. Beretania St. (at Ward Ave.). ☎ 808/532-8700, or 808/532-8701. www.honolulumuseum.org. $10 adults, $5 children 4–17, free for children 3 & under; free the 3rd Sun each month (11am–5pm) & 1st Wed each month. Tues–Sat 10am–4:30pm, Sun 1–5pm.*

Drive 'Ewa on Beretania St. and turn left on Richards St. Park at a meter on the street. TheBus: Walk about a half-mile down Beretania St. to Punchbowl St., then get TheBus 1, 2, 13, or 1L.

4 ★ Hawai'i State Art Museum. This historic building was once the Royal Hawaiian Hotel, built in 1872 during the reign of King Kamehameha V. All 360 works on display were created by living Hawaiian artists. ⏲ *2–3 hr. 250 S. Hotel St. (at Richards St.). ☎ 808/586-0900. http://sfca.hawaii.gov Free. Tues–Sat 10am–4pm, 1st Fri each month 6–9pm.*

From Richards St., turn left on King St., then take a slight right at Kapi'olani Blvd., right on Piikoi, and left on Ala Moana Blvd. into Waikīkī. Bus: 19.

Romantic Honolulu & O'ahu

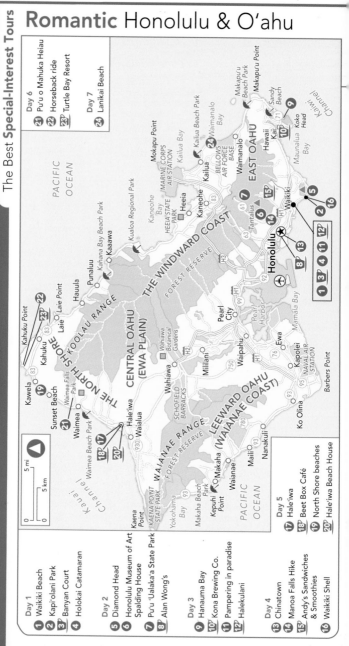

Day 1
1 Waikiki Beach
2 Kapi'olani Park
3 Banyan Court
4 Holokai Catamaran

Day 2
5 Diamond Head
6 Honolulu Museum of Art Spalding House
7 Pu'u 'Ualaka'a State Park
8 Alan Wong's

Day 3
9 Hanauma Bay
10 Kona Brewing Co.
11 Pampering in paradise
12 Halekulani

Day 4
13 Chinatown
14 Manoa Falls Hike
15 Andy's Sandwiches & Smoothies
16 Waikiki Shell

Day 5
17 Hale'iwa
18 Beet Box Café
19 North Shore beaches
20 Hale'iwa Beach House

Day 6
21 Pu'u o Mahuka Heiau
22 Horseback ride
23 Turtle Bay Resort

Day 7
24 Lanikai Beach

What could be more romantic than a vacation in Waikīkī, where the gentle breezes caress your skin, the sensuous aroma of tropical flowers wafts through the air, and the relaxing sound of the surf beckons lovers from around the globe? Below is a suggested tour for discovering the exotic isle of O'ahu, and each other.

Day 1

1 ★★★ Waikīkī Beach. Your vacation starts when the warm sand covers your toes and the salt air kisses your face. Take a stroll hand-in-hand down this famous beach. *See p 161.*

Walk down Kalākaua Ave.

2 ★★ Kapi'olani Park. If you aren't too tired from your trip, explore this tropical park. Stop to smell the flowers and kiss your sweetie. See my tour of the park beginning on p 86.

Walk back to Waikīkī on Kalākaua Ave. and stop just across from Kaiulani St.

3 ★ Banyan Court. Sit oceanside at this outdoor bar and order a tropical cocktail, such as a mai tai. *Moana Surfrider, 2365 Kalākaua Ave. (Kaiulani St.). ☎ 808/921-4600. www.moana-surfrider.com. $$.*

Walk along Waikīkī Beach toward the Halekulani.

4 ★ *Holokai Catamaran.* Spend your first evening in paradise by sailing into the sunset. If it's Friday night, sign up for the Fireworks Sail and watch the weekly Hilton Hawaiian Village fireworks show from the ocean, where it seems like the display explodes right above you. *1–1½. Gray's Beach in front of the Halekulani. www.sailholokai.com.* ☎ ***808/922-2210.*** *All cruises 1½ hr. Sunset Sail $55. Fireworks Sail $50.*

Day 2

From the intersection of Diamond Head Rd. and 18th Ave, follow the road through the tunnel (closed 6pm–6am) and park in the lot. Bus: 22.

5 ★ Diamond Head. You'll probably be up early on your first few days in Hawai'i before you get used to the time difference. So greet the sun by hiking up to Waikīkī's most famous landmark. You'll get a bird's-eye view of the island from atop this 760-foot (232m) extinct volcano. *See p 165.*

Gentle water conditions make Kailua Beach a great place to kayak.

Turn left onto 18th Ave. then left onto Harding Ave. and left onto 11th Ave. Take H-1 west to exit 23/Lunalilo St. Merge onto Lunalilo St. and turn right onto Kewalo St. Turn left onto Nehoa St. Follow Mott Smith Dr. to Makīkī Heights Dr. Bus: 2 to 6 to 15.

6 ★★ Honolulu Museum of Art Spalding House. For a romantic luncheon on the grounds, reserve a Lauhala and Lunch picnic (see p 62–63 1 and 2).

Go back down Makīkī Heights Dr. to Makīkī St. and turn left. Turn left onto Round Top Dr. No bus service.

7 ★ Pu'u 'Ualaka'a State Park. One of the island's most romantic sunset views is from this 1,048-foot (319m) hill named for sweet potatoes. Get there before sunset to see the panoramic view of the entire coastline. *See p 21, 6.*

From Round Top Dr., turn right onto Makīkī St. Turn left onto Nehoa St. Turn right onto Punahou St. Turn left onto Bingham St. Turn right onto Artesian St. Turn left onto S. King St.

The view from the top of Diamond Head

Catamaran cruises depart from several locations along Waikīkī Beach.

8 ★★★ Alan Wong's. This is one of the island's best restaurants. There's no view here, but it hardly matters with such deliciously stunning dishes as the ginger-crusted onaga, steamed clams with kālua pig, and, to finish, a haupia sorbet in a chocolate shell, made to look just like a coconut. *See p 94.*

Return to Waikīkī via McCully St.

Day 3

From Waikīkī, take H-1 East, which becomes Kalaniana'ole Hwy. Look for the Koko Head Regional Park on the left; the beach is on the right (ocean side). The Hanauma Bay Shuttle Bus (TheBus: 22) runs from Waikīkī to Hanauma Bay every half-hour from 8:45am to 1pm. You can catch it at any city bus stop in Waikīkī. It returns every hour from noon to 4pm.

9 ★★★ Hanauma Bay. Rent a mask, snorkel, and fins and head out to O'ahu's premiere snorkeling area to discover the incredible beauty of Hawai'i's underwater world. ***Note:*** The beach is closed on Tuesdays. *See p 155.*

Return to Kalaniana'ole Hwy. (Hwy. 72), heading back to Waikīkī. It's a 1.5-mile walk, or about 30 minutes. TheBus: 22.

10 ★ **Kona Brewing Co.** Stop by this local brewing company to sample some of its beer, such as the Fire Rock Pale Ale or the Liliko'i Wheat Ale (or the nonalcoholic Gingerade, made from organic ginger). *Koko Marina Center, 7192 Kalanianaole Hwy. (Lunalilo Home Rd.). www.konabrewingco.com.* ☎ *808/396-5662. $$.*

Trace your route back to Waikīkī.

⑪ **Pampering in Paradise.** Spend the afternoon at a spa getting pampered. For my top picks, see "Pampering in Paradise" on p 106.

12 ★★★ **Halekulani.** While away the rest of the evening at this exquisitely beautiful resort. Order a cocktail and watch the sunset from House without a Key and then head upstairs to La Mer, O'ahu's most romantic restaurant, where the windows frame swoonfully beautiful views of the ocean and Diamond Head. *See p 105.*

Pamper yourself at the aptly named Halekulani (House Befitting Heaven) Hotel.

Day 4

⑬ ★★★ **Chinatown.** Explore this exotic neighborhood with the help of the tour starting on p 72. Be sure to shop for a lei for your sweetie.

Take H-1 east and take exit 23 for Punahou St. Turn left onto Punahou St. Continue onto Mānoa Rd. Bus 6.

⑭ ★★ **Mānoa Falls Hike.** Take this easy, .75-mile (1.2km) one-way hike in a warm, tropical rainforest just minutes from Waikīkī. In less

The Lei

There's no doubt about it: Getting lei'd in Hawaii is a sensuous experience. The stunning tropical beauty of the delicate garland, the deliciously sweet fragrance of the blossoms, the way the flowers curl softly around your neck. Leis are much more than just a decorative necklace of flowers; they're also one of the nicest ways to say hello, good-bye, congratulations, I salute you, or I love you. The custom of giving leis can be traced back to Hawai'i's very roots; according to chants, the first lei was given by Hiiaka, the sister of the volcano goddess Pele, who presented Pele with a lei of lehua blossoms on a beach in Puna. Leis are the perfect symbol for the islands: even after they fade, their spirit of aloha lives on.

Enjoying a Chinatown art gallery

than an hour, you'll be at the idyllic Mānoa Falls. *See p 167.*

Retrace your route back down Mānoa Rd., turn left on O'ahu Ave., and then turn left again on E. Mānoa Rd.

15 ★ **Andy's Sandwiches & Smoothies.** After hiking in the rainforest, stop by this neighborhood eatery. See p 59, **3**.

Head makai on Mānoa Rd. Turn left on O'ahu Ave. and onto University Ave. Turn right onto the H1 east ramp. Take exit 25B and turn right onto 6th Ave. Turn right onto Hoolulu St. Turn left onto Kapahulu Ave. Turn left onto Kalākaua Ave. and take a slight left onto Monsarrat Ave. Bus 13.

16 ★★ **Waikīkī Shell.** Find out whether anything is playing at Waikīkī's best outdoor venue, this open amphitheater in Kapi'olani Park. *See p 88.*

Day 5

Take H-1 west out of Waikīkī and then take the H-2 north exit (Exit 8A) toward Mililani/Wahiawā. After 7 miles (11km), H-2 becomes Kamehameha Hwy. (Hwy. 80). Look for the turnoff to Hale'iwa town. Bus: 20, then transfer to 55.

17 ★★★ **Hale'iwa.** It's time to take a break from Honolulu and head up to the North Shore. Start your day exploring this famous North Shore surfing town. *See p 137,* **2**.

18 ★ **Beet Box Café.** A cheerful hippie vibe permeates at this vegetarian spot. See p 140, **7**.

Continue down Kamehameha Hwy. Bus: 55.

19 ★★★ **North Shore beaches.** Choose any one of the North Shore beaches to spend the afternoon. If it's winter time and the surf's up, you'll want to head to Pipeline or Sunset to watch the surfers in some of the best waves in the world. If it's summer, head to Waimea to swim in the calm, beautiful bay or Shark's Cove for snorkeling. *See p 159.*

Backtrack on Kamehameha Hwy. to Hale'iwa. Bus: 55.

Shopping for Alohawear in Hale'iwa

Getting Married in Paradise

Honolulu and Waikīkī are great places for a wedding. Not only does the entire island exude romance and natural beauty, but after the ceremony, you're only a few steps away from the perfect honeymoon.

The easiest way to plan your wedding is to let someone else handle it at the resort or hotel where you'll be staying. Most Waikīkī resorts and hotels have wedding coordinators who can plan everything from a simple (relatively) low-cost wedding to an extravaganza that people will talk about for years.

You will need a marriage license: Contact the Marriage License Office, Room 101 (first floor) of the Health Department Building, 1250 Punchbowl St. (corner of Beretania and Punchbowl sts.; ☎ 808/586-4544; http://health.hawaii.gov/; you can download an application for a marriage license from the site); open Monday through Friday from 8am to 4pm. Once in Hawai'i, the prospective bride and groom must go together to the marriage-licensing agent to get a license, which costs $65 and is good for 30 days.

Every year, tens of thousands of couples travel to O'ahu to say their wedding vows.

20 ★ **Hale'iwa Beach House.** Watch the sun set from this newly renovated restaurant, which opens up to a fabulous view of Hale'iwa beach park. Highlights on the menu include the whole fried fish and kālua pig grilled cheese sandwich. *See p 140.*

Spend nights 5 and 6 on the North Shore.

Day 6

21 ★ Pu'u o Mahuka Heiau. Start the day with a quick climb to this sacred heiau and its view overlooking Waimea Bay. *See p 44,* 16.

22 *Horseback Ride.* Explore the North Shore on horseback, from the trails above Pūpūkea Beach or along the beach and through ironwood trees. *See p 174.*

Depending which horseback ride you choose, you'll either head up into Pūpūkea or down Kamehameha Hwy. toward Turtle Bay.

23 ★ **Turtle Bay Resort.** A lively crowd, from pro surfers to tourists, gather at The Point for cocktails and to watch the sunset. If

Postcard-perfect Lanikai Beach

you're here on a Sunday, stay for the free Polynesian show. Otherwise, head to Roy's Beach House, by beloved local chef Roy Yamaguchi, which is set right on the sand. Make sure to order Roy's signature chocolate soufflé. *See p 139.*

Day 7

Spend the day meandering along the coast toward Lanikai, stopping to enjoy the views along the way. Make your way south on Kamehameha Hwy. for about 30 miles (48 km), then merge onto HI-63. Continue onto Kāne'ohe Bay Dr. Continue onto Mokapu Saddle Rd. Turn right onto Oneawa St., then left onto Kainui Dr. Turn right onto N. Kalaheo Ave. Follow the coast about 2 miles (3.2km) to Kailua Beach Park; just past it, turn left and drive uphill on Aalapapa Dr., a one-way street that loops back as Mokulua Dr. Park on Mokulua and walk down any of the eight public-access lanes to the shore. Bus: 55 to 57A to 70.

㉔ ★★ **Lanikai Beach.** Spend your last day luxuriating at this tiny beach with silky white sand and calm turquoise waters. If you're feeling more active, you can kayak to the Mokulua islands offshore (p 181), or climb up to the pillboxes (p 146, ⑫) around dusk. ●

4 The Best of Honolulu & Waikīkī

Historic **Chinatown**

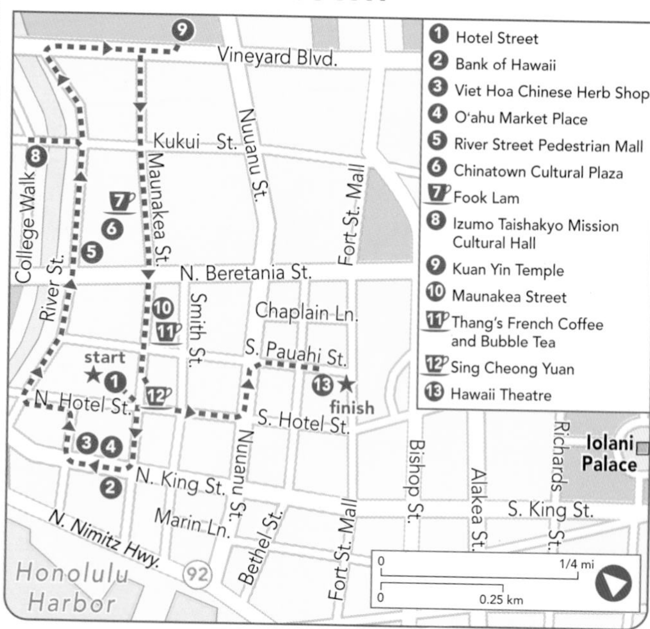

Honolulu's historic Chinatown is a mix of Asian cultures all packed into a small area where tangy spices rule the cuisine, open-air markets have kept out the mini-malls, and acupuncture and herbal remedies have paved the way to good health. Streets bustle with residents and visitors from all over the world and a cacophony of sounds, from the high-pitched bleating of vendors in the market to the lyrical dialects of the retired men "talking story" over a game of mah-jongg. No trip to Honolulu is complete without a visit to this exotic, historic district. Plan at least 2 hours, more if you love to browse.

❶ ★ **Hotel Street.** During World War II, Hotel Street was synonymous with good times. Pool halls and beer parlors lined the blocks, and prostitutes were plentiful. Nowadays, the more nefarious establishments have been replaced with small shops, from art galleries to specialty boutiques. Wander up and down this street and then head to the intersection with Smith Street. On the Diamond Head (east) side of Smith, you'll notice stones in the sidewalk; they were taken from the sandalwood ships, which came to Hawai'i empty of cargo except for these stones, which were used as ballast on the trip over. *Hotel St., btw. Maunakea & Bethel sts.*

When you've finished exploring Hotel St., head back to Maunakea St. and turn toward the ocean.

Previous page: Dining in paradise, Waikīkī Beach

Fresh tropical flowers at a Chinatown lei shop

❷ Bank of Hawaii. This unusual-looking bank is not the conservative edifice you might expect—it's guarded by two fire-breathing-dragon statues. *101 N. King St. (Maunakea St.). ☎ 808/532-2480.*

Head mauka on Maunakea St.

❸ Viet Hoa Chinese Herb Shop. Here, Chinese herbalists act as both doctors and dispensers of herbs. There's a wall of tiny drawers all labeled in Chinese characters; the herbalist pulls out bits and pieces ranging from dried flowers to mashed antelope antler. The patient then takes the concoction home to brew into a strong tea. *1125 Maunakea St. ☎ 808/523-5499. Mon–Sat 8:30am–5pm, Sun 8:30am–2pm.*

Cross to the south side of King St., where, just west of Kekaulike St., you come to the most-visited part of Chinatown, the open-air market.

❹ ★★ O'ahu Market Place. Those interested in Asian cooking will find all the necessary ingredients here, including pigs' heads, poultry (some still squawking), fresh octopuses, pungent fish sauce, and 1,000-year-old eggs. The friendly vendors are happy to explain their wares and give instructions on how to prepare these exotic treats. The market has been at this spot since 1904. 🕓 *1 hr. N. King & Kekaulike sts. Daily 6am–6pm.*

Follow King down to River St. and turn right toward the mountains.

❺ River Street Pedestrian Mall. The statue of Chinese revolutionary leader Sun Yat-sen marks the beginning of this wide mall, which borders the Nu'uanu Stream. It's lined with shade trees, benches, and tables where seniors gather to play mah-jongg and checkers. *N. Beretania St. to Vineyard Blvd.*

❻ Chinatown Cultural Plaza. This modern complex is filled with shops featuring everything from tailors to calligraphers (most somewhat more expensive than their streetside counterparts), as well as numerous restaurants and even a small post office for those who want to mail cards home with the "Chinatown" postmark. The best feature of the plaza is the **Moongate Stage** in the center, the site of many cultural presentations around the Chinese New Year. 🕓 *30 min. 100 N. Beretania St. (Vineyard Blvd.).*

7 ★ Fook Lam. Stop to refuel at this popular dim sum spot, where the servers roll out steam carts so you can see your choices before you decide. My favorites here include the lotus-leaf-wrapped sticky rice, fried taro puffs, and jin dui (fried sesame puffs with red bean inside). Inside Chinatown Cultural Plaza *☎ 808/523-9168. Daily 8am–3pm. $.*

Dragonfruit and other exotic finds at a Chinatown market

Continue up the River Street Mall and cross the Nu'uanu Stream via the bridge at Kukui St.

8 Izumo Taishakyo Mission Cultural Hall. This small wooden Shinto shrine, built in 1923, houses a male deity (look for the X-shaped crosses on the top). Members of the faith ring the bell out front as an act of purification when they come to pray. Inside the temple is a 100-pound sack of rice, symbolizing good health. *15 min. 215 N. Kukui St. ☎ 808/538-7778. Daily 8:30am–5pm.*

Walk a block toward the mountains to Vineyard Blvd.; cross back over Nu'uanu Stream, past the entrance of Foster Botanical Gardens.

9 ★ Kuan Yin Temple. This Buddhist temple, painted in a brilliant red with a green ceramic-tile roof, is dedicated to Kuan Yin Bodhisattva, the goddess of mercy, whose statue towers in the prayer hall. The temple is still a house of worship, not an exhibit, so enter with respect and leave your shoes outside. You may see people burning paper "money" for prosperity and good luck or leaving flowers and fruits at the altar (gifts to the goddess). *15 min. 170 N. Vineyard Blvd. (Nu'uanu St.). ☎ 808/533-6361.*

Continue down Vineyard and then turn right (toward the ocean) on:

10 ★★ Maunakea Street. Numerous lei shops line this colorful street, which is the best place in all of Hawai'i to get a deal on leis. The size, color, and design of the leis made here are exceptional. *Btw. Beretania & King sts.*

11 ★ Thang's French Coffee and Bubble Tea. Head to the courtyard of the bustling Maunakea Marketplace and to this stand that uses fresh fruits (lined up in the case in front of you) for refreshing drinks to cool you down. My favorite is the avocado smoothie, made by blending fresh avocado with condensed milk and ice. It's creamy, like soft serve ice cream. *Maunakea Marketplace, 1120 Maunakea St. ☎ 808/845-2164. Open Mon–Sat 8:30am–6:30pm, Sun 10am–5pm. $.*

Head makai on Maunakea St.

12 ★ Sing Cheong Yuan. Grab an Asian pastry (my picks: moon cakes and peanut candy) at this tempting shop, which also has a wide selection of dried and sugared candies (ginger, pineapple, and lotus root) that you can eat as you stroll or give as a gift to friends back home. *1027 Maunakea St. (near King St.). ☎ 808/531-6688. Daily 6:30am–6pm. $.*

Steaming hot dim sum is a Chinatown specialty.

Plan to spend at least a few hours exploring Honolulu's historic Chinatown.

Head mauka on Maunakea St., turn right onto N. Hotel St. and turn left onto Bethel St.

⑬ ★★★ **Hawaii Theatre.** This restored 1920 Art Deco theater is a work of art in itself. It hosts a variety of programs, from the Hawai'i International Film Festival to Hawaiian concerts. Tours of the theater are available every Tuesday at 11 a.m. ($10 a person). *1130 Bethel St. (at Pauahi St.).* ☎ *808/528-0506. www.hawaiitheatre.com.*

The New Chinatown

In the 1840s, Honolulu's Chinatown began to take shape as many Chinese brought in to work on the sugar plantations opted not to renew their contracts and instead moved to Chinatown to open businesses. Fronting Honolulu harbor, Chinatown catered to whalers and sailors. It reached its zenith in the 1920s, with restaurants and markets flourishing by day, and prostitutes and opium dens doing brisk business at night. As its reputation as a red-light district began to eclipse everything else, the neighborhood slowly declined. That is, until recent decades. Fresh boutiques and restaurants are filling in previously abandoned storefronts—which retain much of their original architectural details from the 1900s—as Chinatown once again attracts the entrepreneurial.

At the original location of **Fighting Eel,** 1133 Bethel St. (www.fightingeel.com; ☎ **808/738-9300**), you'll find bright, easy-to-wear dresses and shirts with island prints—perfect for Honolulu weather, but chic enough to wear back home. **Owens and Co.,** 1152 Nu'uanu Ave. (www.owensandcompany.com; ☎ **808/531-4300**), offers a colorful selection of housewares and accessories, including candles, stationery, jewelry, and totes, many of which are locally made or island inspired. Go treasure hunting at **Tin Can Mailman** (p. 121) and the funky **Hound & Quail,** 920 Maunakea St. (www.houndandquail.com; ☎ **808/779-8436**), where a collection of antiques and curiosities, from a taxidermied ostrich to old medical texts, make for a fascinating perusal. Find nostalgia in a 1950s tiki print dress or red silk kimono at **Barrio Vintage,** 1161 Nu'uanu Ave. (www.barriovintage.com; ☎ **808/674-7156**), one of the island's best shops for vintage clothing. At **Ginger13,** 22 S. Pauahi St. (www.ginger13.com; ☎ **808/531-5311**), local jewelry designer Cindy Yokoyama offers a refreshing change from the delicate jewelry found all over Hawai'i by creating asymmetrical styles with chunky stones such as agate and opal.

Walking the Beach of **Waikīkī**

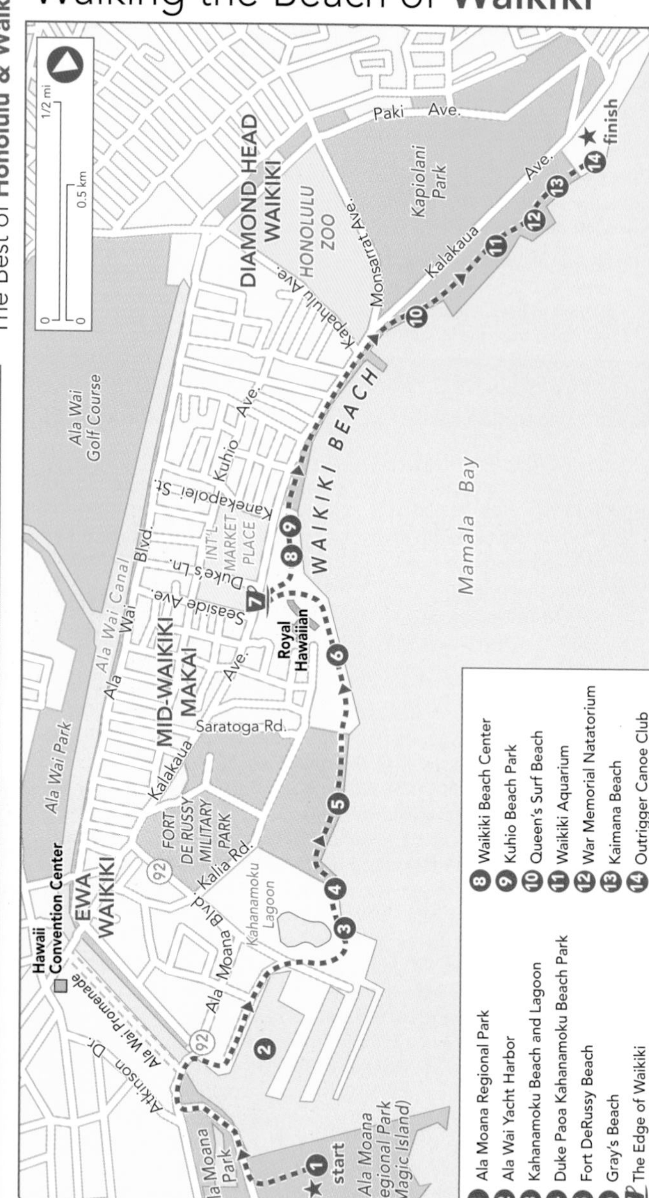
0
1/2 mi
0
0.5 km
Paki Ave.
Kapiolani Park
finish
Ave.
Kalakaua
Monsarrat Ave.
HONOLULU ZOO
DIAMOND HEAD WAIKIKI
Kapahulu Ave.
WAIKIKI BEACH
Kuhio Ave.
Kanekapolei St.
INT'L MARKET PLACE
Duke's Ln.
Seaside Ave.
Ala Wai Golf Course
Ala Wai Canal
Ala Wai Blvd.
Mamala Bay
Royal Hawaiian
MID-WAIKIKI MAKAI
Saratoga Rd.
Kalakaua Ave.
FORT DE RUSSY MILITARY PARK
Kalia Rd.
Kahanamoku Lagoon
Ala Wai Park
EWA WAIKIKI
Hawaii Convention Center
Ala Moana Blvd.
Ala Wai Promenade
Atkinson Dr.
Ala Moana Park
start
Ala Moana Regional Park (Magic Island)
1 Ala Moana Regional Park
2 Ala Wai Yacht Harbor
3 Kahanamoku Beach and Lagoon
4 Duke Paoa Kahanamoku Beach Park
5 Fort DeRussy Beach
6 Gray's Beach
7 The Edge of Waikiki
8 Waikiki Beach Center
9 Kuhio Beach Park
10 Queen's Surf Beach
11 Waikiki Aquarium
12 War Memorial Natatorium
13 Kaimana Beach
14 Outrigger Canoe Club

Just the name Waikīkī conjures images of Paradise. Only the *alii* (royalty) lived on Waikīkī Beach in the 1800s. After the overthrow of the Hawaiian Monarchy in 1893, accommodations for visitors were built. The first large hotel in Waikīkī, the Moana Surfrider (on the spot where the Sheraton Moana Surfrider is today) opened in 1901. During the 20th century, Waikīkī went from a wetland, with ducks and water, to 3 miles (4.8km) of hotels, condominiums, restaurants, and shops. The very word "Waikīkī" translates into spouting water, referring to the numerous springs and streams that flowed (and generally flooded) this now-famous destination. In 1922, the Waikīkī Reclamation project dredged the Ala Wai Canal to drain the area and also buried the springs, ponds, and marshes. The area you see today is surprisingly nearly all man-made—even the famous beach is made from sand shipped in from the island of Molokai. Although most people think of Waikīkī Beach as just one long beach, it actually is a series of small beaches. Plan at least 2 to 3 hours to walk this incredible area (and more if you plan on swimming along the way).

❶ ★ Ala Moana Regional Park. Walk toward the ocean along the peninsula facing Waikīkī. It's hard to believe that this 76-acre (31-ha) park was once a garbage dump. Today, the park is filled with picnickers, joggers, sunbathers, lawn bowlers, tennis players, and model-airplane flyers, and that's just on land. A popular swimming site, the ocean is also attractive to fishermen and surfers (several surf sites offshore include Big Rights, Big Lefts, Bay Haleiwa, Concessions, and Bomboras), and on a calm day, even scuba divers jump into the water. If you're lucky, you may see Hawaiian outrigger canoe paddlers practicing in the Ala Wai Canal.

Trace your steps back to Ala Moana Blvd., turn right toward Waikīkī, and cross the bridge. Turn right at Holomoana St. and head to the harbor.

❷ ★ Ala Wai Yacht Harbor. The largest of all the small boat harbors in Hawai'i, this harbor accommodates slightly more than 700 boats and is the host of one of the longest running ocean yacht races, the Transpac sailing race (which begins in Los Angeles and ends at the harbor), an event that takes place every 2 years.

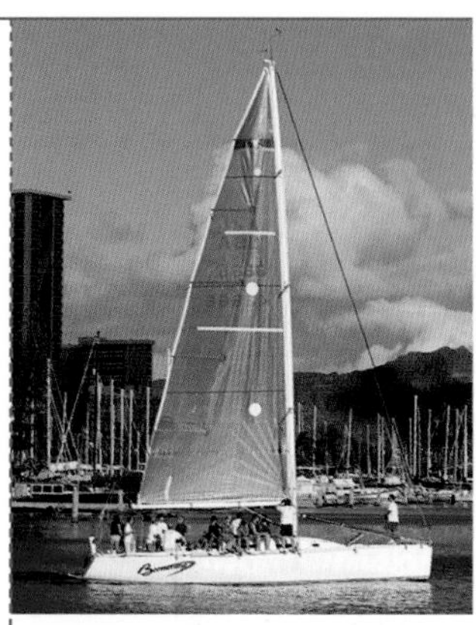

Find a sunset charter or just enjoy a stroll at Ala Wai Yacht Harbor.

At the ocean end of the harbor, continue down the beach on the sand, just before the Hilton Hawaiian Village.

❸ ★ **Kahanamoku Beach and Lagoon.** In 1955, Henry J. Kaiser built Hawai'i's first resort in Hawaii, the Hilton Hawaiian Village. To improve this beautiful site, he also dredged a swimming area and a lagoon inland. The area is named after Duke Paoa Kahanamoku (1890–1968), who spent most of his childhood swimming here and who later became a gold medalist in swimming in the 1912, 1920, and 1924 Olympic Games. He is credited with spreading the sport of surfing to the California coast and to Australia. Offshore is one of Waikīkī's surf sites, Kaisers. If the waves are right, you can see the surfers at the west end of the channel leading to the Ala Wai Harbor.

Continue down the beach toward Diamond Head, on the other side of the Hilton Hawaii Village. At the end of Paoa Place, opposite the catamaran pier, is:

❹ ★ **Duke Paoa Kahanamoku Beach Park.** This tiny (.5-acre/.2-ha) park is also named after Hawai'i's top water man (see ❸). There are restrooms and showers here, and it is a great spot for swimming, and, of course, surfing.

The sheltered waters of Kahanamoku Beach and Lagoon

Continue down the beach toward Diamond Head.

❺ ★ **Fort DeRussy Beach.** One of the best-kept secrets in Waikīkī, this long stretch of sand beach (some say the largest in Waikīkī) is generally less crowded than other parts of Waikīkī. The beach fronts the military reservation of Fort DeRussy Park. The Hale Koa Hotel (for military personnel only) is on the east end of the park, and on the Diamond Head end is the U.S. Army Museum. Food and beach equipment rentals, concessions, picnic tables, restrooms, and showers are on the ocean side of the park. Another popular surf site, Number Threes, or just Threes, lies offshore.

Continue down the beach toward Diamond Head. Look for the sandy area between Halekulani Hotel and the Sheraton Waikīkī that is shaded by a single hau tree.

❻ ★ **Gray's Beach.** Ancient Hawaiians called this area "Kawehewehe" (the removal) and revered the beach and the waters offshore as a sacred healing spot. The Halekulani (house befitting heaven) Hotel site was once a boardinghouse owned in 1912 by La Vancha Maria Chapin Gray, who called her accommodations "Gray's-by-the-Sea." The popular swimming area facing her boardinghouse became known as Gray's. By the 1920s, the boardinghouse had turned into a hotel named Halekulani. One of its guests, Earl Derr Biggers, wrote a murder mystery, *The House Without a Key*, based on Honolulu residents who never locked their doors (at that time). The hero of the book was a Chinese detective named Charlie Chan (based on an actual

Gray's Beach is safe for family swimming and has two popular surfing spots offshore.

detective in the Honolulu Police Department, Chang Apana). The House Without a Key is a restaurant in the Halekulani today. The beach area is a safe swimming spot for families. Two surf sites are offshore: Populars and Paradise.

Continue down the beach toward Diamond Head. At the Sheraton Waikīkī, head toward the swimming pool area.

7 ★ **The Edge of Waikīkī.** If it is after 10am, stop for liquid libation at this hotel bar, overlooking the infinity pool. Be sure to check out the "Vint-Edge" list of cocktails from the 1940s to 1950s. If you are hungry, indulge in island-style food, such as salt and pepper crispy chicken wings and a cornflake crusted corn dog. *Sheraton Waikīkī, 2255 Kalākaua Ave. ☎ 808/922-4422. www.sheraton-waikiki.com. Daily 10am–9pm. $.*

Continue down the beach toward Diamond Head. Just after the Moana Surfrider and before the Waikīkī Wall, look inland for:

8 ★ **Waikīkī Beach Center.** In addition to the police substation here, you'll find the Stones of Kapaemahu, the Duke Kahanamoku statue, and the Prince Kūhiō statue. The Stones represent four famous holy men, legendary for their powers of healing and wisdom. Plus the center has restrooms, showers, picnic tables, and ocean equipment rentals.

Continue down the beach toward Diamond Head to:

9 ★ **Kūhiō Beach Park.** In 1951, this large pedestrian pier was built into the ocean, an extension of the storm drain that runs under Kapahulu Avenue and allows visitors to walk out to a great scenic point to view Waikīkī. The beach is named after Jonah Kūhiō Kalaniana'ole, son of Kekauliki Kinoiki II and High Chief David Kahalepouli Pi'ikoi, born on March 26, 1871, on Kaua'i. His mother died soon after his birth, and he was adopted by Kapi'olani (his mother's sister) and her husband, David Kalākaua. When Kalākaua became king in 1874, Kūhiō

A statue of Jonah Kūhiō Kalaniana'ole, namesake of Kūhiō Beach Park

became prince. He never served as Hawaiian royalty, but he was elected as Hawai'i's delegate to congress in 1902, where he served until his death in 1922. Kūhiō Beach Park fronts the site of Kūhiō's home, Pualeilani (which means flower from a wreath of heaven), where in 1918 he removed the fence around his home and opened the beach to the people of Hawaii. To the west end of the park are two famous surf sites: Queen's and Canoes.

Continue down the beach toward Diamond Head to:

⑩ ★ **Queen's Surf Beach.** King David Kalākaua dedicated this park to his wife, Queen Kapi'olani. Surfing is the most popular activity here, but the area is also great for swimming and fishing. You'll find food stands, picnic tables, restrooms, showers, and ocean equipment concessions here. Surf sites offshore include the Walls, good for bodysurfers and bodyboarders only, no board surfing.

Continue along the pathway toward Diamond Head to:

⑪ ★ **Waikīkī Aquarium.** *See p 33,* ③.

Continue toward Diamond Head to:

⑫ ★ **War Memorial Natatorium.** At the end of World War I, Hawai'i (not yet a state at the time) constructed a memorial to island veterans who had lost their lives in the war. The Natatorium, an Olympic-size swimming pool, was added to the memorial in 1927. Over the years it fell into disrepair and was finally closed in 1979. Even today, there is much political discussion about the question of whether to restore the pool or tear it down. Still, good snorkeling, fishing, and swimming can be found offshore.

Continue toward Diamond Head to:

⑬ ★ **Kaimana Beach.** Named after Kaimana Hila (Diamond Head), this popular beach is also called San Souci Beach, after an old

Monk Seals at the Waikiki Aquarium

An outrigger canoe on Waikīkī Beach

beachfront rental called Sans Souci. I think this is the best family beach in Waikīkī: The wide reef offshore protects the shallow, sandy bottom, making it perfect for small children. You may see a parade of open ocean swimmers and one-man canoe paddlers who enter the water here to get to deep waters offshore. Also offshore is a great surf spot called Old Man's.

Continue to the end of the beach toward Diamond Head to:

⓮ ★ Outrigger Canoe Club. This private club (only members and their guests are allowed on the property) was founded in 1908 to "preserve and promote the sports of surfing and canoe paddling." It started as just two grass houses and went through a few iterations before renowned architect Vladimir Ossipoff designed its current structure. This is the birthplace of beach volleyball, and the club continues to host some of O'ahu's most prestigious water races. The tiny beach fronting the Outrigger marks the end of the Waikīkī Beach area. There are no public amenities here, but the waters offshore are good for snorkeling, swimming, and, when the waves are right, surfing.

Historic Honolulu

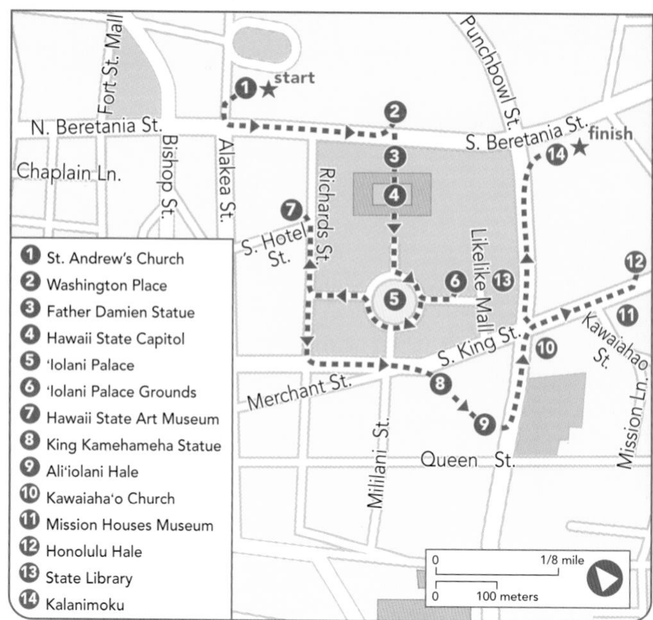

The 1800s were a turbulent time in Hawai'i. By the end of the 1790s, Kamehameha the Great had united all the islands. Foreigners began arriving by ship—first explorers, then merchants, and, in 1820, missionaries. By 1873, the monarchy had run through the Kamehameha line, and David Kalākaua was elected to the throne. Known as "the Merrie Monarch," Kalākaua redefined the monarchy by going on a world tour, building 'Iolani Palace, having a European-style coronation, and throwing extravagant parties. By the end of the 1800s, however, the foreign sugar growers and merchants had become extremely powerful in Hawai'i. With the help of the U.S. Marines, they staged the overthrow of Queen Lili'uokalani, Hawai'i's last reigning monarch, in 1893. The United States declared Hawai'i a territory in 1898. You can witness the remnants of these turbulent years in just a few short blocks. Allow 2 to 3 hours for this tour.

1 ★ St. Andrew's Church. When King Kamehameha IV saw the grandeur of the Church of England, he decided to build his own cathedral. The king, however, didn't live to see the church completed; he died on St. Andrew's Day, 4 years before Kamehameha V oversaw the laying of the cornerstone in 1867. Don't miss the floor-to-eaves hand-blown stained-glass window that faces the setting sun. In the glass is

The stained glass window of St. Andrew's Cathedral on Queen Emma Square

a mural of Reverend Thomas Staley (Hawai'i's first bishop), King Kamehameha IV, and Queen Emma. *229 Queen Sq. (btw. Beretania & Alakea sts.). www.thecathedralofstandrew.org. ☎ 808/524-2822.*

Walk down Beretania St. in the Diamond Head direction.

❷ ★ **Washington Place.** This house, the official residence of the governor, occupies a distinguished place in Hawai'i's history. (Free tours are held Thursdays at 10am by reservation only.) The Greek revival–style home was built in 1842 by a U.S. sea captain named John Dominis. The sea captain's son, also named John, married a Hawaiian princess, Lydia Kapa'akea, who later became Hawai'i's last queen, Lili'uokalani. When the queen was overthrown by U.S. businessmen in 1893, she moved out of 'Iolani Palace and into her husband's inherited home, Washington Place, where she lived until her death in 1917. On the left side of the building, near the sidewalk, is a plaque inscribed with the words to one of the most popular songs written by Queen Lili'uokalani, "Aloha 'Oe" ("Farewell to Thee"). *Beretania St. (btw. Queen Emma & Punchbowl sts.). www.washingtonplacefoundation.org; ☎ 808/586-0240.*

Cross the street and walk to the front of the Hawaii State Capitol.

❸ ★ **Father Damien Statue.** The people of Hawai'i have never forgotten the sacrifice this Belgian priest made to help the sufferers of leprosy when he volunteered to work with them in exile on the Kalaupapa Peninsula on the island of Moloka'i. After 16 years of service, Father Damien died of leprosy at the age of 49. *Beretania St. (btw. Queen Emma & Punchbowl sts.).*

Walk behind Father Damien's statue.

❹ ★ **Hawai'i State Capitol.** This is where Hawai'i's state legislators work from mid-January to the

Built in the 19th-century, Washington Place is now the Governor's Mansion.

The architecture of the Hawaii State Capitol reflects the island's nature and culture.

end of April every year. The building's unusual design has palm tree–shaped pillars, two cone-shaped chambers (representing volcanoes) for the legislative bodies, and, in the inner courtyard, a 600,000-tile mosaic of the sea created by a local artist. A reflecting pool (representing the sea) surrounds the entire structure. You are welcome to go into the rotunda and see the woven hangings and murals at the entrance, or take the elevator up to the fifth floor for a spectacular view. *415 Beretania St. ☎ 808/586-0034.*

Walk down Richards St. toward the ocean.

5 ★★ 'Iolani Palace and 6 ★ Palace Grounds. To really understand Hawai'i's past and present, I suggest taking a tour of this royal palace (*See p 15,* **8**.) You can wander around the grounds at no charge. The domed pavilion on the grounds was originally built as a coronation stand by King Kalākaua. Today, the royal bandstand is still used for concerts, every Friday from noon to 1 pm, by the Royal Hawaiian Band. *At S. King & Richards sts. ☎ 808/522-0832. www.iolanipalace.org.*

Turn in the 'Ewa direction, cross Richards St. and walk to the corner of Richards and Hotel sts.

7 ★ Hawai'i State Art Museum. *See p 63,* **4**.

Walk makai down Richards St. and turn left (toward Diamond Head) on S. King St.

8 ★ King Kamehameha Statue. The striking black-and-gold bronze statue remembers the man who united the Hawaiian Islands. The best day to see the statue is on June 11 (King Kamehameha Day), when it is covered with leis in honor of Hawaii's favorite son. *Juncture of King, Merchant & Mililani sts.*

9 ★ Ali'iōlani Hale. The name translates to "House of Heavenly Kings." This distinctive building, with a clock tower, now houses the State Judiciary Building. King Kamehameha V commissioned Australian architect Thomas Rowe in to build a palace here, though he didn't live to see it completed—King David Kalākaua dedicated the building in 1874. Less than 20 years later, on January 17, 1893, Stanford Dole, backed by other prominent sugar planters, stood on the steps of this building and proclaimed the overthrow of the Hawaiian monarchy and the establishment of a provisional

The Royal Hawaiian Band performs every Friday at noon on the 'Iolani Palace grounds.

Ali'iolani Hale, or House of the Heavenly King, has played an integral role in Hawaii's history.

government. *417 S. King St. (btw. Mililani & Punchbowl sts.). ☎ 808/539-4999. Mon–Fri 8am–4:30pm for guided and self-guided tours.*

Walk toward Diamond Head on King St.; at the corner of King and Punchbowl, stop in at:

⑩ ★ Kawaiaha'o Church. Don't miss this crowning achievement of the first missionaries in Hawai'i—the first permanent stone church, complete with bell tower and colonial colonnade. *See p 22, ⑩.*

Cross the street and you'll see the:

⑪ ★ Hawaiian Mission Houses. Step into 1820 and see what life was like for 19th-century Protestant missionaries. *See p 23, ⑪.*

Cross King St. and walk in the Ewa direction to the corner of Punchbowl and King sts.

⑫ ★ Honolulu Hale. The Honolulu City Hall, built in 1927, was designed by Honolulu's most famous architect, C. W. Dickey. His Spanish mission–style building has an open-air courtyard, which is used for art exhibits and concerts. *530 S. King St. (Punchbowl St.). ☎ 808/523-4385. Mon–Fri 8am–4:30pm.*

Cross Punchbowl St. and walk *mauka* (inland).

⑬ ★ State Library. This main branch of the state's library system is located in a restored historic building. It has an open garden courtyard in the middle, which is great for stopping for a rest on your walk. *478 S. King St. (Punchbowl St.). ☎ 808/586-3617. www.librarieshawaii.org. Mon & Wed 10am–5pm, Thurs 9am–8pm, Tues & Fri–Sat 9am–5pm.*

Head *mauka* up Punchbowl to the corner of Punchbowl and Beretania sts.

⑭ ★ Kalanimoku. A beautiful name, "Ship of Heaven," has been given to this dour state office building. Here you can get information on hiking and camping in state parks from the Department of Land and Natural Resources. *1151 Punchbowl St. (Beretania St.). ☎ 808/587-0320. Mon–Fri 7:45am–4:30pm.*

On King Kamehameha Day (June 11), the ruler's statue is covered in leis.

Kapi'olani Park

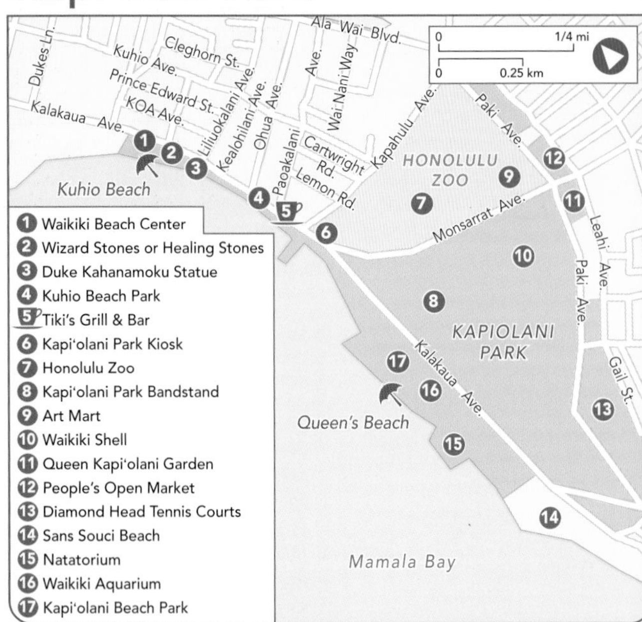

On June 11, 1877 (King Kamehameha Day), King David Kalākaua donated some 140 acres (57 ha) of land to the people of Hawai'i for Hawai'i's first park. He asked that the park be named after his beloved wife, Queen Kapi'olani, and he celebrated the opening of this vast grassy area with a free concert and "high stakes" horse races (the king loved gambling). The horse racing and the gambling that accompanied it were eventually outlawed, but the park lives on. Just a coconut's throw from the high-rise concrete jungle of Waikīkī lies this grassy oasis dotted with spreading banyans, huge monkeypod trees, blooming royal poincianas, and swaying ironwoods. From Waikīkī, walk toward Diamond Head on Kalākaua Avenue. If you're coming by car, the cheapest parking is metered street parking on Kalākaua Avenue adjacent to the park.

1 ★ Waikīkī Beach Center. On the ocean side of Kalākaua Avenue, next to the Westin Moana Surfrider Hotel, are restrooms, showers, surfboard lockers, rental concessions, and the Waikīkī police substation. *2435 Kalākaua Ave., Diamond Head side of the Westin Moana Surfrider Hotel.*

2 ★ Wizard Stones or Healing Stones. These four basalt boulders, which weigh several tons apiece and sit on a lava rock

View of Waikiki from Diamond Head Crater

platform, are held sacred by the Hawaiian people. The story goes that sometime before the 15th century, four powerful healers from Moaulanuiakea (in the Society Islands) lived in Waikīkī. After years of healing the people and the *alii* of O'ahu, they wished to return home. They asked the people to erect four monuments made of bell stone, a basalt rock that was found in a Kaimukī quarry and that produced a bell-like ringing when struck. The healers spent a ceremonious month transferring their spiritual healing power, or *mana,* to the stones. The great mystery is how the boulders were transported from Kaimukī to the marshland near Kūhiō Beach in Waikīkī. *Diamond Head side of the police substation, Kalākaua Ave.*

3 ★ Duke Kahanamoku Statue. Here, cast in bronze, is Hawai'i's most famous athlete, also known as the father of modern surfing. Duke (1890–1968) won Olympic swimming medals in 1912, 1920, and 1924. He was enshrined in both the Swimming Hall of Fame and the Surfing Hall of Fame. He also traveled around the world promoting surfing. *Just west of the stones, Kalākaua Ave.*

4 ★ Kūhiō Beach Park. The two small swimming holes here are great, but heed the warning sign: Watch out for holes in the sandy bottom—you may suddenly find yourself in very deep water. The best pool for swimming is the one on the Diamond Head end, but the water circulation is iffy—there sometimes appears to be a layer of suntan lotion on the surface. If the waves are up, watch the boogie boarders surf by the seawall. They ride toward the wall and at the last minute veer away with a swoosh. *2453 Kalākaua Ave. (btw. Liliuokalani & Paoakalani aves.).*

Cross Kalākaua Ave. and walk toward Paoakalani St.

5 ★ Tiki's Grill & Bar. Stop for lunch at this casual eatery on the second floor of the Aston Waikīkī Beach Hotel overlooking Waikīkī Beach. The menu is American with Pacific Rim influences; seafood dishes are especially good. *2570 Kalākaua Ave. (at Paoakalani St.). http://tikisgrill.com. ☎ 808/923-TIKI (8454). Daily 10:30am–midnight. $$.*

Walk *mauka* down Kalākaua Ave. to Kapahulu Ave. and then walk toward Diamond Head to the entrance of Kapiolani Park.

The Waikīkī Shell entertainment venue

❻ ★ **Kapi'olani Park Kiosk.** This small kiosk contains brochures and photos of the park's history. It also carries information on upcoming events at the sites within the park (the aquarium, the zoo, Waikīkī Shell, and Kapiolani Bandstand). An informative map will help orient you to the park grounds. *Corner of Kalākaua & Kapahulu aves.*

Continue up Kapahulu Ave.

❼ ★ **Honolulu Zoo.** The best time to see the city's 42-acre (17-ha) zoo is as soon as the gates open at 9am—the animals seem to be more active, and it's a lot cooler than walking around at midday in the hot sun. *Open until 4:30pm.* *See p 33,* ❶.

Trace your steps back to Kapahulu and Kalākaua aves. and head *mauka* down Monsarrat Ave.

❽ ★ **Kapi'olani Park Bandstand.** Once upon a time, from 1937 to 2002, the Kodak Hula Show presented the art of hula to visitors, with some 3,000 people filling bleachers around a grassy stage area every day. The show is gone now, but the bandstand is still used for concerts and special events. *Inside Kapi'olani Park.*

Go back to Monsarrat Ave. and look at the fence facing the zoo.

❾ ★ **Art Mart.** The Artists of O'ahu Exhibit is the new official name of this display, where local artisans hang their artwork on a fence for the public to view and buy. You get to meet the artists, and have an opportunity to purchase their work at a considerable discount from the prices you'll see in galleries. *Monsarrat Ave. Sat–Sun 9 am–4:30pm.*

Cross Monsarrat Ave.

❿ ★★ **Waikīkī Shell.** This open-air amphitheater hosts numerous musical shows, from pop acts to

A concert at the Kapi'olani Park Bandstand

traditional Hawaiian music. *2805 Monsarrat Ave.* ☎ *808/768-5400.*

Continue walking down the block to the corner of Monsarrat and Paki aves.

⓫ ★ **Queen Kapi'olani Garden.** You'll see a range of hibiscus plants and dozens of varieties of roses, including the somewhat rare Hawaiian rose. The tranquil gardens are always open and are a great place to wander and relax. *Corner of Monsarrat & Paki aves.*

Walk across the street.

⓬ ★ **People's Open Market.** These farmer's market stalls are great spots to buy produce and flowers. *Monsarrat & Paki aves. Wed 10–11am.*

Continue in the Diamond Head direction down Paki Ave.

⓭ ★ **Diamond Head Tennis Courts.** Located on the *mauka* side of Paki Avenue, the nine free tennis courts are open for play daily during daylight hours. Etiquette suggests that if someone is waiting for a court, limit your play to 45 minutes. *3908 Paki Ave.* ☎ *808/971-2510.*

Turn onto Kalākaua Ave. and begin walking back toward Waikīkī.

⓮ ★ **Sans Souci Beach.** This is one of the best swimming beaches in Waikīkī. The shallow reef, which is close to shore, keeps the waters calm. Farther out there's good snorkeling in the coral reef by the Kapua Channel. Facilities include outdoor showers and a lifeguard. *Next to the New Otani Kaimana Beach Hotel, 2863 Kalākaua Ave.*

Keep walking toward Waikīkī.

Open-air farm markets are held across the island.

⓯ ★ **Natatorium.** This huge concrete structure next to the beach is both a memorial to the soldiers of World War I and a 100-meter saltwater swimming pool. Opened in 1927, when Honolulu had hopes of hosting the Olympics, the ornate swimming pool fell into disuse after World War II and was finally closed in 1979. ***Note:*** At press time, there were plans to raze the Natatorium, but local groups are working to save it. *2815 Kalākaua Ave.*

Go next door.

⓰ ★ **Waikīkī Aquarium.** Try not to miss this tropical aquarium—worth a peek if only to see the only living chambered nautilus born in captivity. *See p 33,* ❸.

⓱ ★ **Kapi'olani Beach Park.** Relax on the grassy lawn alongside the sandy beach, which is much less crowded than the beaches of Waikīkī. It has barbecue areas, picnic tables, restrooms, and showers. The swimming is good year-round, there's a surfing spot offshore, and there's always a game going at the volleyball courts. The middle section of the park, in front of the pavilion, is known as Queen's Beach. *2745 Kalākaua Ave.*

Dining Best Bets

Best **Bistro**
★ 12th Ave Grill $$ 1120 12th Ave. *(p 101)*

Best **Breakfast**
★ Koko Head Café $ 1145c 12th Ave. *(p 98)*

Best **Dim Sum**
★ Fook Lam $ *100 N. Beretania St. (p 96)*

Best for **Families**
★ Diamond Head Market and Grill $ *3158 Monsarrat Ave. (p 96)*

Best **Hamburger**
★ Teddy's Bigger Burgers $ *134 Kapahulu Ave. (p 101)*

Best **Hawaiian**
★★ Helena's Hawaiian Food $ *1240 N. School St. (p 97)*

Best **Vietnamese**
★★★ The Pig and the Lady $$ *83 N. King St. (p 101)*

Best **Hawai'i Regional Cuisine**
★★★ Alan Wong's Restaurant $$$$ *1857 S. King St. (p 94)*

Best for **under $10**
★★ Ono Seafood $ *747 Kapahulu Ave. (p 100)*

Best **Seafood**
★★ Mahina and Sun's $$$ *412 Lewers St. (p 99)*

Best **Steakhouse**
★ Hy's Steakhouse $$$$ *2440 Kūhiō Ave. (p 97)*

Best **Late-Night Meals**
★ Liliha Bakery $ *515 N. Kuakini St. (p 98)*

Most **Romantic**
★★★ La Mer $$$$ *2199 Kalia Rd. (p 98)*

Best **Sunday Brunch**
★★★ Orchids $$$$ *2199 Kalia Rd. (p 100)*

Best **Sushi**
★★★ Izakaya Gaku $$$$ *1329 S. King St. (p 97)*

Best **Sunset Views**
★ Duke's Waikīkī $$ *2335 Kalākaua Ave. (p 96)*

Best **View of Waikīkī**
★ Hau Tree Lanai $$$ *2863 Kalākaua Ave. (p 96)*

Waikīkī's Best Dining

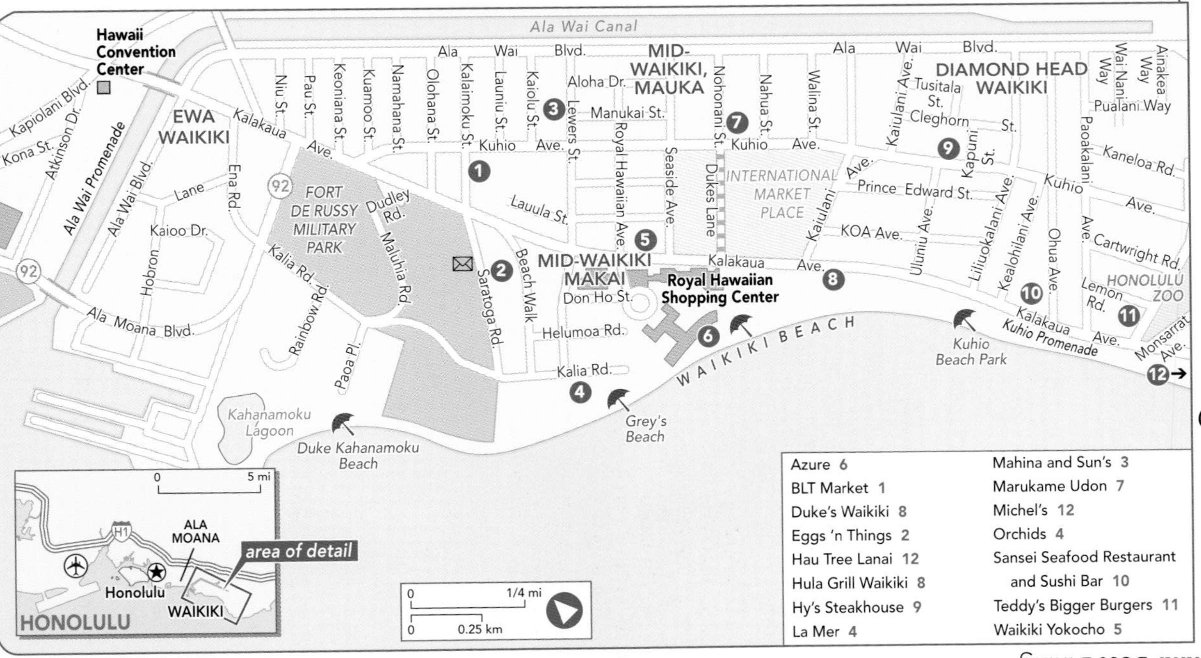
Azure 6
BLT Market 1
Duke's Waikiki 8
Eggs 'n Things 2
Hau Tree Lanai 12
Hula Grill Waikiki 8
Hy's Steakhouse 9
La Mer 4
Mahina and Sun's 3
Marukame Udon 7
Michel's 12
Orchids 4
Sansei Seafood Restaurant and Sushi Bar 10
Teddy's Bigger Burgers 11
Waikiki Yokocho 5
Ala Wai Canal
Hawaii Convention Center
EWA WAIKIKI
MID-WAIKIKI, MAUKA
MID-WAIKIKI MAKAI
DIAMOND HEAD WAIKIKI
Ala Wai Blvd.
Kuhio Ave.
Kalakaua Ave.
FORT DE RUSSY MILITARY PARK
INTERNATIONAL MARKET PLACE
Royal Hawaiian Shopping Center
HONOLULU ZOO
WAIKIKI BEACH
Kuhio Beach Park
Kuhio Promenade
Grey's Beach
Duke Kahanamoku Beach
Kahanamoku Lagoon
Ala Wai Promenade
Ala Moana Blvd.
1/4 mi
0.25 km
5 mi
area of detail
ALA MOANA
Honolulu
WAIKIKI
HONOLULU

Honolulu's Best Dining

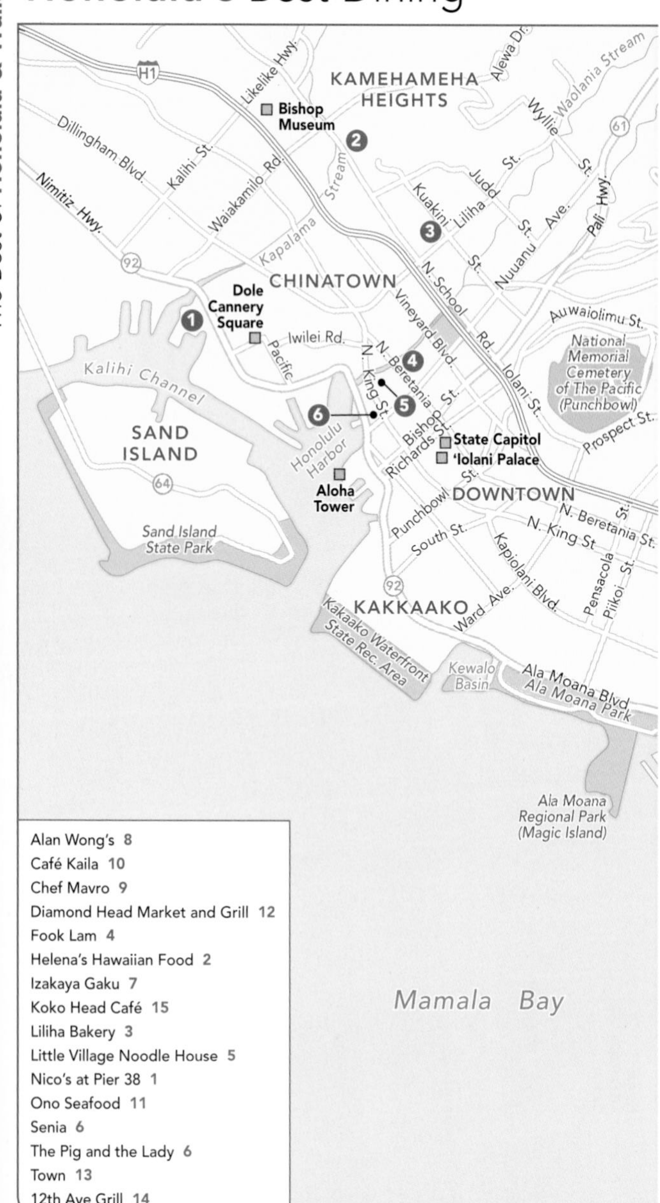

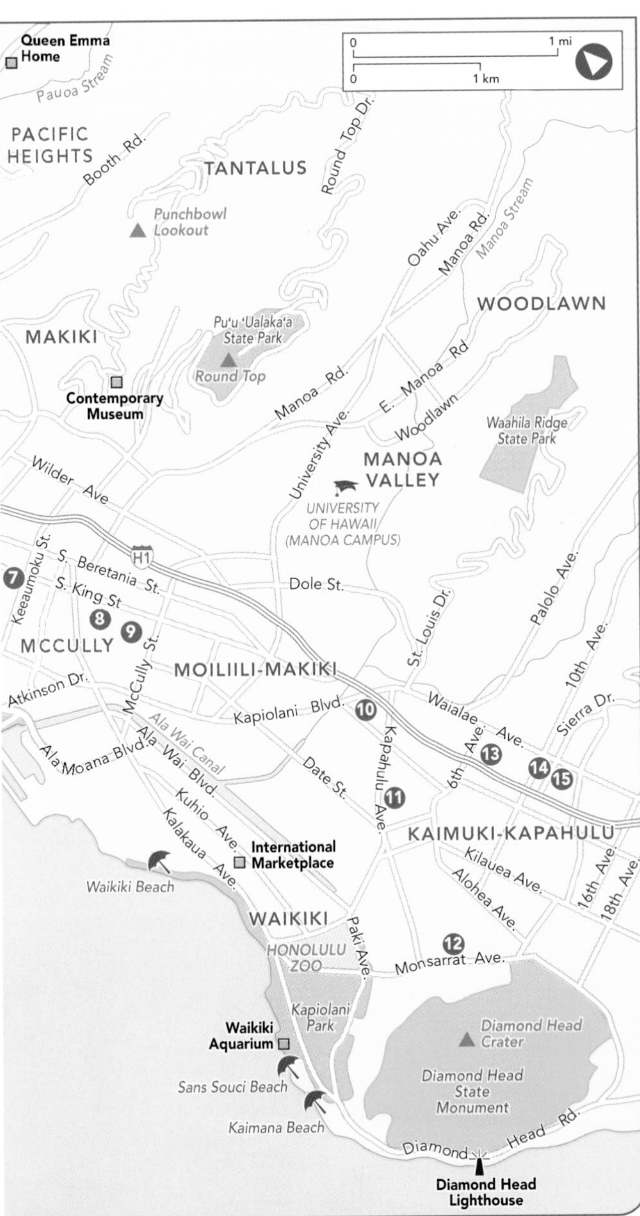
0
1 mi
0
1 km
Queen Emma Home
Pauoa Stream
PACIFIC HEIGHTS
Booth Rd.
TANTALUS
Round Top Dr.
Punchbowl Lookout
Oahu Ave.
Manoa Rd.
Manoa Stream
WOODLAWN
MAKIKI
Pu'u 'Ualaka'a State Park
Round Top
Contemporary Museum
Manoa Rd.
University Ave.
E. Manoa Rd
Woodlawn
Waahila Ridge State Park
MANOA VALLEY
Wilder Ave
UNIVERSITY OF HAWAII (MANOA CAMPUS)
H1
Keeaumoku St.
S. Beretania St.
S. King St
Dole St.
7
8
9
MCCULLY
McCully St.
St. Louis Dr.
Palolo Ave.
10th Ave.
MOILIILI-MAKIKI
Atkinson Dr.
Kapiolani Blvd.
10
Waialae Ave.
Sierra Dr.
Ala Wai Canal
Ala Wai Blvd.
Ala Moana Blvd.
Date St.
Kapahulu Ave.
6th Ave.
13
14
15
11
Kuhio Ave.
Kalakaua Ave.
KAIMUKI-KAPAHULU
International Marketplace
Kilauea Ave.
Alohea Ave.
16th Ave.
18th Ave.
Waikiki Beach
WAIKIKI
Paki Ave.
12
HONOLULU ZOO
Monsarrat Ave.
Kapiolani Park
Waikiki Aquarium
Diamond Head Crater
Sans Souci Beach
Diamond Head State Monument
Kaimana Beach
Diamond Head Rd.
Diamond Head Lighthouse

Honolulu & Waikīkī Restaurants A to Z

★★★ Alan Wong's Restaurant MCCULLY *HAWAII REGIONAL CUISINE* James Beard Award winner Chef Alan Wong, worshiped by foodies across the state, serves brilliantly creative and irresistibly cutting-edge cuisine in a dining room that is always packed, so book in advance. I love the ginger-crusted onaga. *1857 S. King St. (btw. Kalākaua Ave. & McCully St.). ☎ 808/949-2526. www.alanwongs.com. Entrees $36–$55, Tasting menus $85 ($125 w/ wine) and $105 ($165 w/ wine). Dinner daily. Bus: 2. Map p 93.*

★★ Azure Restaurant WAIKĪKĪ *SEAFOOD* This lantern-lit, oceanside restaurant at the Royal Hawaiian Hotel prepares fresh fish with a mixture of French and Hawaiian influences. Dine in plush banquettes with comfy pillows or rent a beachfront cabana and have your own intimate dining area. Hawai'i's fresh fish (most just bought that morning from the Honolulu Fish Market) is the star of the menu. Tasting menus and prix-fixe menus are available. Service is top-notch. *Royal Hawaiian Hotel, 2259 Kalākaua Ave. ☎ 808/923-7311. www.azurewaikiki.com. Reservations recommended. Entrees $26–$52, 5-course tasting menu $75 ($99 w/ wine). Dinner daily. Bus: 8 or 19. Map p 91.*

★ BLT Market WAIKĪKĪ MODERN AMERICAN An oasis on the eighth floor of the Ritz Carlton, with views of the Waikīkī skyline and ocean, this is a pleasant place for breakfast or dinner, especially on Friday nights, when you can catch the weekly fireworks. The menu consists of polished comfort food with classy touches, from fresh pasta and ravioli to tenderloin with a smoked heart of palm puree to a crispy-skinned pork shank that gives way to savory, tender meat. *At the Ritz-Carlton Residences, 383 Kalaimoku St., Waikīkī, Honolulu. www.bltmarket.com. ☎ 808/729-9729. Reservations recommended. Entrees $26–$75. Breakfast, lunch, and dinner daily. Bus: 8 or 19. Map p 91.*

★★ Café Kaila HONOLULU BREAKFAST Hidden in a strip mall next to the freeway is this treasure, where breakfast is always served. Owner/chef Chrissie "Kaila" Castillo serves up all her favorites—do not miss the incredibly fluffy pancakes

The Azure Restaurant at The Royal Hawaiian Hotel

Going Local: Uniquely Hawaiian

Talk to locals who move away from Hawai'i, and these are the foods they miss. Everyone's got their own go-to place and go-to dishes—people here could spend hours arguing over the best. Here are some of my favorites:

POKE Ruby-red cubes of fresh 'ahi (tuna), tossed with limu (seaweed), kukui nut, and Hawaiian chili pepper: Ahi poke (pronounced "*po*-kay") doesn't get better than the Hawaiian-style version at **Ono Seafood ★★** (p. 100).

LOCO MOCO Two sunny-side up eggs over a hamburger patty and rice, all doused in brown gravy. I love it at **Liliha Bakery ★★** (p. 98).

SPAM *(MUSUBI)* Ah yes, Spam. Hawai'i eats more Spam per capita than any other state. A dubious distinction to some, but don't knock it before you try it. Spam *musubi* (think of it as a giant sushi topped with Spam) is so ubiquitous you can find it at convenience stores (where it's pretty good). But for an even finer product, **Mana Bu,** 1618 S. King St. (☎ **808/358-0287**), is the tops. Get there early; the musubi, made fresh daily, are often sold out by 9am.

HAWAIIAN PLATE *Laulau* (pork wrapped in taro leaves), kālua pig (shredded, roasted pork), poi (milled taro), and *haupia* (like coconut Jell-O): It's Hawaiian lū'au food, based on what native Hawaiians used to eat. Find it at **Helena's Hawaiian Food ★★** (p. 97), **Highway Inn ★★** (p. 21), and **Ono Hawaiian Food,** 726 Kapahulu Ave. (☎ **808/737-2275**). (Sorry, I couldn't pick a favorite for this one!)

MALASADAS Hole-less doughnuts, rolled in sugar, by way of Portugal. **Leonard's Bakery,** 933 Kapahulu Ave. (☎ **808/737-5571**), opened in 1952 by the descendants of Portuguese contract laborers brought to work in Hawai'i's sugarcane fields. I love Leonard's malasadas dusted with *li hing mui* powder (made from dried, sweet-tart plums).

SHAVE ICE Nothing cools better on a hot day than powdery-soft ice drenched in tropical fruit syrups. I go to **Waiola Shave Ice,** 3113 Mokihana St. (☎ **808/735-8886**), for the nostalgia factor, but since you'll probably need more than one shave ice while you're in town, also hit up **Uncle Clay's House of Pure Aloha**, 820 W. Hind Dr. #116 (☎ **808/373-5111**), which offers a variety of homemade syrups from real fruit (a rarity).

A daily dose at Waiola Shave Ice

(get them piled on with fruit)—in a relaxed casual atmosphere. ***Warning:*** This place is packed at breakfast and lunch. I suggest going late for breakfast (after 9:30am) and lunch (after 1:30pm) so you won't have to wait for a table. Even if you do run into a long line, grab a latte, read a newspaper, and relax—the food is worth the wait. *Market City Shopping Center, 2919 Kapiolani Rd. ☎ 808/732-3330. Entrees $7–$13. Breakfast & lunch daily. Bus: 9. Map p 93.*

★★ Chef Mavro Restaurant MCCULLLY *PROVENÇAL/HAWAII REGIONAL* Splurge at this intimate dining experience in a non-touristy neighborhood. James Beard Award winner Chef George Mavro's inspired menu (roast pork with apple quinoa or poached fresh fish with sago-coconut nage, Thai herbs, limu, and lime froth) features perfect wine pairings. *1969 S. King St. (McCully St.). ☎ 808/944-4714. www.chefmavro.com. Prix-fixe menu $85–$128 ($140–$191 w/wine pairings). Dinner Tues–Sun. Bus 4. Map p 93.*

★ Diamond Head Market & Grill HONOLULU AMERICAN/ LOCAL Here you'll find some of the island's best plate lunches, near the base of Diamond Head. For breakfast, the pancakes with mac nuts or pineapple are a winner, or start the morning with a savory plate like the kimchi fried rice. Lunch and dinner offer tasty 'ahi steaks and kalbi (Korean-marinated short ribs).

Surfer nostalgia, oceanside dining and a Kalua pork sandwich at Duke's Waikīkī

Don't miss dessert: The lemon crunch cake is the perfect capper to a Diamond Head hike. *3158 Monsarrat Ave., www.diamondheadmarket.com. ☎ 808/732-0077. Plates $6–$17. Breakfast, lunch, and dinner daily. Bus 2. Map p 93.*

★ Duke's Waikīkī WAIKĪKĪ *STEAK/SEAFOOD* This open-air dining room (outfitted in surfing memorabilia) overlooking Waikīkī Beach is the best spot to watch the sunset. Hawaiian musicians serenade diners lingering over a menu ranging from burgers to fresh fish. *Outrigger Waikīkī on the Beach, 2335 Kalākaua Ave. (next door to Royal Hawaiian Shopping Center). ☎ 808/922-2268. www.dukeswaikiki.com. Lunch entrees $10–$16, dinner entrees $20–$40. Breakfast, lunch & dinner daily. Bus: 8 or 19. Map p 91.*

★ Eggs 'n Things WAIKĪKĪ *BREAKFAST* This popular eatery serves breakfast all day: from pancakes and waffles crowned with a tower of whipped cream to hearty plates of 'ahi and eggs. *343 Saratoga Rd. ☎ 808/949-0820. www.eggsnthings.com. Entrees $10–$17. Daily 6am–2pm & 4–10pm. Bus: 8, 19, or 42. Map p 91.*

★ Fook Lam CHINATOWN *DIM SUM* This is my favorite dim sum eatery. It's not fancy, but the dim sum (ranging from deep-fried taro puffs to prawn dumplings to lotus-leaf-wrapped sticky rice) that's rolled out in carts is top notch. The clientele are mainly Chinese-speaking diners, so you know it's authentic. *Chinese Cultural Plaza, 100 N. Beretania St. ☎ 808/523-9168. Dim sum under $7. Daily 8 am–3pm. Bus: 8, 13, or 20. Map p 92.*

★ Hau Tree Lanai WAIKĪKĪ *PACIFIC RIM* Located under a giant hau tree right on the beach (just a few yards from the waves), this informal eatery has the best

All-day breakfast is the specialty at Eggs'n Things.

view of Waikīkī Beach. Breakfast is my favorite—especially the taro pancakes. *New Otani Kaimana Beach Hotel, 2863 Kalākaua Ave. (across from Kapiolani Park).* ☎ *808/921-7066. www.kaimana.com. Breakfast $10–$18, lunch $15–$22, dinner $30–$52. Bus: 19; short walk on Kalākaua to destination. Map p 91.*

★ Helena's Hawaiian Food HONOLULU *HAWAIIAN* When first-generation-Chinese Helen Chock started Helena's in 1946 (she added an "a" at the end to make it sound more "Hawaiian"), she served Chinese and Hawaiian food. Eventually, she pared down the menu to the most popular items—Hawaiian food such as *laulau*, kalua pig, and poi. Sixty years later, her grandson runs the place, and it's as popular as ever. What makes Helena's stand out among other Hawaiian food restaurants? The *pipikaula:* marinated, bone-in short ribs hung above the stove to dry and fried right before they land on your table. *1240 N. School St., www.helenashawaiian food.com.* ☎ *808/845-8044. Full meals $9–$20. Tues–Fri 10am–7:30pm. Cash only. Bus 2. Map p 92.*

★ Hula Grill Waikīkī WAIKĪKĪ *HAWAIIAN REGIONAL* This bistro has a terrific ocean view (clear to Diamond Head), the food is also fabulous (crab cake eggs Benedict, Maui pineapple-and-coconut pancakes), and prices are reasonable. *Outrigger Waikīkī on the Beach, 2335 Kalākaua Ave.* ☎ *808/923-HULA (4852). www.hulagrillwaikiki.com. Breakfast $8–$14, dinner entrees $20–$33. Breakfast & dinner daily. Bus: 8. Map p 91.*

★ Hy's Steakhouse WAIKĪKĪ *STEAKHOUSE* Bask in the old-school cool of this steakhouse, almost four decades old. Bow-tied waiters carve kiawe-broiled steaks and flambé desserts tableside in a dining room that's all white tablecloths, mahogany, and chocolate brown leather. *2440 Kūhiō Ave.* ☎ *808/922-5555. www.hyswaikiki.com. Entrees $44–$89. Dinner daily. Bus 8. Map p 91.*

★★★ Izakaya Gaku HONOLULU *JAPANESE* There is life beyond maguro and hamachi nigiri, and the best place to experience it is at Izakaya Gaku. The izakaya restaurants embrace small plates as the best

Hau Tree Lanai serves up casual fare and shaded views of Waikīkī Beach

Helena's Hawaiian Food is famous for its pipikaula: marinated, bone-in short ribs.

way to eat and drink with friends; although Honolulu offers many of them, Izakaya Gaku is the best. Here you can get uncommon seasonal sushi and seafood, such as wild yellowtail and grilled ray. One of the best dishes here is a hamachi tartare, with hamachi scraped off the bones and topped with tobiko and raw quail egg, served with sheets of crisp nori. But you're not likely to be disappointed with any dish. *1329 S. King St. ☎ 808/589-1329. Reservations highly recommended. Sashimi $12–$40; small plates $4–$13. Bus 2. Dinner Mon–Sat. Map p 93.*

★ **Koko Head Café** KAIMUKĪ *BRUNCH* This "island-style brunch house" offers inspired takes on breakfast favorites. There's the cornflake French toast, extra crunchy on the outside and custardy on the inside, crowned with frosted flake gelato, and the Don Buri Chen, a rice bowl for carnivores, with miso-smoked pork, five-spice pork belly and eggs. *1145c 12th Ave., www.kokoheadcafe.com.*

Innovative sushi at Izakaya Gaku

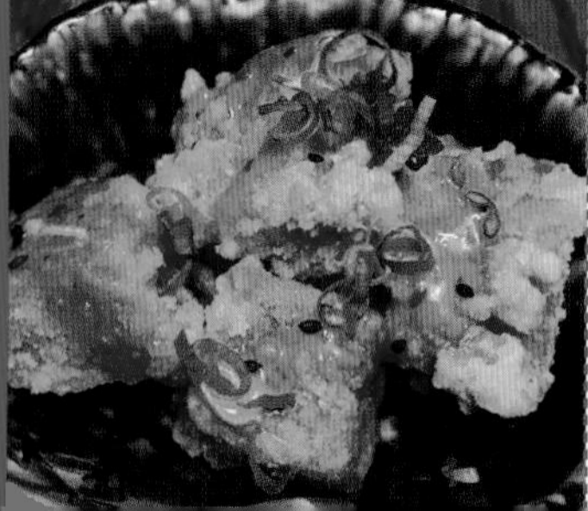

☎ 808/732-8920. Breakfast $9–$16. Bus 9. Map p 93.

★★★ **La Mer** WAIKĪKĪ *NEOCLASSIC FRENCH* This second-floor oceanfront bastion of haute cuisine is the place to go for a romantic evening. Michelin Award–winning chef Alexandre Trancher prepares classical French dishes with fresh island ingredients (hamachi with pistachio, shrimp on black risotto, and scallops with ratatouille served with a saffron sauce). *Halekulani Hotel, 2199 Kalia Rd. (Lewers St.). ☎ 808/923-2311. www.halekulani.com. Prix-fixe menu $110 for 3 courses, $145 for 4 courses; tasting menu $175. Dinner daily. Bus: 8. Map p 91.*

★ **Liliha Bakery** HONOLULU *LOCAL/AMERICAN* Open 24-hours, this is one of O'ahu's favorite old-school diners, beloved by young and old alike. Sit at the Formica counter and watch the ladies expertly man the grill, turning out light and fluffy pancakes, crispy and seriously buttery waffles, loaded country-style omelets, and satisfying hamburgers and hamburger steaks. There's a newer location on Nimitz, but I prefer the ambience of the original. *515 N. Kuakini St. www.lilihabakeryhawaii.com. ☎ 808/531-1651. Most items under $10. Open 24 hr. from Tues at 6am to Sun at 8pm. Bus 13. Map p 92.*

★★ **Little Village Noodle House** CHINATOWN *CHINESE* My pick for the best Chinese food served "simple and healthy" (its motto) is this tiny neighborhood restaurant with helpful waitstaff and even parking in the back (unheard of in Chinatown). Try the honey-walnut shrimp or the garlic eggplant. The menu includes Northern, Canton, and Hong Kong–style dishes. *1113 Smith St. (btw. King & Pauahi sts.). ☎ 808/545-3008. www.littlevillagehawaii.com. Entrees under $21. Lunch & dinner daily. Bus: 13 or 20. Map p 92.*

★★ **Mahina and Sun's** WAIKĪKĪ *HAWAI'I REGIONAL* The sad truth is that in Waikīkī, it's hard to find good local seafood. Most of the stuff on menus, from shellfish to salmon, is imported. But you won't find any of that here. Order the Family Feast for the best Mahina and Sun's experience—a whole, mochiko fried local fish arrives to the table, surrounded by fixin's: roasted roots with ogo (seaweed), pohole (fiddlehead fern) salad, buttered 'ulu (breadfruit), plus oysters, raised on the Windward side of O'ahu, and to finish, a salted mac nut pavlova. *At Surfjack Hotel, 412 Lewers Street, Waikīkī. www.surfjack.com. ☎ 808/924-5810. Breakfast $10–$16, lunch $13–$17, dinner entrees $17–$35. Breakfast, lunch, and dinner daily. Bus 8. Map p 91.*

A breakfast/brunch skillet at Koko Head Café

★★ **Marukame Udon** WAIKĪKĪ *JAPANESE/UDON* There's always a massive line out the door at this cafeteria-style noodle joint, but it moves quickly. Pass the time by watching the cooks roll out and cut the dough for udon right in front of you. Bowls of udon, hot or cold, with toppings such as a soft poached egg or Japanese curry, are all under $7. *2310 Kūhiō Ave., Waikīkī, Honolulu. ☎ 808/931-6000. Noodles $4–$7. Lunch and dinner daily. Bus 8, 19, or 20. Map p 91.*

★★ **Michel's** WAIKĪKĪ *FRENCH/HAWAI'I REGIONAL* One side of this 45-year-old classic French restaurant opens to the ocean view (get there for sunset), but the food is the real draw. Tuxedo-clad waiters serve classic French cuisine with an island infusion (lobster bisque, steak Diane, and a Caesar salad made at your table) in an elegantly

Romantic French dining at the acclaimed La Mer Restaurant

casual atmosphere. *Colony Surf Hotel, 2895 Kalākaua Ave.* ☎ *808/923-6552. www.michelshawaii.com. Entrees $45–$80. Dinner daily. Bus: 19 or 20. Map p 91.*

★ **Nico's at Pier 38** IWILEI *FRESH FISH* This spot, on the pier next to the fish auction, serves up, you guessed it, fresh fish. My favorite is the furikake-pan-seared ahi with the addicting ginger garlic cilantro dip, served with greens or macaroni salad for $13. *Pier 38, 1129 N. Nimitz Hwy. (Alakawa St.).* ☎ *808/540-1377. www.nicospier38.com. Breakfast $7–$9, lunch $9–$17, dinner $10–$28. Breakfast Mon–Sat, lunch & dinner daily. Bus: 19 or 20. Map p 92.*

★★ **Ono Seafood** WAIKĪKĪ *LOCAL* This little seafood counter serves some of Honolulu's freshest and best poke—cubes of ruby-red 'ahi (tuna) seasoned to order with soy sauce and onions for the *shoyu* poke or *limu* (seaweed) and Hawaiian salt for Hawaiian-style poke. *747 Kapahulu Ave., Apt. 4,* ☎ *808/732-4806. Everything under $10. Mon and Wed–Sat 8am–6pm; Sun 10am–3pm. Bus 2. Map p 93.*

★★★ **Orchids** WAIKĪKĪ *INTERNATIONAL/SEAFOOD* This is the best Sunday brunch in Hawai'i, with a whole, roasted suckling pig, and an outstanding array of dishes from popovers to sushi to an omelet station. The setting is extraordinary (right on Waikīkī Beach), and the food is excellent. You'll need to book at least a month in advance

Beef udon from Marukame Udon

Nico's at Pier 38

for brunch reservations. *Halekulani Hotel, 2199 Kalia Rd. (Lewers St.).* ☎ *808/923-2311. www.halekulani.com. Dinner entrees $24–$59; Sun brunch $69 adults, $34 children 5–12. Breakfast, lunch & dinner Mon–Sat, brunch & dinner Sun. Bus: 8, 19, or 42. Map p 91.*

★ **Sansei Seafood Restaurant & Sushi Bar** WAIKĪKĪ *SUSHI/ASIAN–PACIFIC RIM* Perpetual award winner D. K. Kodama's Waikīkī restaurant is known not only for its extensive menu but also for Kodama's outrageous sushi creations. Examples include seared foie gras nigiri sushi (duck liver lightly seared over sushi rice, with caramelized onion and ripe mango) or the wonderful mango crab salad hand roll (mango, blue crab, greens, and peanuts with a sweet Thai-chili vinaigrette). *Waikīkī Beach Marriott Resort, 2552 Kalākaua Ave.* ☎ *808/931-6286. www.sanseihawaii.com. Sushi $4–$20, entrees $16–$32. Dinner daily. Bus: 8 or 19. Map p 91.*

★★ **Senia** CHINATOWN *MODERN AMERICAN* This is one of Honolulu's newest and most exciting restaurants, where something as ordinary as cabbage can surprise and delight. Senia, deriving from "xenia," the Greek word for hospitality, is a rare mesh of the fine dining and comfort food worlds. As in, the food is fancy—bone marrow custard, foie gras terrine, and pretty presentations of smoked salmon with date and cauliflower—but the flavors are accessible, the setting leans casual and the prices are moderate. The menu changes frequently at Senia, but it will always be a combination of surprise and comfort. *75 N. King St., Honolulu. www.restaurantsenia.com ☎ 808/200-5412. Reservations recommended. Small plates $12–$22. Dinner Mon–Sat. Bus: 19 or 20. Map p 92.*

★ Teddy's Bigger Burgers WAIKĪKĪ *AMERICAN* This casual burger joint is voted Honolulu's best, year after year. It's deserved: here, you'll get juicy patties on buns that are soft, yet sturdy enough to hold the meat and fixin's all together. Get the Cajun fries as a side. *134 Kapahulu Ave. ☎ 808/926-3444. www.teddysbb.com. Sandwiches and burgers $7–$12. Lunch and dinner daily. Bus 8, 19, or 20. Map p 91.*

★ The Pig and the Lady CHINATOWN *MODERN VIETNAMESE* Welcome to a world of Vietnamese noodle soups beyond pho—such as one with oxtail, another with crab and tomato. Chef Andrew Le applies creative twists to Southeast Asian food for unique eats like a pho French dip banh mi—an absolute must with its melting slices of braised brisket, smeared with a bright Thai basil chimichurri and served with a side of pho broth for dipping. Everything is en pointe here, from the cocktails to the dessert. *83 N. King St., www.thepigandthelady.com. ☎ 808/383-2152. Reservations recommended. Entrees $11–$30. Lunch and dinner Mon–Sat. Bus 19 or 20. Map p 92.*

★ Town KAIMUKI *CONTEMPORARY ITALIAN* Dine on ahi tartar on risotto cakes or outstanding gnocchi in this restaurant that combines Italian flavors with local ingredients. Lunches consist of sandwiches, salads, and pastas. *3435 Waialae Ave. (at 9th St.). ☎ 808/735-5900. www.townkaimuki.com. Lunch $11–$16, dinner $16–$26. Breakfast, lunch & dinner Mon–Sat. Bus: 2L. Map p 93.*

★ 12th Avenue Grill KAIMUKI *CONTEMPORARY AMERICAN* Here, the menu leans towards comfort food, like baked mac 'n' cheese, and locally raised meat, such as pork chops with potato pancakes and ribeye on fresh pappardelle. ***Tip:*** Sit in the bar area during opening or closing hours, when the bar serves a special menu of terrific hamburgers and meatloaf sandwiches, and nothing costs more than $10. *1120 12th Ave., Honolulu. http://12thavegrill.com. ☎ 808/732-9469. Reservations recommended. Small plates $7–$13; large plates $23–$36 Dinner daily. Bus: Walk to Kala̅kaua Ave., then catch 2L bus & transfer to 1. Map p 93.*

★ Waikiki Yokocho WAIKĪKĪ *JAPANESE* What used to be nondescript basement food court has been reimagined as *yokocho*—literally, alleyways off to the side of a main street, but often referring to the small bars and eateries in these narrow lanes. Here, you'll find tiny restaurants—some with just a few tables—dishing out tempura, sushi, and ramen, as well as a Japanese whisky and cocktail bar in the center. For dessert, finish off with a matcha parfait or soft serve at Nana's Green Tea. *At the Waikīkī Shopping Plaza, 2250 Kala̅kaua Ave., Waikı̅kı̅, Honolulu. www.waikiki-yokocho.com. ☎ 808/926-8093. Items from $10. Lunch and dinner daily. Bus 8, 19, or 20. Map p 91.*

Teddy's Bigger Burgers is a local favorite.

Lodging Best Bets

Most **Romantic**
★★ Royal Hawaiian $$$$ *2259 Kalākaua Ave. (p 109)*

Most **Historic**
★★ Moana Surfrider, a Westin Resort $$$$ *2365 Kalākaua Ave. (p 107)*

Most **Luxurious**
★★★ Halekulani $$$$ *2199 Kalia Rd. (p 105)*

Best **Moderately Priced**
★ Park Shore Waikīkī $$ 2586 Kalākaua Ave. *(p 109)*

Best **Budget Hotel**
Royal Grove Hotel $ *151 Uluniu Ave. (p 109)*

Best **for Kids**
★★★ Embassy Suites Waikīkī Beach Walk $$$$ *201 Beach Walk (p 105)*

Best **Value**
★ The Breakers $$ *250 Beach Walk (p 104)*

Hippest Hotel
★★ Waikīkī Parc $$$ *2233 Helumoa Rd. (p 111)*

Best **View of Waikīkī Beach**
★★ Hilton Hawaiian Village Waikīkī Beach Resort $$$ *2005 Kalia Rd. (p 105)*

Best **View of Ala Wai Harbor**
★★ Prince Hotel Waikīkī $$$$ *100 Holomoana St. (p 109)*

Best **View of Fort DeRussy Park**
★ Luana Waikīkī $$ *2045 Kalākaua Ave. (p 107)*

Most **Trendy**
★★ The Modern Honolulu $$$ *1775 Ala Moana Blvd. (p 108)*

Best **Hi-Tech Gadgets**
★★ Hotel Renew $$$ *129 Paoakalani Ave. (p 106)*

Best **Hidden Gem**
★ New Otani Kaimana Beach Hotel $$$ *2863 Kalākaua Ave. (p 108)*

Best **Boutique Hotel**
★★ Surfjack Hotel & Swim Club $$ 412 Lewers St. *(p 110)*

Best **View of Diamond Head**
★★ Lotus Honolulu $$$ 2885 Kalākaua Ave. *(p 107)*

Waikīkī's Best Lodging

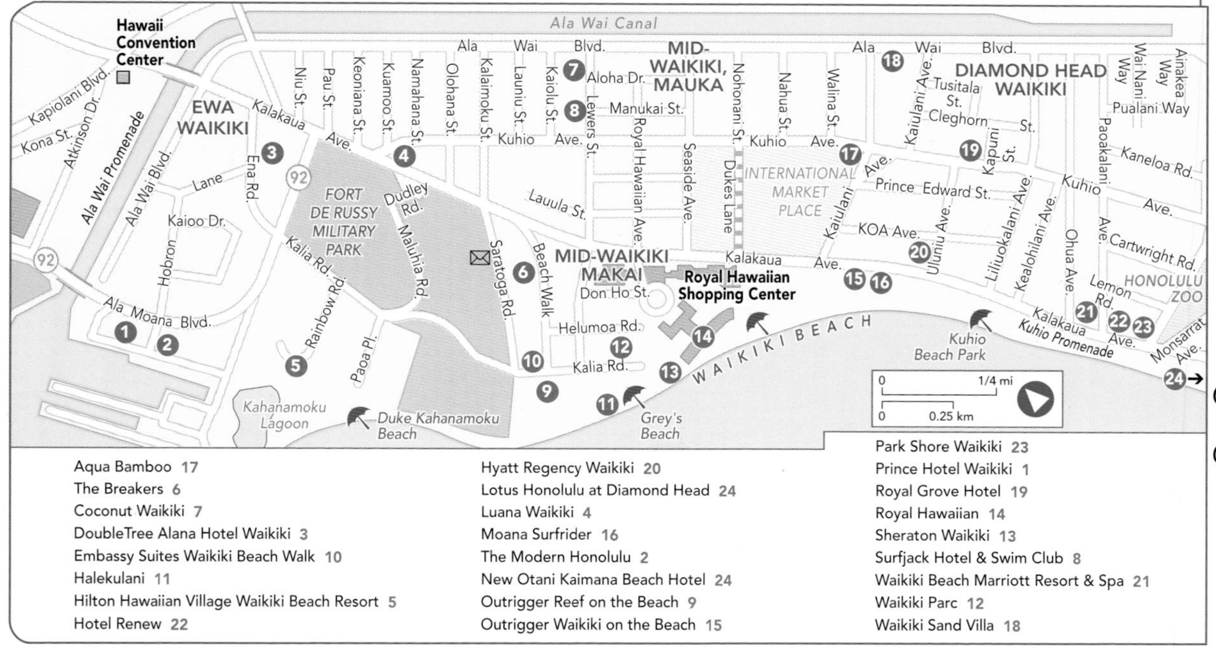

Waikīkī Hotels A to Z

★ **Aqua Bamboo** MID-WAIKĪKĪ MAUKA An intimate boutique hotel, decorated with Asian flair (with kitchenettes or kitchens). Other pluses: only a block from Waikīkī beach, free continental breakfast, spa on property, and personal service. Minus: not enough parking for all rooms. *2425 Kūhiō Ave. (at Kaiulani Ave.). ☎ 866/406-2782 or 808/922-7777. www.aquaresorts.com. 90 units. Doubles $169–$260. Bus: 19 or 20. Map p 103.*

★ **The Breakers** MID-WAIKĪKĪ MAKAI This two-story 1950s budget hotel is a terrific buy for families (kitchenettes in all rooms) and just 2 minutes' walk to the beach, restaurants, and shopping. Expect comfortable budget accommodations with tropical accents. *250 Beachwalk (btw. Kalākaua Ave. & Kalia Rd.). ☎ 800/426-0494 or 808/923-3181. www.breakers-hawaii.com. 64 units. Doubles $160–$180; suites $235. Bus: 19 or 20. Map p 103.*

★ **Coconut Waikīkī** MID-WAIKĪKĪ MAKAU Rooms at this family-friendly, mid-range hotel are immaculate and come with a small lānai and wet bar. The tiny pool is kind of wedged between the hotel and a fence—better to grab the free beach-towel rental and head to the ocean sands. Its sister hotel, **Shoreline Hotel Waikīkī** (http://shorelinehotelwaikiki.com), is a few blocks away, with similar amenities and a midcentury modern vibe. Check out **Heavenly** at the Shoreline, with its surfer-chic decor and delicious brunch. *450 Lewers St. (at Ala Wai Blvd.). coconutwaikikihotel.com. ☎ 808/923-8828. 81 units. Doubles $169–$219; suites from $249. Bus 19 or 20. Map p 103.*

★ **DoubleTree Alana Hotel Waikīkī** EWA This boutique hotel (operated by the Hilton Hawaiian Village) is an oasis of small but comfortable rooms, with amenities of a more luxurious hotel at more affordable prices. Waikīkī Beach is a 10-minute walk away, and the convention center is about a 7-minute walk. *1956 Ala Moana Blvd. (near Kalākaua Ave.). ☎ 808/941-7275. www.doubletree.com. 317 units. Doubles $209–$239; suites from $249. Bus 19 or 20. Map p 103.*

Halekulani Hotel, where 90 percent of the rooms face the ocean

ton Hawaiian Village Waikīkī Beach Resort

★★★ Embassy Suites Waikīkī Beach Walk MID-WAIKĪKĪ MAKAI This ultraluxe one- and two-bedroom hotel, famous for its cooked to order breakfast and evening cocktail reception, has a great location just 1 block from the beach. The newly opened Waikīkī Beach Walk provides plenty of shops and restaurants on property. Prices may seem high, but it pencils out to a deal for families. *201 Beach Walk (at Kalia Rd.). ☎ 808/921-2345. www.embassysuiteswaikiki.com. 421 suites. 1-br suites $309–$639, 2-br suites $549–$849. Bus: 19 or 20. Map p 103.*

★★★ Halekulani MID-WAIKĪKĪ MAKAI This is my favorite hotel in all Hawai'i—the ultimate heavenly Hawai'i luxury accommodations, spread over 5 acres (2 ha) of prime Waikīkī beachfront. Some 90 percent of the large rooms (620 sq. ft./58 sq. m) face the ocean, and all have furnished lanais and top-drawer amenities. This is the best Waikīkī has to offer. *2199 Kalia Rd. (at Lewers St.). ☎ 808/923-2311. www.halekulani.com. 455 units. Doubles $555–$835; suites from $1,260. Bus: 19 or 20. Map p 103.*

★★ Hilton Hawaiian Village Waikīkī Beach Resort EWA This sprawling resort is like a microcosm of Waikīkī—on good days it feels like a lively little beach town with hidden nooks and crannies to discover and great bars in which to make new friends, and on bad days it's just an endless traffic jam, with lines into the parking garage, at the front desk, and in the restaurants. A wide choice of accommodations,

Waikīkī Neighborhoods

The neighborhoods in Waikīkī can be divided into four districts: **Ewa** (the western end of Waikīkī from Ala Wai Canal to Fort DeRussy Park), **Mid-Waikīkī Makai** (from the ocean up to Kalākaua Ave. and from Fort DeRussy Park to Kaiulani St.), **Mid-Waikīkī Mauka** (mountain side of Kalākaua Ave. to Ala Wai Blvd. and from Kalaimoku St. to Kaiulani St.), and **Diamond Head** (from the ocean to Ala Wai Blvd. and from Kaiulani to Diamond Head).

Pampering in Paradise

Hawai'i's spas have raised the art of relaxation and healing to a new level, as traditional Greco-Roman–style spas have evolved into airy, open facilities that embrace the tropics. Today's spas offer a wide diversity of treatments, many including traditional Hawaiian massages and ingredients. There are even side-by-side massages for couples and duo massages—two massage therapists working on you at once.

Of course, all this pampering doesn't come cheap. Massages are generally $175 to $300 for 50 minutes and $250 to $350 for 80 minutes; body treatments are in the $175 to $275 range; and alternative healthcare treatments can be as high as $200 to $300. But for many, a spa visit is an essential part of a Hawaiian vacation.

My picks for Waikīkī's best spas:

- **Most Relaxing: SpaHalekulani** From the time you step into the elegantly appointed, intimate spa until the last whiff of fragrant maile, the spa's signature scent, you will be transported to nirvana. Spa connoisseurs should try something unique, such as the Polynesian Nonu, a Samoan-inspired massage using stones. Halekulani Hotel, ☎ **808/923-2311;** www.halekulani.com.
- **Best Facial: Abhasa Waikīkī Spa** This contemporary spa, spread out over 7,000 square feet (650 sq. m), concentrates on natural, organic treatments in a soothing, outdoor atmosphere, where the smell of eucalyptus wafts through the air. Try the anti-aging facial for a refreshed, revitalized face immediately. Royal Hawaiian Hotel, ☎ **808/922-8200;** www.abhasa.com.
- **Best Day Spa: Moana Lani Spa** It's hard to beat the ocean views from the elegant, oceanfront treatment rooms and the relaxation lounges, where you can indulge in steam rooms and saunas before and after your massage. Moana Surfrider ☎ **808/237-2535;** www.moanalanispa.com.

from simple hotel rooms to ultradeluxe, are housed in five towers. An oasis in the middle of it all is the Ali'i Tower, with its own lobby lounge, reception, and concierge, and even its own pool and bar; it's like a hotel within a hotel. There's something for everyone here: tropical gardens dotted with exotic wildlife (flamingos, peacocks, and even penguins), nine restaurant and bars, 100 different shops, six pools, two minigolf courses, and a gorgeous stretch of Waikīkī Beach *2005 Kalia Rd. (at Ala Moana Blvd.).* ☎ *808/949-4321. www.hiltonhawaiianvillage.com. 2,860 units. Doubles $279–$479; suites from $499. Bus: 19 or 20. Map p 103.*

★★ **Hotel Renew** DIAMOND HEAD This boutique is a gem among aging Waikīkī hotels, an oasis of tranquility and excellent taste in a sea of schlock. Rooms have a quiet, Zen-like décor and lots of high-tech gadgets. Other perks include a location just a block from

Enjoy a sunset cocktail at Banyan Courtyard at the Moana Surfrider.

the beach, complimentary breakfast, and a free fitness center and yoga classes. *129 Paoakalani Ave. (at Lemon Rd.). ☎ 866/774-2924. www.hotelrenew.com. 72 units. Doubles $190–$350. Bus: 19 or 20. Map p 103.*

★ Hyatt Regency Waikīkī DIAMOND HEAD This is one of Waikīkī's largest hotels, with two 40-story towers covering nearly an entire city block, located across the street from Waikīkī Beach. The location is great, there's a good children's program, and guest rooms are large and luxuriously furnished, but personally I find it too big and too impersonal, with service to match. *2424 Kalākaua Ave. (btw. Kaiulani St. & Uluniu Ave.). ☎ 808/923-1234. www.waikiki.regency.hyatt.com. 1,230 units. Doubles $300–$610, Club level doubles $425–$660. Bus: 19 or 20. Map p 103.*

★★ Lotus Honolulu at Diamond Head DIAMOND HEAD You can sleep with the windows open here, on the quiet side of Waikīkī, between Kapi'olani Park and Diamond Head. Recently updated rooms offer dark hardwood floors, platform beds, granite-tiled bathrooms, and—in the corner units—a lānai and window that frame Diamond Head beautifully. Little touches, like music and cookies in your room when you first check in and morning yoga classes in the park make for a welcoming boutique experience. *2885 Kala¯kaua Ave., www.www.lotushonoluluhotel.com. ☎ 808/922-1700. 51 units. $219–$339 double. Bus: 2 or 14. Map p 103.*

★ Luana Waikīkī EWA Families take note: This midsize hotel offers studios with kitchenettes and 1-bedrooms with full kitchens. You also get terrific views of Fort DeRussy park and the ocean in the distance. *2045 Kalākaua Ave. (at Kūhiō Ave.). ☎ 808/955-6000. www.outrigger.com. 205 units. Doubles $149–$219; studios $169–$239; 1-bedroom $209–$269. Bus: 19 or 20. Map p 103.*

★★ Moana Surfrider, a Westin Resort MID-WAIKĪKĪ MAKAI Old Hawai'i reigns here; I recommend staying in the historic Banyan Wing, where rooms are modern replicas of Waikīkī's first hotel (built in 1901). Outside is a prime stretch of beach and an oceanfront courtyard centered on a 100-year-old banyan tree, where there's live music in the evenings. *2365 Kalākaua Ave. (across from Kaiulani St.). ☎ 808/922-3111. www.moana-surfrider.com. 793 units. Doubles $340–$625; suites from $970. Bus: 19 or 20. Map p 103.*

★★ The Modern Honolulu EWA Waikīkī's trendiest hotel offers comfy, yet stylish rooms with huge windows overlooking the yacht club and ocean. Bucking the trend in Waikīkī, this new-in-2010 hotel is *not* on Waikīkī Beach but overlooks the Ala Wai Harbor. Because there is no white sand beach, the hotel designers decided on a cruise ship–inspired view: You can look out at the third floor's large pool and deck area and see all ocean. Terrific spa. *1775 Ala Moana Blvd. (at Hobron Lane). ☎ 866/811-4163 or 808/943-5800. www.themodernhonolulu.com. 353 units. Doubles $289–$519; suites from $629. Bus: 19 or 20. Map p 103.*

★ New Otani Kaimana Beach Hotel DIAMOND HEAD This is one of Waikīkī's best-kept secrets: a boutique hotel nestled on the beach at the foot of Diamond Head, with Kapiolani Park just across the street. Skip the inexpensive, barely-room-for-two rooms and go for the oceanfront rooms. *2863 Kalākaua Ave. (near Waikīkī Aquarium, across from Kapiolani Park). ☎ 800/356-8264 or 808/923-1555. www.kaimana.com. 124 units. Doubles $148–$344; studios from $184; suites $272–$470 and up. Bus: 19 or 20. Map 103.*

★ Outrigger Reef on the Beach MID-WAIKĪKĪ MAKAI This three-tower megahotel's prime beachfront location and loads of facilities (including a 5,000-sq.-ft./465-sq.-m spa) make it one of the chain's most attractive properties. A recent multimillion-dollar renovation upgraded furniture and spruced up the bathrooms. Even the standard rooms are large and comfortable. *2169 Kalia Rd. (at Beach Walk). ☎ 800/OUTRIGGER (688-7444) or 808/923-3111. www.outrigger.com. 883 units. Doubles $249–$549; suites from $275. Bus: 19 or 20. Map p 103.*

★★ Outrigger Waikīkī on the Beach MID-WAIKĪKĪ MAKAI I'd pick this Outrigger to stay in: Not only does it have an excellent location on Waikīkī Beach, but it also invested $20 million into guest room renovations and upgrades (oversize Jacuzzi bathtubs with ocean views in some rooms). These upgrades, coupled with the great dining (**Duke's** and **Hula Grill;** see p 96, 97), mean more for your money. *2335 Kalākaua Ave. (btw. the Royal Hawaiian Shopping Center &*

The Modern Honolulu's Sunrise Pool

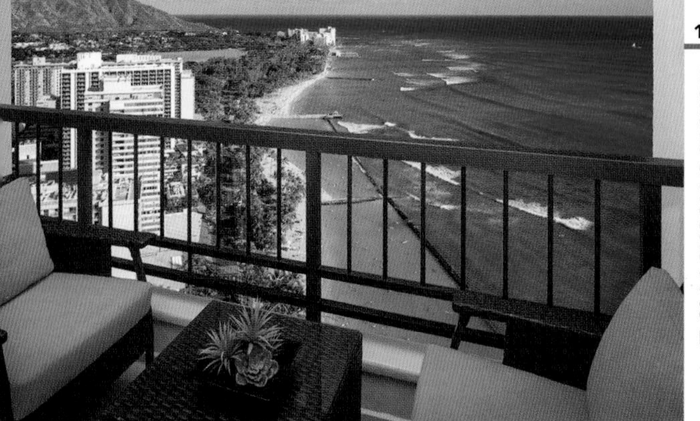

A balcony room at Hyatt Regency Waikīkī Beach Resort and Spa

Moana Surfrider). ☎ *800/OUTRIGGER (688-7444) or 808/923-0711. www.outrigger.com. 525 units. Doubles $259–$829; suites from $559. Bus: 19 or 20. Map p 103.*

★ **Park Shore Waikīkī** DIAMOND HEAD This hotel has a great location, on the quieter end of Waikīkī, and yet it's still close to the water. A number of the rooms have oceanfront views, making this option terrific for the price. 2586 Kalākaua Ave. (☎ **808/954-7426**), *www.parkshorewaikiki.com. 226 units. Doubles $169–$249; suites from $289. Bus: 19 or 20. Map p 103.*

★★ **Prince Hotel Waikīkī** EWA For accommodations with a view and the feel of a palace, stay in these striking twin 33-story high-tech towers, where service is priority. All bedrooms face the Ala Wai Yacht Harbor, with floor-to-ceiling sliding-glass windows (sorry, no lanai). The higher the floor, the higher the price. Ala Moana Center is a 10-minute walk away, and Waikīkī's beaches are just a 5-minute walk. Check out the spare **Katsumidori Sushi Tokyo** restaurant for impeccable sushi. *100 Holomoana St. (just across Ala Wai Canal Bridge).* ☎ *800/321-O'AHU (6248) or 808/956-1111. www.princeresortshawaii.com. 521 units. Doubles $294–$444; suites from $544. Bus: 19 or 20. Map p 103.*

★ **Royal Grove Hotel** DIAMOND HEAD This is a great bargain for frugal travelers and families; the budget accommodations are no-frill (along the lines of a Motel 6), but the family-owned hotel has genuine aloha for all the guests, and Waikīkī Beach is a 3-minute walk. *151 Uluniu Ave. (btw. Prince Edward & Kūhiō aves.).* ☎ *808/923-7691. www.royalgrovehotel.com. 85 units. Doubles $57–$75; 1-bedroom $100–$150. Bus: 19 or 20. Map p 103.*

★★ **Royal Hawaiian** MID-WAIKĪKĪ MAKAI The symbol of Waikīkī, this flamingo-pink oasis, nestled in tropical gardens, offers rooms in both the 1927 historic wing (my favorites, with carved

All rooms at the Prince Hotel Waikīkī face the Ala Wai Yacht Harbor.

The Royal Hawaiian Suite at the Royal Hawaiian Hotel

wooden doors, four-poster canopy beds, flowered wallpaper, and period furniture) and modern oceanfront towers. The beach outside is the best in Waikīkī for sunbathing. *2259 Kalākaua Ave. (at Royal Hawaiian Ave.). ☎ 800/325-3535 or 808/923-7311. www.starwoodhotels.com. 527 units. Doubles $430–$670; suites from $775. Bus: 19 or 20. Map p 103.*

★ **Sheraton Waikīkī** MID-WAIKĪKĪ MAKAI It's hard to get a bad room here—the hotel sits right on Waikīkī Beach: A whopping 1,200 units have ocean views, and 650 overlook Diamond Head. However, this is a megahotel, with two 30-story towers and an immense lobby. It's a frequent favorite of conventions and can be crowded, noisy, and overwhelming (not to mention the long wait at the bank of nearly a dozen elevators). *2255 Kalākaua Ave. (at Royal Hawaiian Ave.). ☎ 800/325-3535 or 808/922-4422. www.starwoodhotels.com. 1,852 units. Doubles $325–$588; club level from $370; suites from $701. Bus: 19 or 20. Map p 103.*

★★ **Surfjack Hotel & Swim Club** MID-WAIKĪKĪ MAKAI Remade from a 1960s budget hotel, the Surfjack is achingly retro-hip and screams midcentury-beach house cool, from the "Wish You Were Here" mosaic on the swimming pool floor to the pretty blue and white tiling in the bathrooms to the vintage headboard upholstery

The Royal Hawaiian Hotel's iconic pink building dates to 1927.

by Tori Richard. It's not close to the beach, and the views are mostly of buildings, and yet, it will be hard to leave this soulful enclave, where you can get excellent cocktails by the pool, or a perfect cup of coffee while you browse the onsite clothing boutique. *412 Lewers St., Honolulu. www.surfjack.com. ☎ 855/945-4082 or 808/564-7608. 112 units. Doubles $227–$287; suites from $340. Bus: 19 or 20. Map p 103.*

★ Waikīkī Beach Marriott Resort & Spa DIAMOND HEAD Pluses: It's across the street from the beach, has renovated rooms, and boasts great restaurants (**Sansei Seafood Restaurant & Sushi Bar** and **d.k. Steakhouse;** see p 100). The minus: Rack rates are way too high—check its website for 40 percent off. *2552 Kalākaua Ave. (at Ohua Ave.). ☎ 800/367-5370 or 808/922-6611. www.marriott.com. 1,310 units. Doubles $209–$419. Bus: 19 or 20. Map p 103.*

★★ Waikīkī Parc MID-WAIKĪKĪ MAKAI Recently redesigned and renovated, especially for the 20s and 30s crowd, this "hidden" luxury hotel (operated by the Halekulani) offers lots of bonuses: It's just 100 yards (91m) from the beach, has modern high-tech rooms, hosts frequent wine-party receptions, and offers first-class service. *2233 Helumoa Rd. (at Lewers St.). ☎ 800/422-0450 or 808/921-7272. www.waikikiparchotel.com. 297 units. Doubles $221–$425. Bus: 19 or 20. Map p 103.*

The lagoon-style pool at the Sheraton Waikīkī

★ Waikīkī Sand Villa MID-WAIKĪKĪ MAUKA Budget travelers, take note: This very affordable 10-story hotel is located on the quieter side of Waikīkī, with medium-size rooms and studio apartments with kitchenettes (fridge, stove, and microwave). It's a 10-minute walk to the beach. *2375 Ala Wai Blvd. (at Kanekapolei Ave.). ☎ 800/247-1903 or 808/922-4744. www.sandvillahotel.com. 214 units. Doubles $88–$145; studios kitchenette $148–$185. Bus: 19 or 20. Map p 103.*

Shopping Best Bets

Best **Traditional Alohawear**
★★ Bailey's Antiques & Aloha Shirts, *517 Kapahulu Ave. (p 116)*

Best **Modern Alohawear**
★ Roberta Oaks, *19 N. Pauahi St, (p 117)*

Best **Curios and Vintage**
★ Hound and Quail, *920 Maunakea St. (p 117)*

Best **Antiques**
★ T. Fujii Japanese Antiques, *1016 Kapahulu Ave. (p 117)*

Best **Place to Browse**
★★★ Native Books/Na Mea Hawai'i, *1050 Ala Moana Blvd. (p 121)*

Best **Mochi**
★ Nisshodo Candy Store, *1095 Dillingham Blvd. (p 118)*

Best **Gifts**
★★★ Nohea Gallery, *1050 Ala Moana Blvd. (p 121)*

Best **Place for Edible Gifts**
Whole Foods, *4211 Wai'alae Ave. and 629 Kailua Rd., Kailua. (p 119)*

Best **Place for a Lei**
★ Cindy's Lei Shoppe, *1034 Maunakea St. (p 120)*

Best **Shopping Center**
★★ Ala Moana Center, *1450 Ala Moana Blvd. (p 122)*

Best **Shopping-as-Entertainment**
★★ Honolulu Fish Auction, *Pier 38, 1131 N. Nimitz Hwy. (p 120)*

Best **Bean-to-Bar Chocolate**
★★ Madre Chocolate., *8 N. Pauahi St. (p 118)*

Best **Chocolate Truffles**
★ Padovani's Chocolates, *650 Iwilei Rd. #280. (p 119)*

Best **Wine & Liquor**
Fujioka's Wine Times, *2919 Kapiolani Blvd. (p 117)*

Best **Vintage Clothing**
★ Barrio Vintage, *1161 Nu'uanu Ave. (p 119)*

Waikīkī's Best Shopping

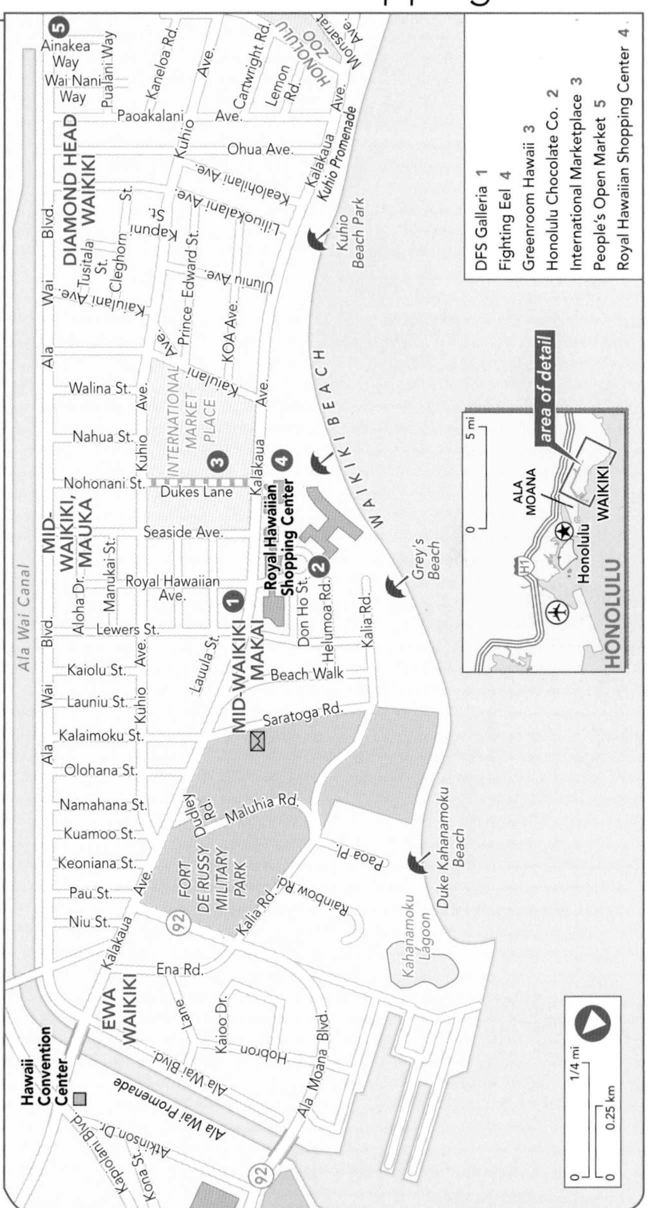

Honolulu's Best Shopping

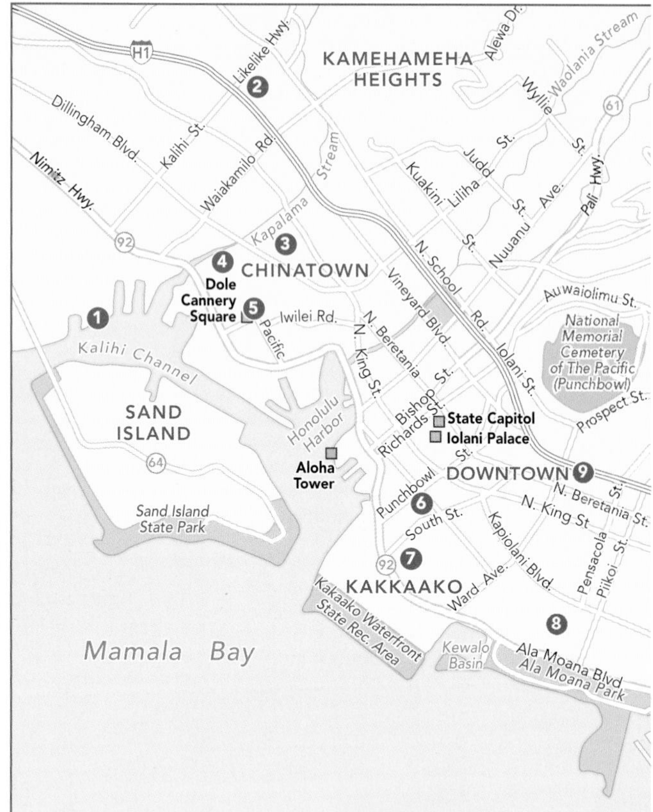

Ala Moana Center 12
Bailey's Antiques & Aloha Shirts 19
Don Quijote 11
Down to Earth 14
Fujioka's Wine Times 16
Hawaiian Island Creations 12
Honolulu Chocolate Co. 7
Honolulu Fish Auction 1
Honolulu Museum of Art Shop 9
Kamaka Ukulele 6
Kicks 11
Kokua Market 15
Local Motion 12
Native Books/Na Mea Hawaii 7
Nisshodo Candy Store 4
Nohea Gallery 7
Padovani's Chocolates 5
Rainforest at Kilohana Square 18
Reyn Spooner 12
R. Field Wine Co. 10
Salt at Kaka'ako 7
Shop Pacifica 2
Tamashiro Market 3
T. Fujii Japanese Antiques 17
Ward Village Shops 8
Whole Foods 20
Yama's Fish Market 13

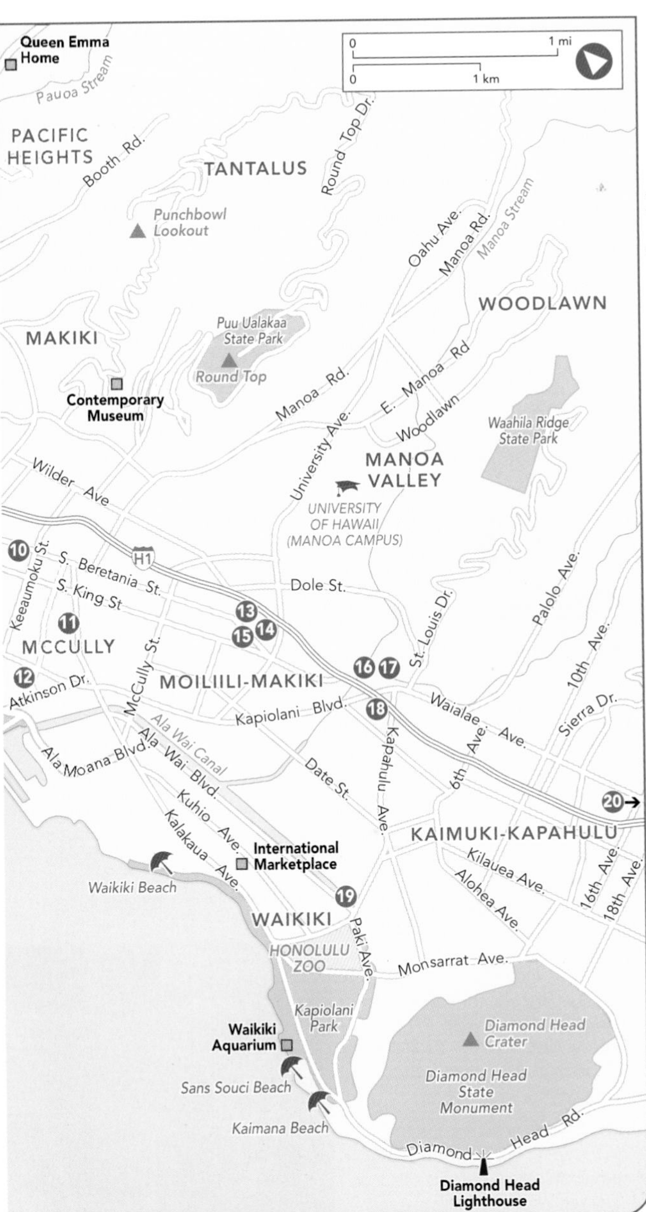
0 1 mi
0 1 km
Queen Emma Home
Pauoa Stream
PACIFIC HEIGHTS
Booth Rd.
TANTALUS
Round Top Dr.
Punchbowl Lookout
Oahu Ave.
Manoa Rd.
Manoa Stream
WOODLAWN
MAKIKI
Puu Ualakaa State Park
Round Top
Contemporary Museum
Manoa Rd.
University Ave.
E. Manoa Rd
Woodlawn
Waahila Ridge State Park
MANOA VALLEY
Wilder Ave
UNIVERSITY OF HAWAII (MANOA CAMPUS)
H1
10
S. Beretania St.
S. King St
Keeaumoku St.
Dole St.
13
11
15
14
MCCULLY
Palolo Ave.
St. Louis Dr.
10th Ave.
16
17
12
Atkinson Dr.
McCully St.
MOILIILI-MAKIKI
Kapiolani Blvd.
18
Waialae Ave.
Sierra Dr.
6th Ave.
Ala Wai Canal
Ala Moana Blvd.
Ala Wai Blvd.
Date St.
Kapahulu Ave.
20
Kuhio Ave.
Kalakaua Ave.
International Marketplace
KAIMUKI-KAPAHULU
Kilauea Ave.
Alohea Ave.
16th Ave.
18th Ave.
Waikiki Beach
19
WAIKIKI
Paki Ave.
HONOLULU ZOO
Monsarrat Ave.
Kapiolani Park
Diamond Head Crater
Waikiki Aquarium
Diamond Head State Monument
Sans Souci Beach
Kaimana Beach
Diamond Head Rd.
Diamond Head Lighthouse

Chinatown's Best Shopping

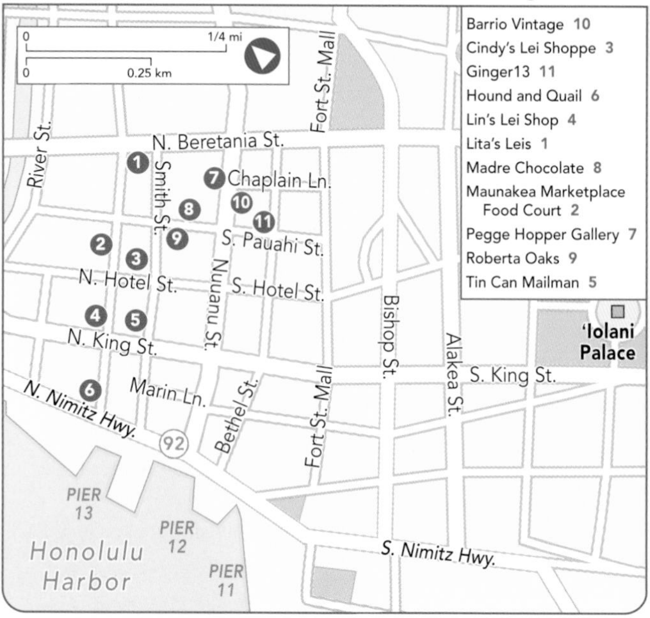

0
1/4 mi
0
0.25 km
Barrio Vintage 10
Cindy's Lei Shoppe 3
Ginger13 11
Hound and Quail 6
Lin's Lei Shop 4
Lita's Leis 1
Madre Chocolate 8
Maunakea Marketplace Food Court 2
Pegge Hopper Gallery 7
Roberta Oaks 9
Tin Can Mailman 5
River St.
N. Beretania St.
Smith St.
Chaplain Ln.
S. Pauahi St.
N. Hotel St.
S. Hotel St.
Nuuanu St.
N. King St.
Marin Ln.
N. Nimitz Hwy.
92
Bethel St.
Fort St. Mall
Bishop St.
Alakea St.
S. King St.
'Iolani Palace
S. Nimitz Hwy.
PIER 13
PIER 12
PIER 11
Honolulu Harbor

Honolulu & Waikīkī Shopping A to Z

Alohawear

★★ Bailey's Antiques & Aloha Shirts KAPAHULU Honolulu's largest selection (thousands) of vintage, secondhand, and nearly new aloha shirts and other collectibles fill this eclectic emporium, as do old ball gowns, feather boas, fur stoles, leather jackets, 1930s dresses, and scads of other garments. *517 Kapahulu Ave. (at Castle St.). ☎ 808/734-7628. www.alohashirts.com. Bus: 2 or 13. Map p 115.*

Reyn Spooner ALA MOANA Reyn Spooner used to be a prosaic line but has stepped up its selection of women's and men's alohawear with contemporary fabric prints and stylings that appeal to a trendier clientele. *Ala Moana Center, 1450 Ala*

Alohawear at Bailey's Antiques & Aloha Shirts

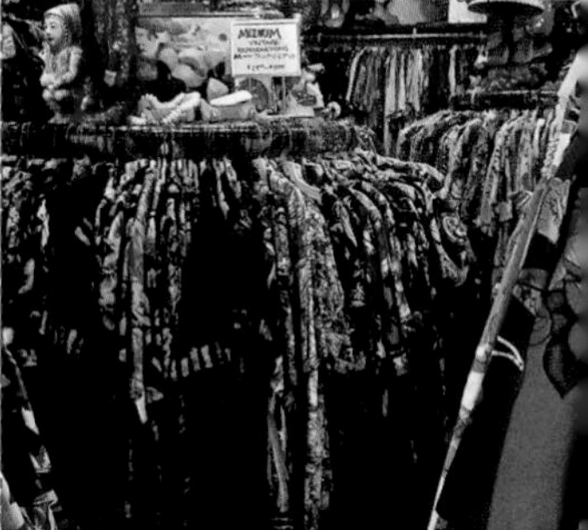

Artist Pegge Hopper is known for her paintings of Hawaiian women.

Moana Blvd. (at Piikoi). ☎ *808/949-5929. Also at the Sheraton Waikīkī and the Kahala Mall. www.reyns.com. Bus: 19 or 20. Map p 115.*

★ **Roberta Oaks** CHINATOWN The hippest guys and gals come here. Roberta Oaks ditches the too-big aloha shirt for a more stylish, fitted look, but keeps the vintage designs. Plus, she even has super-cute, tailored aloha shirts for the ladies. *19 N. Pauahi St.* ☎ *808/428-1214. www.robertaoaks.com. Bus 19 or 20. Map p 116.*

Antiques & Collectibles

★ **Hound and Quail** CHINATOWN A funky collection of antiques and curiosities, from a taxidermied ostrich to old medical texts, make for a fascinating perusal. The bottom floor hosts a gallery of young and local artists. *920 Maunakea St.* ☎ *808/779-8436. www.houndandquail.com. Bus 19 or 20. Map p 116.*

T. Fujii Japanese Antiques MO'ILI'ILI This is a long-standing icon in Hawai'i's antiques world and an impeccable source for ukiyo-e prints, scrolls, obis, Imari porcelain, tansus, tea-ceremony bowls, and screens as well as contemporary ceramics from Mashiko and Kasama, with prices from $25 to $18,000. *1016-B Kapahulu Ave. (King St. & H1).* ☎ *808/732-7860. www.tfujiiantiques.com. Bus: 13 to 14. Map p 115.*

Art

★ **Greenroom Hawaii** WAIKĪKĪ Stop into this gallery for the best of Hawai'i's surf art and photography. You'll find Clark Little's snaps of pounding beach breaks, Zak Noyle's breathtaking surf photos, Nick Kuchar's vintage-styled Hawai'i travel posters, Heather Brown's bold and bright prints, and Kris Goto's quirky drawings combing manga sensibilities with Hawai'i beach culture. *At International Marketplace. 2330 Kalākaua Ave.* ☎ *808/377-6766 and Sheraton Waikīkī, 2255 Kalākaua Ave.* ☎ *808/931-8908 www.greenroomhawaii.com. Bus: 19 or 20. Map p 113.*

★ **Pegge Hopper Gallery** CHINATOWN One of Hawai'i's most popular artists, Hopper displays her widely collected paintings in her attractive gallery, which has become quite the gathering place for exhibits ranging from Tibetan sand painting by saffron-robed monks to the most avant-garde printmaking in the islands. *1164 Nu'uanu Ave. (btw. Beretania & Pauahi sts.).* ☎ *808/524-1160. www.peggehopper.com. Bus: B, 19, or 20. Map p 116.*

Edibles

Don Quijote KAKA'AKO You can find everything at this huge emporium, ranging from takeout sushi, Korean *kal bi*, pizza, and Chinese food to Kau navel oranges, macadamia nuts, Kona coffee, Chinese taro, and other Hawai'i products. *801 Kaheka St. (at Kahunu St.).* ☎ *808/973-4800. Bus: 2. Map p 115.*

Fujioka's Wine Times MO'ILI'ILI Oenophiles flock here for the fine selection of wines,

Take-out sashimi at Don Quijote

single-malt Scotches, craft beers, and cigars—libations for all occasions. *Market City Shopping Center, 2919 Kapi'olani Blvd. (at S. King St.), lower level. www.timessupermarkets.com/fujiokas-wine-times.* ☎ *808/739-9463. Bus: 14. Map p 115.*

★ **Honolulu Chocolate Co.** ALA MOANA Life's greatest pleasures are dispensed here with abandon: boulder-size turtles (caramel and pecans covered with chocolate), truffles, dark chocolate and macadamia nut clusters, and my favorites—the chocolate-dipped dried apricot and candied oranges. *Ward Village Shops, 1200 Ala Moana Blvd. (at Auahi St.).* ☎ *808/591-2997. Sheraton Waikīkī, 2255 Kalākaua Ave.* ☎ *808/931-8937. www.honoluluchocolate.com. Bus: 19 or 20. Map p 114.*

★ **Madre Chocolate** CHINATOWN Ethnobotanist Nat Bletter started this bean-to-bar chocolate business, where he carefully sources cacao from around the world, focusing on organic and fair-trade beans, as well as grown-in-Hawai'i chocolate (Hawai'i is the only state that grows cacao commercially.) The result is unique bars that incorporate hibiscus, liliko'i, coconut milk and caramel, and even the fruity pulp of the cacao. *8 N. Pauahi St.* ☎ *808/377-6440. www.madrechocolate.com. Bus 19 or 20. Map p 116.*

Maunakea Marketplace Food Court CHINATOWN Hungry patrons line up for everything from pizza and plate lunches to quick, authentic, and inexpensive Vietnamese, Thai, Chinese, Japanese, and Filipino dishes. Join in the spirit of discovery at the produce stalls (pungent odors, fish heads, and chicken feet on counters—not for the squeamish). Vendors sell everything from fresh 'ahi and whole snapper to yams and taro, seaweed, and fresh fruits and vegetables. *1120 Maunakea St. (btw. N. Hotel & Pauahi sts.), Chinatown.* ☎ *808/524-3409. No credit cards. Bus: 2. Map p 116.*

Nisshodo Candy Store IWILEI Mochi (Japanese sticky rice cake) is so essential to locals' lives that even the drugstores sell it. But for the freshest and widest variety, go straight to the source: Nisshodo, an almost century-old business. Choose among pink-and-white *chichi dango* (or milk mochi), mochi filled with smooth azuki bean, *monaka* (delicate rice wafers sandwiching sweetened lima-bean paste), and much more. *1095 Dillingham Blvd.* ☎ *808/847-1244. nisshodomochicandy.com. Bus: 2. Map p 114.*

★ **People's Open Market** WAIKĪKĪ Truck farmers from all over the island bring their produce to O'ahu's neighborhoods in regularly scheduled, city-sponsored open markets, held Monday

Rocky Road bites from Honolulu Chocolate Co.

Pan-Asian fare at Maunakea Marketplace Food Court

through Saturday at various locations. *Paki/Monsarrat aves. ☎ 808/527-5167. www.honolulu.gov/parks/programs/pom/index1.htm. Bus 19 or 20. Map p 113.*

★ Padovani's Chocolates IWILEI Brothers Philippe and Pierre Padovani are two of Hawai'i's best chefs, involved with the Hawai'i Regional Cuisine movement. In recent years, they've been devoting their attention to chocolate truffles. Their edible gems come in delightful flavors such as a calamansi (a small Filipino lime) and pirie mango ganache, flavored with fragrant, local mangoes picked at the height of the season. Other favorites incorporate ginger, Mānoa honey, and *liliko'i* (Hawaiian passionfruit). *650 Iwilei Rd., #280. ☎ 808/536-4567. padovanichocolates.com. Bus 19 or 20. Map p 114.*

R. Field Wine Co. KAKA'AKO Richard Field—oenophile, gourmet, and cigar aficionado—moved his wine shop and thriving gourmet store into this grocery store. You'll find all manner of epicurean delights, including wines and single-malt Scotches. *Foodland Super Market, 1460 S. Beretania St. (btw. Kalākaua Ave. & Makiki St.). ☎ 808/596-9463. For other locations, see the website. www.foodland.com. Bus: 2. Map p 115.*

Whole Foods KAHALA Whole Foods does a great job of sourcing local, both in produce and in specialty items such as honey, jams, hot sauces, coffee, and chocolate. It's also got one of the best selections of locally made soaps, great for gifts to take home. *4211 Wai'alae Ave at Kahala Mall ☎ 808/738-0820 and 629 Kailua Rd., Kailua. ☎ 808/263-6800. www.wholefoodsmarket.com/stores/honolulu. Bus 4 to 1. Map p 115.*

Fashion

Barrio Vintage CHINATOWN At the island's best shop for vintage clothing, you might find a 1950s tiki print dress or red silk kimono, but the specialty is retro-alohawear in psychedelic colors. *1161 Nu'uanu Ave. www.barriovintage.com; ☎ 808/674-7156. Bus 19 or 20. Map p 116.*

Fighting Eel WAIKĪKĪ At this local designer's boutique, you'll find bright, easy-to-wear, rayon and cotton dresses and shirts with island prints that are in every local fashionista's closet—perfect for Honolulu weather, but chic enough to wear back home. *At the Royal Hawaiian Shopping Center 2233*

Chichi dango candy made from sweet, sticky rice cake at Nisshodo Candy Store

Kalākaua Ave. *Check www.fightingeel.com for other locations;* ☎ *808/738-9295. Bus 8. Map p 113.*

Ginger13 CHINATOWN Local jewelry designer Cindy Yokoyama offers a refreshing change from the delicate jewelry found all over Hawai'i by creating asymmetrical styles with chunky stones such as agate and opal. Find mismatched earrings and statement pieces in this that also brims with green, glossy, tropical plants. *22 S. Pauahi St. www.ginger13.com;* ☎ *808/531-5311. Bus 19 or 20. Map p 116.*

Kicks KAKA'AKO Attention sneaker aficionados, collectors, and those looking for shoes as a fashion statement: This is your store. You'll find limited editions and classic footwear by Nike and Adidas, plus trendy clothing lines. *1530 Makaloa St. (btw. Ke'eaumoku & Amana sts.).* ☎ *808/941-9191. www.kickshawaii.com. Bus: 13. Map p 115.*

Fish Markets

★★ Honolulu Fish Auction IWILEI If you want to experience the high drama of fish buying, head to this auction at the United Fishing Agency, where fishermen bring their fresh catch in at 5:30am (sharp) Monday through Saturday, and buyers bid on a variety of fish, from fat tuna to weird-looking hapupu. *Pier 38, 1131 N. Nimitz Hwy.* ☎ *808/536-2148. www.hawaii-seafood.org. No credit cards. Bus: 19. Map p 114.*

Fresh fruit at the People's Open Market

★ Tamashiro Market IWILEI Good service and the most extensive selection of fresh fish in Honolulu have made this the randdaddy of fish markets. You'll find everything from live lobsters and crabs to fresh slabs of 'ahi to whole *onaga* and *ehu*. *802 N. King St. (btw. Palama St. & Austin Lane), Kalihi.* ☎ *808/841-8047. www.tamashiromarket.com. Bus: 2 or 42. Map p 114.*

Yama's Fish Market MOILI-ILI Known for its inexpensive fresh fish, tasty poke, lomi salmon, and many varieties of prepared seafood, Yama's also makes a terrific Hawaiian plate lunch. Finish it off with kulolo, a traditional Hawaiian sweet made with taro and coconut. *2332 Young St. (Hoawa Lane).* ☎ *808/941-9994. www.yamasfishmarket.com. Bus: 2, transferring to 1 . Map p 113.*

Flowers & Leis

★ Cindy's Lei Shoppe CHINATOWN I love this lei shop because it always has unusual leis, such as feather dendrobiums, firecracker combinations, and everyday favorites like ginger, tuberose, orchid, and pikake. Its "curb service" allows you to phone in your order and pick up your lei curbside—a great convenience on this busy street. *1034 Maunakea St. (at Hotel St.).* ☎ *808/536-6538. www.cindysleishoppe.com. Bus: 2 or 19. Map p 116.*

★ Lin's Lei Shop CHINATOWN Features creatively fashioned, unusual leis. *1017-A Maunakea St. (at King St.).* ☎ *808/537-4112. linsleishop.com. Bus: 2 or 19. Map p 116.*

The Honolulu Fish Auction

★ **Lita's Leis** CHINATOWN This small lei shop features fresh puakenikeni, gardenias that last, and a supply of fresh and reasonable leis. *59 N. Beretania St. (btw. Maunakea & Smith sts.). ☎ 808/521-9065. Bus: 2, 19, or 42. Map p 116.*

★ **Rainforest at Kilohana Square** KAPAHULU For special-occasion designer bouquets or leis, this is the place. Custom-designed leis and special arrangements come complete with cards in Hawaiian, with English translations. *1016 Kapahulu Ave. (btw. H-1 & Kehei Place). ☎ 808/738-0999. rainforesthawaii.com. Bus 13. Map p 115.*

Hawaiiana Gifts

★★★ **Kamaka Ukulele** KAKA'AKO Forget the cheap plastic ukulele found all over the island. Come to this ukulele factory, which just celebrated 100 years, to see these beautiful, made-in-Hawa'i instruments. The body is made with Hawaiian koa wood, aged for four years, the necks are made of mahogany, and the fingerboards and bridges are rosewood. Each one is a work of art, and priced accordingly (they will run upwards of $1,000). Even if you don't intend on buying a ukulele, stop by for the free guided tour, Tuesdays through Fridays from 10:30 am to 11:30 am. *550 South St. ☎ 808/531-3165. www.kamakahawaii.com. Bus: 19 or 20. Map p 114.*

★★★ **Native Books/Na Mea Hawai'i** ALA MOANA Recently joined by the Hula Supply Center, the space is now a one-stop shop and resource for all things local and Hawaiian. This is a browser's paradise, featuring a variety of Hawaiian items from musical instruments to calabashes, jewelry, leis, books, contemporary Hawaiian clothing, Hawaiian food products, and other high-quality gift items. Regular classes in lauhala weaving, Hawaiian featherwork, 'ukulele, the Hawaiian language, and more are also held here. Call for the schedule. *Ward Village Shops, 1050 Ala Moana Blvd. (at Ward Ave.). ☎ 808/596-8885. www.nativebookshawaii.com. Bus: 19 or 42. Map p 114.*

★★★ **Nohea Gallery** ALA MOANA/WAIKĪKĪ A fine showcase for contemporary Hawai'i art, Nohea celebrates the islands with thoughtful, attractive selections, such as pit-fired raku (ceramics), finely turned wood vessels, jewelry, handblown glass, paintings, prints, fabrics (including Hawaiian-quilt cushions), and furniture. *Ward Village Shops, 1050 Ala Moana Blvd. (at Ward Ave.). ☎ 808/596-0074. www.noheagallery.com. Bus: 19 or 42. Map p 114.*

★ **Tin Can Mailman** CHINATOWN What, not looking for a 1950s oil hula lamp? Check out this shop anyway. It's packed with vintage Hawaiiana to emulate old-school

A Chinatown lei shop

general stores. The emphasis is on ephemera, such as pinups, postcards, old sheet music and advertisements, and the elusive Betty Boop hula girl bobblehead. *1026 Nu'unau Ave. ☎ 808/524-3009. tincanmailman.net. Bus: 19 or 20. Map p 116.*

Health Food Stores

Down to Earth MO'ILI'ILI Located near the University of Hawai'i, this locally owned store sells organic vegetables and vegetarian bulk foods. It offers a strong selection of supplements and herbs for good prices and a vegetarian juice-and-sandwich bar. *2525 S. King St. ☎ 808/947-7678. www.downtoearth.org. Bus: 2, transferring to 1. Map p 115.*

Kokua Market HONOLULU This health food cooperative is one of Honolulu's best sources for organic vegetables. It also has an excellent variety of cheeses, pastas, bulk grains, sandwiches, salads, prepared foods, organic wines, and an expanded vitamin section. *2643 S. King St. (at University Ave.). ☎ 808/941-1922. www.kokua.coop. Bus: 2, transferring to 1. Map p 115.*

Museum Stores

★ Honolulu Museum of Art Shop MAKIKI The place to go for art books, jewelry, basketry, ethnic fabrics, native crafts from all over the world, posters, books, and fiber vessels and accessories. *Honolulu Museum of Art, 900 S. Beretania St. (at Ward Ave.). ☎ 808/532-8703. www.honolulumuseum.org. Bus: 2. Map p 114.*

Each handmade instrument from Kamaka Ukulele is a work of art.

Organic produce at the Kokua Market cooperative

★★ Shop Pacifica KALIHI Plan to spend time browsing through the local crafts (including terrific Ni'ihau shell leis), lauhala and Cook Island woven products, Hawaiian music tapes and CDs, pareu, and a vast selection of Hawaii-themed books that anchor this gift shop. *Bishop Museum, 1525 Bernice St. (btw. Kalihi St. & Kapalama Ave.). ☎ 808/848-4158. www.bishopmuseum.org. Bus: 2 or 19. Map p 114.*

Shopping Centers

★★ Ala Moana Center ALA MOANA Nearly 400 shops and restaurants sprawl over several blocks, making this Hawai'i's largest shopping center catering to every imaginable need, from upscale (**Neiman Marcus, Tiffany,** and **Chanel**) to mainland chains (**Gap, Banana Republic, lululemon,** and **Old Navy**), to department stores

Farmers' Markets in Paradise

Have you ever peeled a dragon's eye? Or kissed a passion fruit or tasted a just-picked mangosteen? Diverse cultures have brought their favorite fruits, vegetables, and other culinary products to Hawai'i, and the best place to taste these interesting and unusual foods is at one of the island's farmers' markets.

- **Hawai'i Farm Bureau Federations Farmers' Markets** One of the most popular farmers' markets takes place next door to Waikīkī at the Kapiolani Community College's parking lot (4303 Diamond Head Rd.) every Saturday from 7:30 to 11am. Some 8,000 residents and visitors flock to this bountiful market to buy the locally grown produce and to sample the prepared food. The key feature of this market is that the majority of the vendors are actual farmers, so this is a great place to get information about products and the farms themselves. For additional information on Kapi'olani Community College Farmers' Market and other Hawaii Farm Bureau Federation Farmers' Markets, see **www.hfbf.org.**
- **Farm Lovers Farmers' Markets** This market takes place on Saturdays from 8am to noon in Kaka'ako. It's filled with local vendors (all produce and products sold have to be grown in Hawai'i) and is a wonderful place to eat at impromptu, temporary cafes, where patrons sit family style. If you are in town in October, when taro is celebrated, or in January, when cacao is featured, the market turns into a big festival. For information on other Farm Lovers Farmers' Markets around the island (on the North Shore, in Hawai'i Kai, and Kailua), see **www.farmloversmarkets.com.**
- **People's Open Market Program** This is the island's oldest farmers' market, started in 1973 by the City and County of Honolulu, and has spread across the island (the closest to Waikīkī is located in Queen Kapi'olani Park parking lot, Monsarrat and Paki Streets, open Wed 10–11am). The County started the markets as a way for people to get low-cost produce, but be aware that the fruits and vegetables do not have to be grown on the island or even in the state. The theory in the beginning was that farmers could sell their off-grade or even surplus products here and local residents would get a bargain. For a list of the 23 different markets, their locations, and times, see **www1.honolulu.gov/parks/programs/pom/schedules.htm.**

(**Macy's, Nordstrom**), to practical touches, such as banks, a foreign-exchange service (**Travelex**), a U.S. Post Office, several optical companies (including 1-hr. service by **LensCrafters**), and a handful of smaller locally owned stores (**Pacific Sunwear** and **Splash! Hawaii**). The **food court** is abuzz with dozens of stalls purveying Cajun food, pizza, plate lunches, vegetarian fare, green tea, panini, and countless other treats.

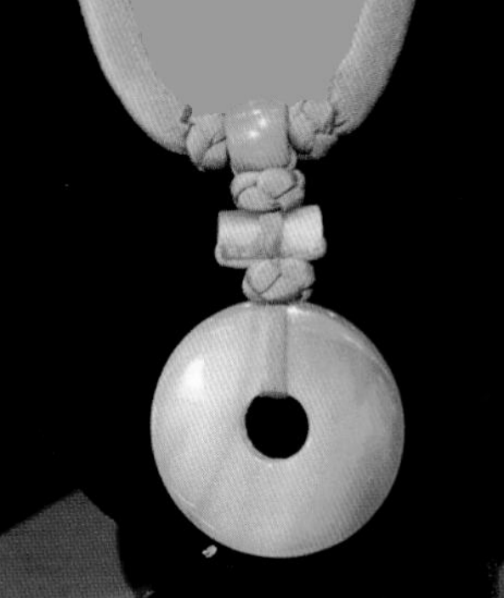

A one-of-a-kind gift at the Honolulu Museum of Art Shop

Also check out the **Shirokiya Japan Village Walk**, where you'll find everything from ramen to udon to tempura. *1450 Ala Moana Blvd. (btw. Kaheka & Pi'ikoi sts.).* ☎ *808/955-9517. www.alamoanacenter.com. Bus: 8, 19, or 42. Map p 115.*

DFS Galleria WAIKĪKĪ This Waikīkī emporium is a three-floor extravaganza of shops ranging from the superluxe (like **Kate Spade** and **Coach**) to the very touristy, with great Hawai'i food products, aloha shirt and T-shirt shops, surf and skate equipment, a terrific Hawaiian music selection, and a labyrinth of fashionable stores thrown in to complete the retail experience. *330 Royal Hawaiian Ave. (at Kalākaua Ave.).* ☎ *808/931-2655. www.dfsgalleria.com. Bus: 19 or 20. Map p 113.*

★ International Marketplace WAIKĪKĪ Gone is the open-air, decaying warren of kitschy vendors and dive bars, and in its place is this new, gleaming behemoth. The only thing that remains of the old is the banyan tree, thankfully. You'll find primarily luxury brands here, anchored by a **Saks Fifth Avenue**, as well as **Greenroom Hawaii**. Stop by **Kona Coffee Purveyors** for excellent espresso and pastries. *2330 Kalākaua Ave.* ☎ *808/931-6105. www.shopinternationalmarketplace.com. Bus: 19 or 20. Map p 113.*

★ Royal Hawaiian Shopping Center WAIKĪKĪ This is a 293,000 upscale square feet (27,220-sq.-m) of open-air mall with 110 stores, restaurants, and entertainment options on four levels, including a nightclub and theater, entry porte-cochere, and even a garden grove of 70 coconut trees. Shops range from Aloha Aina Boutique to **Cartier, Hermès,** and **Salvatore Ferragamo.** *2201 Kalākaua Ave. (at Royal Hawaiian Ave.).* ☎ *808/922-0588. www.royalhawaiiancenter.com. Bus: 19 or 20. Map p 113.*

★ Salt at Kaka'ako KAKA'AKO There are grand plans for Kaka'ako, the neighborhood between WAIKĪKĪ and downtown. Mostly, it's a lot of new, hi-rise luxury condos, but developers are also trying to create an interesting mix of restaurants and retailers. Here, you'll find **Milo**, a hip surf shop that also carries accessories for the home; **Paiko**, an adorable tropical botanical boutique, and **Treehouse**, a must for any photography lover, especially those with a penchant for vintage and film**.** *660 Ala Moana Blvd. www.saltatkakaako.com. Bus: 19. Map p 114.*

There are nearly 400 retailers, from standard to upscale, at the Ala Moana Center.

Skateboards, surf gear and beachwear at Hawaiian Island Creations

★ Ward Village Shops WARD Great restaurants (**Piggy Smalls, Goma Tei**) and shops (**Red Pineapple, Honolulu Chocolate Co., Native Books, Nohea Gallery**) make this a popular place, bustling with browsers. The focus at these Ward Village Shops is smaller, independent stores and designers. The South Shore Market building houses a lot of young Hawai'i fashion designers, including **Kealopiko**'s breezy clothing inspired by the natural and cultural landscapes of Hawai'i, as well as **Salvage Public**, with its line of menswear for surfers in and out of the water. *1240 Ala Moana Blvd. ☎ 808/591-8411. www.wardvillageshops. Bus: 19 or 20. Map p 114.*

T-Shirts

Hawaiian Island Creations ALA MOANA This supercool surf shop offers sunglasses, sun lotions, surf wear, surfboards, skateboards, and accessories galore. *Ala Moana Center, 1450 Ala Moana Blvd. (btw. Piikoi & Kaheka sts.). ☎ 808/973-6780. 298 Beachwalk Ave. ☎ 808/923-0442. www.hicsurf.com. Bus: 19 or 20. Map p 114.*

★ Local Motion ALA MOANA This icon of surfers and skateboarders, both professionals and wannabes, has everything from surfboards, T-shirts, alohawear, and casual wear, to countless accessories for life in the sun. *Ala Moana Shopping Center, 1450 Ala Moana Blvd. (btw. Kaheka & Piikoi sts.). ☎ 808/979-7873. www.localmotionhawaii.com. Bus: 19 or 20. Map p 114.*

Gourmet and local specialties at the Food Hall at DFS Galleria

Nightlife & Performing Arts Best Bets

Best Place to **Celebrate St. Patrick's Day**
★ Murphy's Bar & Grill, *2 Merchant St. (p 129)*

Best for **Cocktails**
★ Tchin Tchin, *39 N. Hotel St. (p 129)*

Best **Intimate Bar**
★ Lewers Lounge, *Halekulani 2199 Kalia Rd. (p 129)*

Best for **Hawaiian Music**
★★★ Kana Ka Pila Grille, *Outrigger Reef on the Beach, 2169 Kalia Rd. (p 131)*

Best **Club for Jazz**
★★ Blue Note Hawai'i, Outrigger Waikīkī, 2335 *Kalākaua* Ave. *(p 132)*

Most **Romantic Place for Sunset**
★★★ House Without a Key, *Halekulani 2199 Kalia Rd. (p 131)*

Best Place to **People-Watch at Sunset**
★★ Duke's Canoe Club, *Outrigger Waikīkī on the Beach Hotel, 2335 Kalākaua Ave. (p 130)*

Best **Lū'au**
★★ Royal Hawaiian Hotel, *2259 Kalākaua Ave. (p 132)*

Best **Performing Arts Center**
★★ Neal Blaisdell Center, *777 Ward Ave. (p 132)*

Best for **Outdoor Concerts**
★★ Waikīkī Shell, *2805 Monsarrat Ave. (p 133)*

Best for **Film Buffs**
★★ The Movie Museum, *3566 Harding Ave. (p 130)*

Most **Historic Theater**
★★★ Hawai'i Theatre, *1130 Bethel St. (p 133)*

Best Place to See **Locally Written and Produced Plays**
★★ Kumu Kahua Theatre, *46 Merchant St. (p 133)*

Hawaiian music and a casual dress code at Duke's Canoe Club

Waikīkī's Best Nightlife

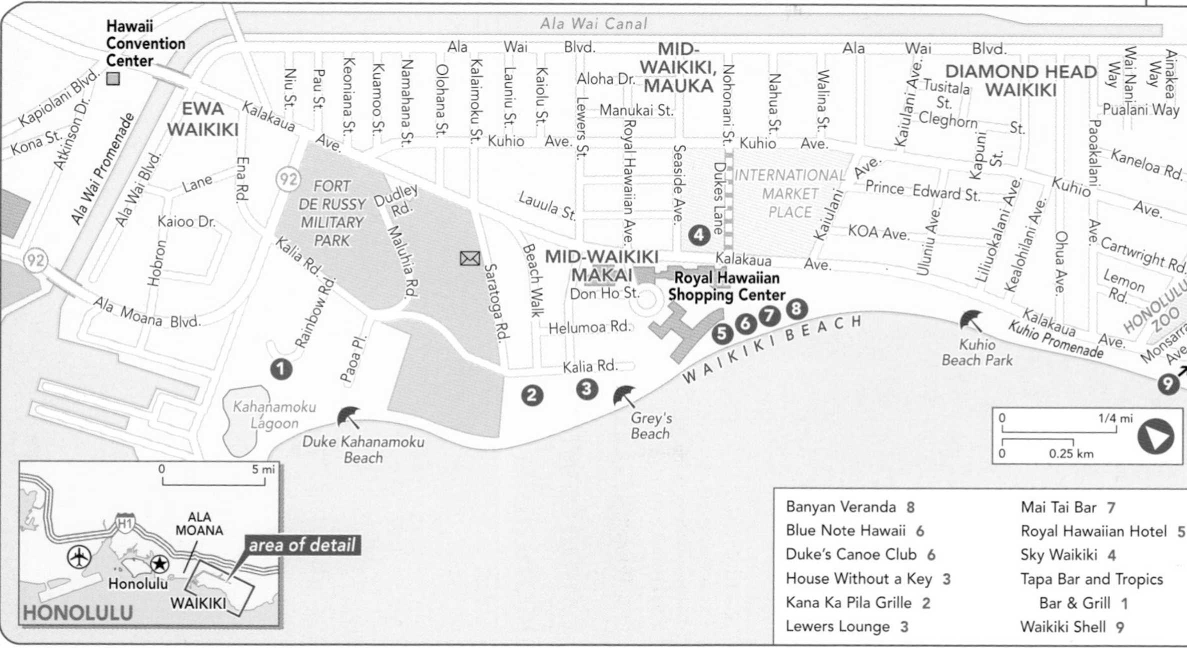

Honolulu's Best Nightlife

Diamond Head Theatre 6
Doris Duke Theatre 2
Manoa Valley Theatre 4
The Movie Museum 5
Neal Blaisdell Center 1
Rumours Nightclub 3

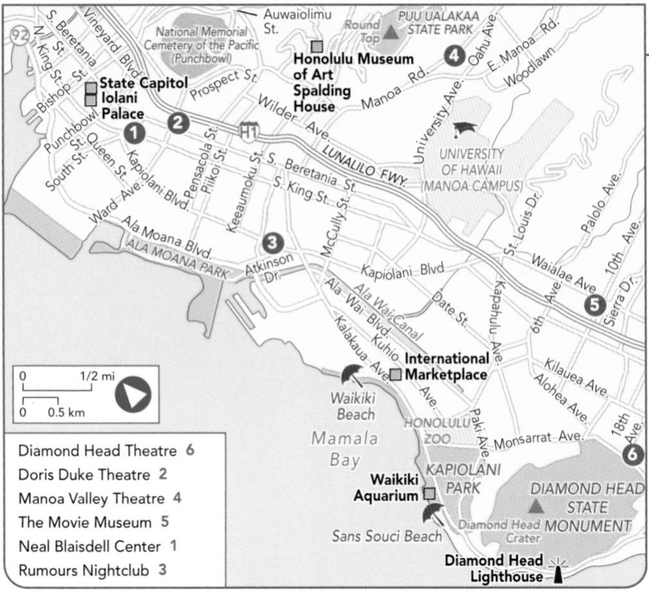

Chinatown & Downtown Honolulu's Best Nightlife

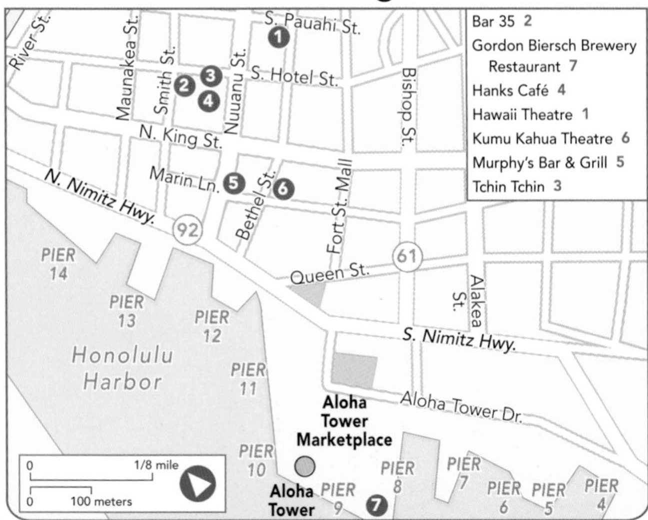

Nightlife & Performing Arts A to Z

Bars & Cocktail Lounges

Gordon Biersch Brewery Restaurant ALOHA TOWER A large stage area allows diners to swing to jazz, blues, and island riffs. *1 Aloha Tower Dr., on the waterfront btw. piers 8 & 11, Honolulu Harbor (at Bishop St.). ☎ 808/599-4877. www.gordonbiersch.com. Bus: 19 or 20. Map p 128.*

Hanks Café DOWNTOWN This tiny, kitschy, friendly pub has live music nightly, open-mic nights, and special events that attract great talent and a supportive crowd. On some nights, the music spills out into the streets, and it's so packed you have to press your nose against the window to see what you're missing. *1038 Nu'uanu Ave. (btw. Hotel & King sts.). ☎ 808/526-1410. www.hankscafehonolulu.com. Bus: 2, 19, or 42. Map p 128.*

★Lewers Lounge WAIKĪKĪ Tops in taste and ambience is this intimate lounge in the Halekulani. Comfy intimate seating around the pillars makes this a great spot for contemporary live jazz nightly from 8:30pm to midnight. *Halekulani Hotel, 2199 Kalia Rd. (at Lewers St.). ☎ 808/923-2311. www.halekulani.com. No cover. Bus: 19 or 20. Map p 127.*

★ Murphy's Bar & Grill DOWNTOWN One of Honolulu's most popular downtown ale houses and media haunts. More than a dozen beers on tap, including (of course) Murphy's and Guinness. *2 Merchant St. (at Nu'uanu Ave.). ☎ 808/531-0422. www.gomurphys.com. Bus: 19, 20, or 42. Map p 128.*

★ Tchin Tchin CHINATOWN This bar and lounge offers an incomparable wine list and some of the best cocktails in town. Revel in the outdoor courtyard among the rooftops of Chinatown, anchored by a living wall of ferns and orchids. This is urban Honolulu at its best. Enter through an unmarked door and up a flight of stairs. *39 N. Hotel St. ☎ 808/528-1888. www.thetchintchinbar.com. Bus: 19, 20, or 42. Map p 128.*

Live Top 40 music at Rumours Nightclub

Clubs

Bar 35 CHINATOWN If you are looking for a brew, its claim to fame is the 110 beers available, plus wine, cocktails, and even pizzas. You must be at least 21 to enter (strictly enforced). *35 N. Hotel St. (btw. Smith St. & Nu'uanu Ave.). ☎ 808/537-3535. www.bar35hawaii.com. Bus: 2, 19, or 42. Map p 128.*

Rumours Nightclub ALA MOANA The disco of choice for those who remember Paul McCartney as something other than Stella's father, with "themes" that change monthly. A spacious dance floor, a good sound system, and Top-40 music draw a mix of generations. *Lobby, Ala Moana Hotel, 410 Atkinson Dr. (next to Ala Moana Shopping Center). ☎ 808/955-4811. www.alamoanahotelhonolulu.com. Only open Fri–Sat nights. Cover $10. Bus: 19 or 20. Map p 128.*

Sky Waikīkī WAIKĪKĪ This rooftop lounge and nightclub brings in DJs and attracts a youthful, well-dressed crowd. If all the dancing and music gets too much, escape to the lounge, which has spectacular views of WAIKĪKĪ. *2270 Kalākaua Ave., 19th floor. ☎ 808/979-7590. www.skywaikiki.com. Cover charge varies. Bus: 19 or 20. Map p 127.*

The sun sets behind the 100-year-old banyan tree at the historic Moana Surfrider.

Film

★ Doris Duke Theatre MAKIKI This is the film-as-art center of Honolulu, offering special screenings, guest appearances, and cultural performances as well as noteworthy programs in the visual arts. *900 S. Beretania St. (at Ward Ave.). ☎ 808/532-8703. www.honolulumuseum.org. Ticket prices vary. Bus: 2 or 13. Map p 128.*

★★ The Movie Museum KAIMUKI Film buffs and esoteric movie lovers can enjoy special screenings as they recline comfortably on brown-vinyl stuffed recliners or rent from a collection of 3,000 vintage and hard-to-find films. *3566 Harding Ave. (btw. 11th & 12th aves.). ☎ 808/735-8771. www.kaimukihawaii.com. Tickets $5. Reservations recommended. Bus: 2, transferring to 1. Map p 128.*

Hawaiian Music

★★ Banyan Veranda WAIKĪKĪ Enjoy a romantic evening sitting on the back porch of this historic hotel, overlooking an canopy of banyan trees as you watch the sun set and sip a liquid libation to the sounds of live Hawaiian music playing softly in the background. You'll be in good company; Robert Louis Stevenson once loved to linger here. *Moana Surfrider, 2365 Kalākaua Ave. (btw. Duke's Lane & Kaiulani Ave.). ☎ 808/922-3111. www.moana-surfrider.com. 2-drink minimum. Bus: 19 or 20. Map p 127.*

★★ Duke's Canoe Club WAIKĪKĪ The outside Barefoot Bar is perfect for sipping a tropical drink, watching the waves and sunset, and listening to music. It can get crowded, so get there early. Hawaii sunset music is usually from 4 to 6pm daily, and live entertainment occurs

Legendary hula dancer Kanoelehua Miller performs at the Halekulani Hotel's House Without a Key.

nightly from 9:30pm to midnight. *Outrigger Waikīkī on the Beach Hotel, 2335 Kalākaua Ave. (btw. Duke's Lane & Kaiulani Ave.). ☎ 808/922-2268. www.dukeswaikīkī.com. No cover & no drink minimum. Bus: 19 or 20. Map p 127.*

★★★ House Without a Key WAIKĪKĪ This is my favorite place to relax at sunset. Watch the breath-taking Kanoelehua Miller dance hula to the riffs of Hawaiian steel-pedal guitar with the sunset and ocean glowing behind her—a romantic, evocative, nostalgic scene. It doesn't hurt, either, that the Halekulani happens to make the best mai tais in the world. *Halekulani Hotel, 2199 Kalia Rd. (at Lewers St.). ☎ 808/923-2311. www.halekulani.com. No cover. Bus: 19 or 20. Map p 127.*

★ Kana Ka Pila Grille WAIKĪKĪ *Kana ka pila* means to make music, so it makes sense then that this poolside, outdoor restaurant at the Outrigger Reef on the Beach has one of the city's best Hawaiian-music lineups, including slack key guitarists Cyril Pahinui (son of famed guitarist Gabby Pahinui). *Outrigger Reef on the Beach, 2169 Kalia Rd. ☎ 808/924-4990. www.outrigger.com/events/music/kani-ka-pila-grille. No cover. Bus: 19 or 20. Map p 127.*

★ Mai Tai Bar WAIKĪKĪ This circular bar, right down at beach level,

Get Down with ARTafterDark

The last Friday of every month (except Nov and Dec), the place to be after the sun goes down is **ARTafterDark,** a *pau-hana* (after-work) mixer at the **Honolulu Museum,** 900 S. Beretania St. Each gathering has a theme combining art with food, music, and dancing. In addition to the exhibits in the gallery, ARTafterDark features visual and live performances. Entry fee is $10; the party gets going about 6pm and lasts to 10pm, the crowd age ranges from 20s to 50s, and the dress is everything from jeans and T-shirts to designer cocktail party attire. For more information, call ☎ **808/532-8700** or visit www.artafterdark.org.

features live Hawaiian music and hula from 6 to 9:30pm Tuesday through Sunday. *Royal Hawaiian Hotel, 2259 Kalākaua Ave. (at Seaside Ave.). ☎ 808/923-7311. www.royal-hawaiian.com. 1-drink minimum. Bus: 19 or 20. Map p 127.*

★ **Tapa Bar and Tropics Bar & Grill** WAIKĪKĪ Impromptu hula and spirited music from the family and friends of the performers are an island tradition nightly. *Hilton Hawaiian Village, 2005 Kalia Rd. (at Ala Moana Blvd.). ☎ 808/949-4321. www.hiltonhawaiianvillage.com. 2-drink minimum. Bus: 19 or 20. Map p 127.*

Jazz

Blue Note Hawai'i WAIKĪKĪ From the owner of the Blue Note jazz club in New York City, this venue offers jazz, blues, and favorite local entertainers. It has a great, old-school jazzy vibe, with intimate booths as well as standing-room tickets by the bar. The restaurant offers hearty plates like a hamburger and braised short rib. Past performers have included Dee Dee Bridgewater and 'ukulele virtuoso Jake Shimabukuro. *Outrigger Waikīkī 2335 Kalākaua Ave. ☎ 808/777-4890. www.bluenotehawaii.com. Ticket prices vary. Bus: 19 or 20. Map p 127.*

Lū'au

★★ **Royal Hawaiian Hotel** WAIKĪKĪ WAIKĪKĪ's only oceanfront lū'au features a variety of traditional Hawaiian as well as continental American dishes: roasted kālua pig, mahimahi, teriyaki steak, poi, sweet potatoes, rice, vegetables, haupia (coconut pudding), and a selection of desserts. Entertainment includes songs and dances from Hawai'i and other Polynesian island nations. *Royal Hawaiian Hotel, 2259 Kalākaua Ave. (at Seaside Ave.). ☎ 888/808-4668. www.royal-hawaiianluau.com/. Mon 5:30pm. $190 adults, $106 children 5–12. Bus: 19 or 20. Map p 127.*

The hula show at the Royal Hawaiian Hotel's Mai Tai Bar

Symphony, Opera & Dance Performances

★★ **Neal Blaisdell Center** WARD Hawai'i's premier performance center for the best in entertaining. This arena/concert hall/exhibition building can be divided into an intimate 2,175-seat concert hall or an 8,805-seat arena, serving everyone from symphony-goers to punk rockers. The **Hawai'i Symphony Orchestra** (☎ 808/593-9468; www.hawaiisymphonyorchestra.org) plays here. From October to April, the highly successful **Hawai'i Opera Theatre** takes to the stage with such hits as *La Bohème*, *Carmen*, *Turandot*, *Romeo and Juliet*, *Rigoletto*, and *Aïda* (www.hawaiiopera.org). Also performing at this concert hall are Hawaii's four ballet companies: **Hawaii Ballet Theatre** (www.hawaiiballettheatre.org), **Ballet Hawaii** (www.ballethawaii.org), **Hawaii State Ballet** (www.hawaiistateballet.com), and **Honolulu Dance Company** (www.honoluludanceco.com). *Neal Blaisdell Center, 777 Ward Ave. (btw. Kapiolani Ave. & King St.). ☎ 808/768-5433. www.blaisdellcenter.com. Bus: 2 or 13. Map p 128.*

★★ **Waikīkī Shell** WAIKĪKĪ This outdoor venue in the middle of Kapi'olani Park allows concertgoers to watch the sunset and see the stars come out before the concert begins. A range of performers from Hawaiian to jazz musicians has graced this stage. *2805 Monsarrat Ave. (btw. Kalākaua & Paki aves.). ☎ 808/768-5433. www.blaisdellcenter.com. Bus: 19 or 20. Map p 127.*

Theater

★ **Diamond Head Theatre** DIAMOND HEAD Hawai'i's oldest theater (since 1915), this community theater presents a sort of "Broadway of the Pacific," producing a variety of performances from musicals to comedies to classical dramas. *520 Makapu'u Ave. (at Alohea Ave.). ☎ 808/733-0274. www.diamondheadtheatre.com. Tickets $12–$42. Bus: 2 or 23. Map p 128.*

★★★ **Hawai'i Theatre** CHINATOWN Audiences here have enjoyed performances ranging from the big off-Broadway percussion hit *Stomp* to the talent of Norah Jones; the Hawaii International Jazz Festival, the American Repertory Dance Company, barbershop quartets, and John Ka'imikaua's *halau* (hula school). The neoclassical Beaux Arts landmark features a 1922 dome, 1,400 plush seats, a hydraulically elevated organ, and gilt galore. *1130 Bethel St. (btw. Hotel & Pauahi sts.). ☎ 808/528-0506. www.hawaiitheatre.com. Ticket prices vary. Bus: 2, 8, 19, or 42. Map p 128.*

★ **Kumu Kahua Theatre** DOWNTOWN For an intimate glimpse at island life, take in a show at Kumu Kahua. This tiny theater (100 seats) produces plays dealing with today's cultural experience in Hawai'i, often written by residents. *46 Merchant St. ☎ 808/536-4441. www.kumukahua.org. Tickets $5–$20. Bus: 2 or 19. Map p 128.*

An open-air concert at the Waikīkī Shell

Popular Hawaiian group The Brothers Cazimero performs in various venues around Waikīkī and Oahu.

Mānoa Valley Theatre
MāNOA Honolulu's equivalent of off-Broadway, with performances of well-known shows—anything from *Urinetown* to *Who's Afraid of Virginia Woolf*. *2833 E. Manoa Rd. (btw. Keama Place & Huapala St.). ☎ 808/988-6131. www.manoavalleytheatre.com. Tickets $15–$30.* *Map p 128.*

Comedy Tonight

Local comics tend to move around a lot, so the best way to see comedy is to check their websites. The best in comedy acts are **Andy Bumatai, Augie T** (www.augiet.com), and **Frank Delima** (www.frankdelima.com), who perform "local" stand-up sketches that will have you not only understanding local residents but also screaming with laughter.

5 The Best **Regional Tours**

The North Shore

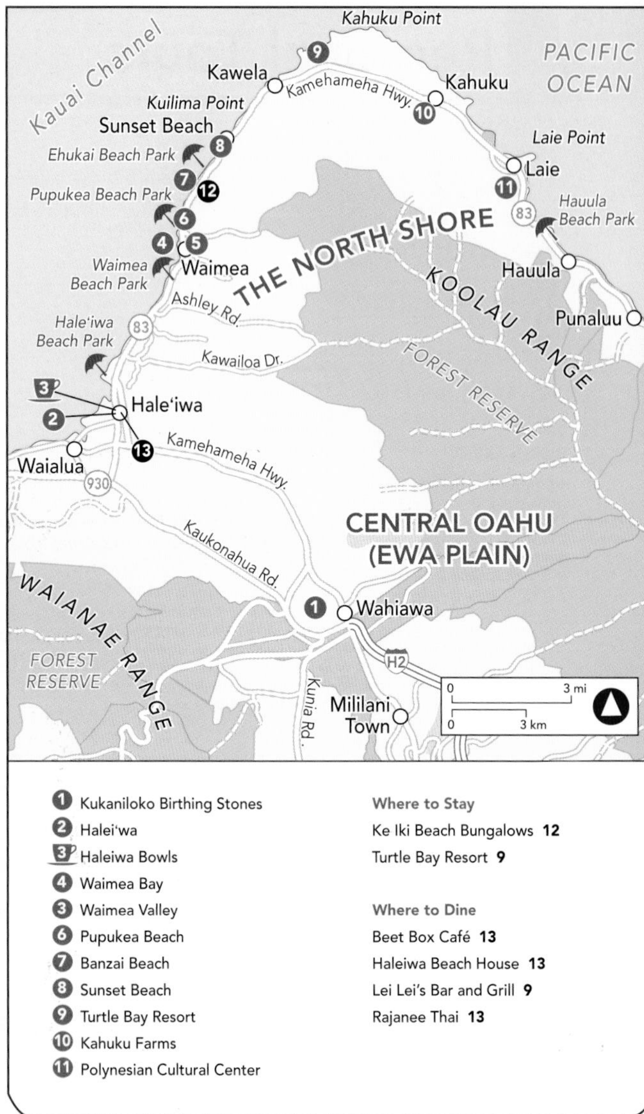
Kahuku Point
PACIFIC OCEAN
Kauai Channel
Kawela
Kamehameha Hwy.
Kahuku
Kuilima Point
Sunset Beach
Ehukai Beach Park
Laie Point
Laie
Pupukea Beach Park
Hauula Beach Park
THE NORTH SHORE
Waimea Beach Park
Waimea
Hauula
KOOLAU RANGE
Ashley Rd.
Punaluu
Hale'iwa Beach Park
83
Kawailoa Dr.
FOREST RESERVE
Hale'iwa
Kamehameha Hwy.
Waialua
930
Kaukonahua Rd.
CENTRAL OAHU (EWA PLAIN)
WAIANAE RANGE
Wahiawa
H2
FOREST RESERVE
Kunia Rd.
Mililani Town
0 3 mi
0 3 km
1 Kukaniloko Birthing Stones
2 Halei'wa
3 Haleiwa Bowls
4 Waimea Bay
5 Waimea Valley
6 Pupukea Beach
7 Banzai Beach
8 Sunset Beach
9 Turtle Bay Resort
10 Kahuku Farms
11 Polynesian Cultural Center
Where to Stay
Ke Iki Beach Bungalows 12
Turtle Bay Resort 9
Where to Dine
Beet Box Café 13
Haleiwa Beach House 13
Lei Lei's Bar and Grill 9
Rajanee Thai 13

Previous page: The lookout near the Makapu'u Point Lighthouse

On O'ahu, don't just stay in Waikīkī—get out and see the island. Drive up through the center of O'ahu to the famous North Shore. If you can afford the splurge, rent a bright, shiny convertible—the perfect car for O'ahu, so you can tan as you go. Majestic sandalwood trees once stood in the central plains; the Hawaiian chiefs ordered them cut down, and now the area is covered with tract homes, malls, and factory outlets. Beyond the plains is the North Shore and Hawai'i's surf city: Hale'iwa, a turn-of-the-20th-century sugar-plantation town that has been designated a historic site. Once a collection of faded clapboard stores, Hale'iwa has evolved into a surfer outpost and major roadside attraction with art galleries, restaurants, and shops that sell breezy dresses and aloha wear, jewelry, and, of course, surfboards.

Take H-1 West to H-2 North, which becomes Hwy. 99. Stay on Hwy. 99, and then make a left at Whitmore Ave. Bus: 52.

❶ ★ Kukaniloko Birthing Stones. This is the most sacred site in central O'ahu. Two rows of 18 lava rocks once flanked a central birthing stone, where women of ancient Hawai'i gave birth to potential *ali'i* (royalty). Used by O'ahu's *ali'i* for generations of births, many of the *pohaku* (rocks) have bowl-like shapes. Some think the site also may have served ancient astronomers—like a Hawaiian Stonehenge. Look for the two interpretive signs, one explaining why this was chosen as a birth site and the other telling how the stones were used to aid in the birth process. ⏲ *30 min. Whitmore Ave and Hwy. 80.*

Continue on Kamehameha Hwy. Bus: 52.

❷ ★★★ Hale'iwa. Only 34 miles (55km) from Waikīkī is Hale'iwa, the funky ex-sugar-plantation town that's the world capital of big-wave surfing. This beach town really comes alive in winter, when waves rise up, light rain falls, and temperatures dip into the 70s; then, it seems, every surfer in the world is here to see and be seen. Officially designated a historic cultural and

A surfer in Haleiwa

scenic district, Hale'iwa's architecture recalls the turn of the 20th century, when it was founded by sugar baron Benjamin Dillingham. He opened a Victorian hotel overlooking Kaiaka Bay and named it Hale'iwa, or "house of the Iwa," the tropical seabird often seen here. The hotel is gone, but Hale'iwa, which was rediscovered in the late 1960s by hippies, resonates with rare rustic charm. Arts and crafts studios, boutiques, and burger stands line both sides of the town. There's also a busy fishing harbor full of charter boats. 🕔 *2–3 hr.*

3 ★**Haleiwa Bowls.** Shave ice isn't your only option for cooling down in Hale'iwa. Surfers, locals, and visitors alike love acai bowls: the purple fruit, acai berry, which usually comes frozen from Brazil, is blended and topped with granola, fresh bananas, and drizzled with honey. Sweet, tart, cold, crunchy—it makes for a great pick me up. This truck is the best place to try it. Haleiwa Bowls also dispenses kombucha on tap in flavors like liliko'i, ginger, or mango. Check www.haleiwabowls.com for current location. *Daily 7:30am–6:30pm. $.*

Continue on Kamehameha Hwy. Transfer to Bus 55.

4 ★★ **Waimea Bay.** From November to March, monstrous waves—some 30 feet (9m) tall—roll into Waimea. When they break on the shore, the ground actually shakes. The best surfers in the world paddle out to challenge these freight trains—it's amazing to see how small they appear in the lip of the giant waves. *See p 162.*

Turn toward the mountain on Waimea Valley Rd.

Waimea Bay

5 ★ **Waimea Valley.** The 150-acre (61-ha) Arboretum and Botanical Garden contains more than 5,000 species of tropical plants. Walk through the gardens (take the paved paths or dirt trails) and wind up at 45-foot-high (14m) Waimea Falls—bring your bathing suit, and you can dive into the cold, murky water. The public is invited to hike the trails and spend a day in this quiet oasis. There are cultural activities, such as lei-making, kappa demonstrations, hula lessons, Hawaiian games and crafts, and music and storytelling. *See p 60,* 8.

Continue on Kamehameha Hwy. and spend some time at one of the following three beaches. Bus: 55.

6 ★ **Pūpūkea Beach.** This 80-acre (32-ha) beach park, excellent for snorkeling and diving, is a Marine Life Conservation District with strict rules about taking marine life, sand, coral, shells, and rocks. *See p 159.*

Continue on Kamehameha Hwy.; access is via Ehukai Beach Park, off Kamehameha Hwy. on Ke Nui Rd. in Pupukea. Bus: 55.

❼ ★ **Banzai Beach.** In the winter, this is a very popular beach with surfers, surf fans, curious residents, and visitors; it's less crowded in the summer months. *See p 155.*

Continue on Kamehameha Hwy. Bus: 55.

❽ ★★ **Sunset Beach.** If it's winter, just people-watch on this sandy beach, as the waves are huge. During the summer, it's safe to go swimming. *See p 161.*

Continue on Kamehameha Hwy. Bus: 55.

❾ ★★★ **Turtle Bay Resort.** The resort is spectacular—an hour's drive from Waikīkī but eons away in its country feeling. Sitting on 808 acres (327 ha), this place is loaded with activities and 5 miles (8km) of shoreline with secluded white-sand coves. Even if you don't stay here, check out the beach activities, golf, horseback riding, tennis, surf lessons, and spa. See chapter 7 for a full list. You can also grab a bite or drink here; during the wintertime, all the pros come to **Lei Lei's Bar and Grill**, and **Surfer, The Bar**—a collaboration between the resort and *Surfer* magazine—offers Surf Talk Story nights, bringing in pro surfers and watermen to share their tales. Dine poolside at **The Point** or beachside at **Roy's Beach House**. 🕓 *Depends on your activity. 57–091 Kamehameha Hwy., Kahuku.* ☎ *808/293-6000. www.turtlebayresort.com.*

Snorkeling at Pūpūkea Beach

Continue on Kamehameha Hwy. Bus: 55.

❿ ★ **Kahuku Farms.** Take a tractor-pulled wagon ride through the tropical fruit groves of this working farm. You'll learn about the apple banana (short and tart), *liliko'i* (passionfruit), and pineapple, and then taste them all in a smoothie made on the spot at the café. Oh, and definitely don't miss the grilled banana bread topped with made-on-the-farm ice cream and *haupia* (coconut) and caramel sauce. 🕓 *30 min. to 1 hr. 56-800 Kamehameha Hwy. www.kahukufarms.com;* ☎ *808/628-0639.Tours $16–$32 for adults, $14 to $22 for ages 5-12.*

⓫ ★ **Ha: Breath of Life at the Polynesian Cultural Center.** Catch the evening show at the Polynesian Cultural Center. *See p 17,* ⓮.

Continue on Kamehameha Hwy. Turn right on Likelike Hwy. Take the Kalihi St./H-1 exit and continue on H-1 to Waikīkī. Bus: 55, then transfer to 8 or 19.

The North Shore's Best Spa

The Zen-like **Nalu Kinetic Spa,** at the Turtle Bay Resort, has a beautiful outdoor relaxation room and a thatched-hut treatment room right on the water, where you'll hear the waves crashing as you melt into your massage.

Where to **Stay**

★ Ke Iki Beach Bungalows KE IKI BEACH This collection of studio, one-, and two-bedroom cottages, located on a 200-foot (61m) stretch of beautiful white-sand beach, is affordable and perfect for families (plus all units have full kitchens and their own barbecue areas). *59–579 Ke Iki Rd. (off Kamehameha Hwy.). ☎ 866/638-8229 or 808/638-8829. www.keikibeach.com. 11 units. Studios $160; 1-bedroom $145–$225, 2-bedroom $160 –$245. Bus: 55.*

★★★ Turtle Bay Resort KAHUKU Located in the "country" on 5 miles (8km) of shoreline with secluded white-sand coves, this is the place to stay to get away from everything. The resort offers lots of activities, and all rooms have ocean views and balconies. It also boasts one of the best spas on the island. *57–091 Kamehameha Hwy. (at Kuhuku Dr.). ☎ 800/203-3650 or 808/293-6000. www.turtlebayresort.com. 477 units. Doubles $319–$389; cottages from $599; suites from $499; villas from $1,169. Bus: 55.*

Where to **Dine**

★ Beet Box Café HALE'IWA *VEGETARIAN* Warm wood paneling (upcycled, of course) welcomes you into this vegetarian restaurant. Flavors pack a punch in the form of satisfying sandwiches with portobello and feta or avocado and local greens. The breakfast burritos and smoothies are popular, too. *66-437 Kamehameha Hwy., www.thebeetboxcafe.com. ☎ 808/637-3000. Entrees $8–$12. Breakfast and lunch daily. Bus: 55.*

★ Haleiwa Beach House HALE'IWA *AMERICAN/LOCAL* When you tire of the North Shore food trucks, come here. This newly renovated restaurant opens up to a fabulous view of Hale'iwa beach park; come during pau hana (happy hour) when you can watch the sun set. Highlights on the menu include the whole fried fish and the kālua pig grilled cheese. *62-540 Kamehameha Hwy., Hale'iwa. ☎ 808/637-3435. Lunch $12–$29; dinner $26–$36. Lunch and dinner daily.*

Secluded, full-service Turtle Bay Resort

Kahuku Food Spots

Kahuku is famous for its shrimp trucks—you can practically smell the garlic wafting in the air as you approach. **Giovanni's Original White Shrimp Truck,** 56-505 Kamehameha Hwy. (☎ ***808/293-1839***) (see p. 27) is the most popular, but head north from Giovanni's about a mile, and you'll hit **Romy's,** 56-781 Kamehameha Hwy. (☎ ***808/232-2202***), a shrimp shack instead of a truck. Here the shrimp actually come from the farm behind it. Romy's is my favorite for the sauce—tons of sautéed and fried garlic over a half-pound of head-on shrimp, plus a container of spicy soy sauce for dipping. The shrimp, however, are inconsistent—sometimes firm and sweet, sometimes mealy.

Giovanni's Shrimp Truck

But Kahuku isn't just about shrimp. Head to the back of the nondescript **Kahuku Superette,** 56-505 Kamehameha Hwy. (☎808/293-9878) for some of the best poke (raw, seasoned cubes of 'ahi) on the island. The shoyu poke is legendary, infused with ginger, and the limu 'ahi poke, tossed with local Hawaiian seaweed, showcases the fresh fish. For something different, try the **Fiji Market & Curry Shop**, 56-565 Kamehameha Hwy. (☎808/293-7120), another hole-in-the-wall with unexpectedly delicious food. The short menu consists of Fijian curry (influenced by Indian spices): get the lamb or vegetable curry.

★ Lei Lei's Bar and Grill

KAHUKU *AMERICAN* At this casual spot overlooking the Turtle Bay golf course, you'll get solid and hearty dishes from the seafood cobb salad to the baby back ribs. If you've got a big appetite for dinner, go for the prime rib. *Turtle Bay Resort, 57–091 Kamehameha Hwy.* ☎ *808/293-2662. www.turtlebayresort.com. Lunch $14–$35; dinner $26–$45. Breakfast, lunch, and dinner daily. Bus: 55.*

★ Rajanee Thai HALE'IWA *THAI*

This cheery little spot serves some of the best Thai food on the island. There are the staples like pad thai and green curry, which are solid, but also try the zingy ginger salad, the crisp, battered fish, and the garlicky Bangkok night noodles. *66–111 Kamehameha Hwy. #1001* ☎ *808/784-0023. Entrees $8–$12. Lunch & dinner Tue–Sun. Bus: 55.*

Southern O'ahu & the Windward Coast

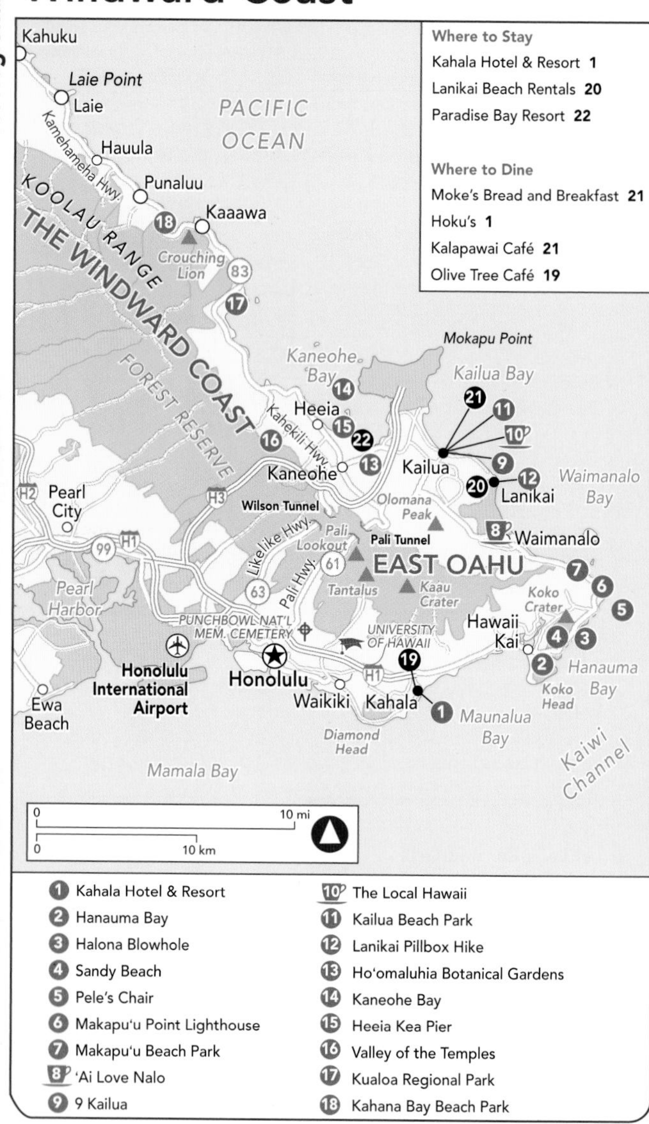

Where to Stay
Kahala Hotel & Resort 1
Lanikai Beach Rentals 20
Paradise Bay Resort 22
Where to Dine
Moke's Bread and Breakfast 21
Hoku's 1
Kalapawai Café 21
Olive Tree Café 19
Kahuku
Laie Point
Laie
PACIFIC OCEAN
Kamehameha Hwy.
Hauula
Punaluu
Kaaawa
KOOLAU RANGE
THE WINDWARD COAST
Crouching Lion
FOREST RESERVE
Mokapu Point
Kaneohe Bay
Kailua Bay
Heeia
Kahekili Hwy.
Kaneohe
Kailua
Lanikai
Waimanalo Bay
Pearl City
Wilson Tunnel
Olomana Peak
Pali Lookout
Pali Tunnel
Waimanalo
Likelike Hwy.
Pali Hwy.
EAST OAHU
Pearl Harbor
Tantalus
Kaau Crater
Koko Crater
PUNCHBOWL NAT'L MEM. CEMETERY
UNIVERSITY OF HAWAII
Hawaii Kai
Honolulu International Airport
Honolulu
Waikiki
Kahala
Hanauma Bay
Koko Head
Ewa Beach
Maunalua Bay
Diamond Head
Mamala Bay
Kaiwi Channel
0
10 mi
0
10 km
1 Kahala Hotel & Resort
2 Hanauma Bay
3 Halona Blowhole
4 Sandy Beach
5 Pele's Chair
6 Makapu'u Point Lighthouse
7 Makapu'u Beach Park
8 'Ai Love Nalo
9 9 Kailua
10 The Local Hawaii
11 Kailua Beach Park
12 Lanikai Pillbox Hike
13 Ho'omaluhia Botanical Gardens
14 Kaneohe Bay
15 Heeia Kea Pier
16 Valley of the Temples
17 Kualoa Regional Park
18 Kahana Bay Beach Park

From the high-rises of Waikīkī, venture to a very different O'ahu, the arid south shore and lush windward coast. The landscape on the south side is like a moonscape, with prickly cactuses on shore and, in winter, spouting whales cavorting in the water. Hawaiians call this area *Ka Iwi,* which means "the bone"—no doubt because of all the bone-cracking shore breaks along this popular bodyboarding coastline. The South gives way to the Windward side, where lots of rain keeps the vegetation green and growing, and a string of white-sand cove beaches promises a great outing.

From Waikīkī, take Kalakaua Ave. to Poni Moi Rd. and turn left. Go right on Diamond Head Rd., which becomes Kahala Ave.; go to the end of the street. Bus: 22, plus a 9-min. walk.

❶ ★★ Kahala Hotel & Resort. Stop by this lush, tropical resort where the grounds include a crescent-shaped beach, alagoon (home to two bottlenose dolphins, sea turtles, and tropical fish), plus a fabulous spa. You can start off your day with the brunch buffet at the oceanside Plumeria Beach House. *🕓 1 hr. 5000 Kahala Ave. (next to the Wai'alae Country Club). ☎ 800/367-2525 or 808/739-8888.*

Backtrack on Kahala Ave., then turn right on Kealaolu Ave. Take a slight right at Wai'alae Ave., which becomes Kalaniana'ole Hwy., and then go right at Hanauma Bay. Bus: Walk about 1 mile (1.6km) to Kilauea Ave. and Makaiwa St. to catch Bus 22.

❷ ★★★ Hanauma Bay. This marine preserve is a great place to stop for a swim; you'll find the friendliest fish on the island here. The beach park is closed on Tuesdays. *See p 155.*

Continue about a mile down Kalaniana'ole Hwy. (Hwy. 72) to around mile marker 11. Bus: 22, plus a 9-min. walk.

❸ Halona Blowhole. I'll give you two reasons to pull over at this scenic lookout: You get to watch

Aerial view of Hanauma Bay

The pull-off and observation deck at the Halona Blowhole

the ocean waves forced through a hole in the rocks shoot up 30 feet (9m) in the air, and there's a great view of Sandy Beach and across the 26-mile (42km) gulf to neighboring Moloka'i, with the faint triangular shadow of Lanai on the far horizon. Be sure to obey all the signs warning you to stay away from the blowhole. 🕓 *15 min. Kalaniana'ole Hwy. (Hwy. 72) around mile marker 11.*

Continue about a half mile (.8km) down Kalaniana'ole Hwy.

❹ ★ **Sandy Beach.** This is O'ahu's most dangerous beach—it's the only one with an ambulance always standing by to whisk injured wave catchers to the hospital. Bodyboarders just love it. I suggest you just sit on the sand and watch. *See p 160.*

Continue on Kalaniana'ole Hwy. No bus service.

❺ **Pele's Chair.** Just after you leave Sandy's, look out to sea for this famous formation, which from a distance looks like a mighty throne; it's believed to be the fire goddess's last resting place on O'ahu before she flew off to continue her work on other islands.

Continue on Kalaniana'ole Hwy. No bus service.

❻ ★★ **Makapu'u Point Lighthouse.** As you round the bend, ahead lies a 647-foot-high (197m) hill, with a lighthouse that once signaled safe passage for steamship passengers arriving from San Francisco. Today it lights the south coast for passing tankers, fishing boats, and sailors. You can take a short hike up here for a spectacular vista view. During the winter, you can spot cavorting whales off shore.

Continue on Kalaniana'ole Hwy. No bus service.

❼ ★ **Makapu'u Beach Park.** In summer, the ocean here is as gentle as a Jacuzzi, and swimming and diving are perfect; come winter, however, Makapu'u is hit with big, pounding waves that are ideal for expert bodysurfers but too dangerous for regular swimmers. *See p 158.*

Cross Kalaniana'ole Hwy. No bus service. Bus 57.

8 ★ **'Ai Love Nalo.** This roadside gem offers vegetarian takes on local favorites, such as the laulau, here a package of kalo (taro, a staple in the Hawaiian diet), 'ulu (breadfruit), Okinawan sweet potato, and carrot, all bundled in a lū'au leaf (taro leaf) and slow-cooked in coconut milk. Everything is full of flavor. Try the poi parfait or the soft serve, both topped with fresh, seasonal fruit and toasted cacao coconut flakes. *41-1025 Kalaniana'ole Hwy., Waimānalo. www.ailovenalo.com. Wed–Mon 9am–5pm. $.*

Continue on Kalaniana'ole Hwy. and turn right at Kailua Dr. Bus: 57.

9 **Kailua.** This is Hawai'i's biggest beach town, with more than 50,000 residents and two special beaches, Kailua and Lanikai, begging for visitors. Funky little Kailua is lined with million-dollar houses next to tar-paper shacks, antiques shops, and a great little boutique scene selling beachy wear.

From Kailua Dr., turn left on Hahani St. and right on Hekili St. Bus: 70.

Look for migrating whales on the hike up to the Makapu'u Point Lighthouse.

10 ★ **The Local Hawai'i.** Inside the boutique Aloha Beach Club is this shave ice stand, which uses locally grown fruit syrups (a rarity in the artificially flavored and colored shave ice world). The liliko'i and lychee are tops. *131 Hekili St. www.thelocalhawaii.com. $.*

Turn left on Kailua Dr., which becomes Kuulei Rd., then left on Kalaheo Ave., which becomes Kawailoa Rd. Bus: 70.

11 ★★ **Kailua Beach Park.** Windward O'ahu's premier beach is a 2-mile-long (3.2km), wide golden strand with dunes, palm trees, panoramic views, and offshore islets that are home to seabirds and

Lanikai Beach as seen from the Pillbox Hike

Ho'omaluhia Botanical Gardens

every type of ocean activity you can think of. *See p 156.*

From the beach, walk on Kawailoa Rd., away from the canal. Turn left onto Mokulua Dr. Stay on Mokulua Dr. and turn right onto Aalapapa Dr. Turn right onto Kaelepulu Dr.

⓬ ★ **Lanikai Pillbox Hike.** This short hike up to the Ka Iwi ridge is only about 30 minutes each way up the steep, dirt trail, but the payoff is great: picture-perfect views of Kailua, the Ko'olau mountains, and the Mokulua islands. It makes you realize why the pillboxes were built up here in the first place (they were constructed around WWII as observation posts and later abandoned). 🕒 *1 hr. Kaelepulu Dr.*

Retrace your route back to Kalaheo Ave., then turn left on Kuulei Rd., right on Oneawa St., and left at Mokapu Blvd., which becomes Mokapu Saddle Rd. Make a slight left on Kāne'ohe Bay Dr., go left on Kamehameha Hwy., and turn right on Luluku Rd. No bus service.

⓭ ★ **Ho'omaluhia Botanical Gardens.** If you have had enough time under the hot sun, stop by this 400-acre (162-ha) botanical garden, the perfect place for a picnic or hike. *See p 61,* ❿.

Retrace your route back to Kamehameha Hwy., turn right, and immediately get on H-3 East. Take the Kāne'ohe Bay Dr. exit. Drive down Kāne'ohe Bay Dr. and then turn right on Kamehameha Hwy. No bus service.

⓮ ★ **Kāne'ohe Bay.** Take an incredibly scenic drive around Kāne'ohe Bay, which is spiked with islets and lined with gold-sand beach parks. The bay has a barrier reef and four tiny islets, one of which is known as *Moku o loe,* or Coconut Island. Don't be surprised if it looks familiar—it appeared in *Gilligan's Island.* 🕒 *15 min.*

Turn right on Heeia Kea Pier off Kamehameha Hwy.

⓯ ★ **He'eia Kea Pier.** This old fishing pier jutting out into Kāne'ohe Bay is a great place to view the bay. Take a snorkel cruise here or sail out to a sandbar in the middle of the bay for an incredible view of O'ahu. 🕒 *30 min., longer if you snorkel or sail. See chapter 7 for details.*

Retrace your route on Kamehameha Hwy. and then turn right at Haiku Rd. Take a right at Kahekili Hwy. (Hwy. 83) and then a left at Avenue of the Temples. Bus: 56 to 65 from Kailua.

O'ahu's Best Spa

The Kahala Hotel & Resort has taken the concept of spa as a journey into relaxation to a new level with **Spa Suites at the Kahala** (www.kahalaresort.com; ☎ **808/739-8938**). The former garden guest rooms have been converted into personal spa treatment rooms, each with a glass-enclosed shower, private changing area, infinity-edge deep-soaking Jacuzzi tub, and personal relaxation area. No detail is overlooked, from the warm foot bath when you arrive to the refreshing hot tea served on your personal enclosed garden lanai after your relaxation treatment. Treatments range from $170 to $185 for 60 minutes and $255 to $270 for 90 minutes.

16 ★ Valley of the Temples. This famous site is stalked by wild peacocks and about 700 curious people a day, who pay to see the 9-foot (2.7m) meditation Buddha, 2 acres (.8 ha) of ponds full of more than 10,000 Japanese koi fish, and a replica of Japan's 900-year-old Byodo-In Temple. A 3-ton (2,722kg) brass temple bell brings good luck to those who can ring it. ⏱ *1 hr. 47–200 Kahekili Hwy. (across the street from Temple Valley Shopping Center).* ☎ *808/239-8811. www.byodo-in.com. $3 adults, $2 seniors 65 & over, $1 children 11 & under. Daily 9am–5pm.*

A replica of Japan's 900-year-old Byodo-In Temple at the Valley of the Temples

Continue on Kahekili Hwy., which becomes Kamehameha Hwy. Bus: 65, transfer to 55.

17 ★★ Kualoa Regional Park. This 150-acre (61-ha) coconut palm–fringed peninsula is the biggest beach park on the windward side and one of Hawai'i's most scenic. The long, narrow, white-sand beach is perfect for swimming, walking, beachcombing, kite flying, or just sunbathing. *See p 157.*

Continue on Kamehameha Hwy. about 10 miles (16km). Bus: 55.

18 ★★ Kahana Bay Beach Park. This white-sand, crescent-shaped beach has a picture-perfect backdrop: a huge, jungle-cloaked valley with dramatic, jagged cliffs. The bay's calm water and shallow, sandy bottom make it a safe swimming area for children. *See p 156.*

Retrace your route on Kamehameha Hwy. to Kahekili Hwy. Turn right on Likelike Hwy. Take the Kahilli St./H-1 exit. Merge onto H-1 and continue into Waikīkī. Bus: 55, then transfer to 8, 20, or 42.

Hawai'i Seafood Primer

The seafood in Hawai'i has been described as the best in the world. And why not? Without a doubt, the islands' surrounding waters and a growing aquaculture industry contribute to the high quality of the seafood here.

Although some menus include the Western description for the fresh fish used, most often the local nomenclature is listed. To help familiarize you with the menu language of Hawai'i, here's a basic glossary of island fish:

ahi yellowfin or big-eye tuna, important for its use in sashimi and poke at sushi bars and in Hawai'i Regional Cuisine

aku skipjack tuna, heavily used in home cooking and poke

ehu red snapper, delicate and sumptuous, yet lesser known than opakapaka

hapuupuu grouper, a sea bass whose use is expanding

hebi spearfish, mildly flavored, and frequently featured as the "catch of the day" in upscale restaurants

kajiki Pacific blue marlin, also called *au,* with a firm flesh and high fat content that make it a plausible substitute for tuna

mahimahi dolphin fish (the game fish, not the mammal) or dorado, a classic sweet, white-fleshed fish

monchong big-scale or sickle pomfret, an exotic, tasty fish, scarce but gaining a higher profile on Hawaiian Island menus

nairagi striped marlin, also called *au;* good as sashimi and in poke, and often substituted for ahi in raw-fish products

onaga ruby snapper, a luxury fish, versatile, moist, and flaky

ono wahoo, firmer and drier than the snappers, often served grilled and in sandwiches

opah moonfish, rich and fatty, and versatile—cooked, raw, smoked, and broiled

opakapaka pink snapper, light, flaky, and luxurious, suited for sashimi, poaching, sautéing, and baking

papio jack trevally, light, firm, and flavorful

shutome broadbill swordfish, of beeflike texture and rich flavor

tombo albacore tuna, with a high fat content, suitable for grilling

uhu parrotfish, most often encountered steamed, Chinese style

uku gray snapper of clear, pale-pink flesh, delicately flavored and moist

ulua large jack trevally, firm fleshed and versatile

Fresh-caught fish in Oahu

Where to **Stay**

★★★ Kāhala Hotel & Resort KāHALA Located in one of O'ahu's most prestigious residential areas, the Kāhala offers elegant rooms and peace and serenity away from Waikīkī, with the conveniences of central Honolulu just a 10-minute drive away. The lush, tropical grounds include a small beach with a private feel. There's a pool, too, but what makes the Kahala unique is the Dolphin Quest, which allows you to get up close and personal with the dolphins in the lagoon. Activities range from Hawaiian sailing canoe tours to stand-up paddleboard yoga. Yeah, you read that right. *5000 Kāhala Ave. (next to the Wai'alae Country Club).* ☎ *800/367-2525 or 808/739-8888. www.kahalaresort.com. 343 units. Doubles from $595; suites from $1,750.*

★ Lanikai Beach Rentals LANIKAI Choose from a 1,000-square-foot (93-sq.-m) two-bedroom apartment or a 540-square-foot (50-sq.-m) honeymooner's studio in this B&B tucked away in the swank beach community. They also have a booking agency to help you with other B&B and vacation rentals nearby. *1277 Mokulua Dr. (btw. Onekea & Aala drives).* ☎ *808/261-7895. www.lanikaibeachrentals.com. Doubles from $249.*

★ Paradise Bay Resort KĀNE'OHE Nestled in the tranquil, tropical setting on Kāne'ohe Bay, with views of the surrounding Ko'olau and Kualoa Mountains, this cluster of cabins (all with kitchens) also has terrific views of the calm waters of the bay and, in the distance, the small islets off shore. ***Tip:*** When booking, ask for a unit with a lanai; that way you'll end up with at least a partial view of the bay. The resort also features an array of ocean-oriented activities. *47–039 Lihikai Dr. (off Kamehameha Hwy.).* ☎ *800/735-5071 or 808/239-5711. www.paradisebayresorthawaii.com. 20 units. 1-bedroom $250–$419, 2-bedroom $249–$419, 3-bedroom from $674, 4-bedroom $758; all rates include breakfast.*

A studio apartment from Lanikai Beach Rentals

Where to Dine

★ **Moke's Bread and Breakfast** KAILUA *BREAKFAST/BRUNCH* Of all the pancake joints in Kailua, Moke's is my pick—their *liliko'i* pancakes are unparalleled. A light passionfruit cream sauce cascades over tender, fluffy pancakes, a perfect blend of tart and sweet, simple and decadent. Other staples, such as the loco moco and omelets, are also spot-on. *27 Ho'olai St., Kailua. www.mokeskailua.com. ☎ 808/261-5565. Entrees $8–$14. Breakfast Wed–Mon.*

★★ **Hoku's** KAHALA *HAWAIIAN REGIONAL* Elegant without being stuffy and creative without being overwrought, the upscale dining room of the Kahala Hotel & Resort combines European finesse with an island touch, with such dishes as the fried whole fresh fish, black-pepper roasted venison, rack of lamb, and the full range of East-West specialties. Sunday brunch is not to be missed. *Kahala Hotel, 5000 Kahala Ave. (end of street). ☎ 808/739-8780. www.kahalaresort.com. Entrees $28–$69. Dinner Wed–Sun; brunch Sun.*

A salmon entrée at Hoku's at the Kahala Hotel

Olive Tree Café is a favorite for casual Greek dining.

★ **Kalapawai Café** KAILUA *MEDITERRANEAN* This tiny neighborhood bistro features everything from gourmet espresso coffee (it opens at 6am) to breakfast goodies to lunch treats (to take to the beach) to elegant cuisine for dinner. Combination deli, market, and cafe, you can sit inside or in the garden lanai outside. *750 Kailua Rd. (at Kihapai St.). ☎ 808/262-3354. www.kalapawaimarket.com. Dinner entrees $19–$24. Breakfast, lunch & dinner daily.*

★★ **Olive Tree Café.** KAHALA *GREEK/EASTERN MEDITERRANEAN* This is Honolulu's best restaurant for a meal under $20, a totally hip hole-in-the-wall eatery with divine Greek fare. There are umbrella tables outside and a few seats indoors, and you order and pay at the counter. Winners include mussel ceviche; fish souvlaki; and the generous Greek salad. *4614 Kilauea Ave. (across from Kāhala Mall). ☎ 808/737-0303. Entrees $10–$15. No credit cards.* ●

6 The Best Beaches

O'ahu's Best Beaches

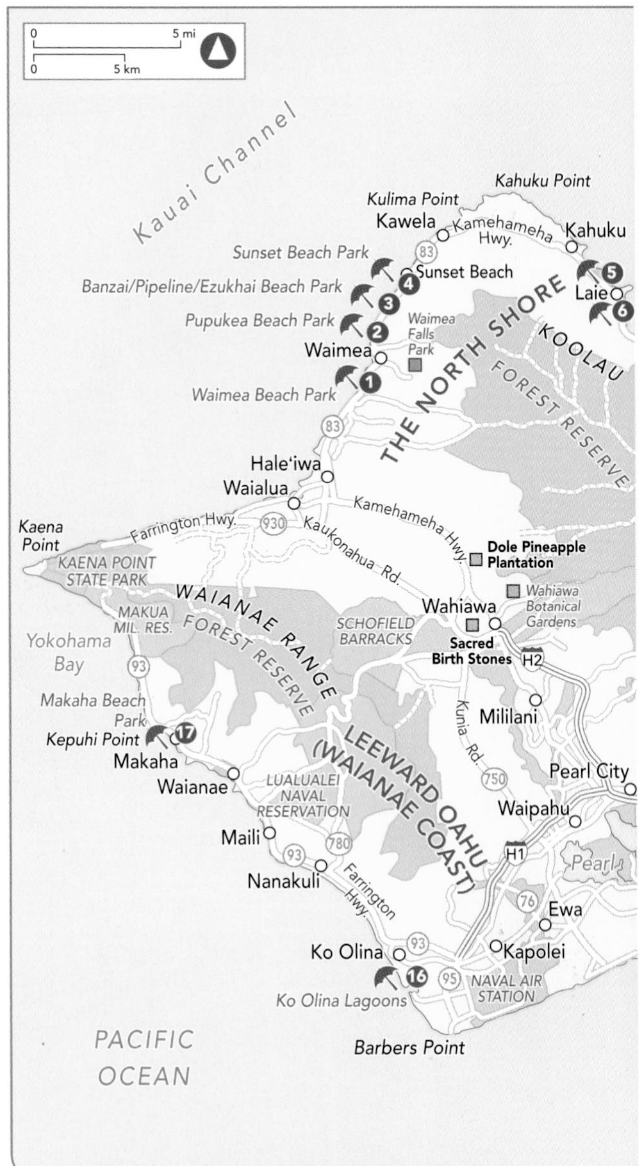
0
5 mi
0
5 km
Kauai Channel
Kahuku Point
Kulima Point
Kawela
Kamehameha Hwy.
Kahuku
Sunset Beach Park
Sunset Beach
Banzai/Pipeline/Ezukhai Beach Park
Laie
Pupukea Beach Park
Waimea Falls Park
Waimea
THE NORTH SHORE
KOOLAU FOREST RESERVE
Waimea Beach Park
Hale'iwa
Waialua
Kaena Point
Farrington Hwy.
Kamehameha Hwy.
Kaukonahua Rd.
Dole Pineapple Plantation
KAENA POINT STATE PARK
WAIANAE RANGE
Wahiawa Botanical Gardens
Wahiawa
MAKUA MIL. RES.
FOREST RESERVE
SCHOFIELD BARRACKS
Yokohama Bay
Sacred Birth Stones
Makaha Beach Park
Mililani
Kepuhi Point
LEEWARD OAHU (WAIANAE COAST)
Kunia Rd.
Makaha
Pearl City
Waianae
LUALUALEI NAVAL RESERVATION
Waipahu
Maili
Pearl
Nanakuli
Farrington Hwy.
Ewa
Ko Olina
Kapolei
NAVAL AIR STATION
Ko Olina Lagoons
PACIFIC OCEAN
Barbers Point

Previous page: The Duke Kahanamoku statue on Waikīkī Beach

Ala Moana Beach Park 15
Banzai/Pipeline/Ehukai Beach Park 3
Hanauma Bay 13
Kahana Bay Beach Park 7
Kailua Beach 9
Ko Olina Lagoons 16
Kualoa Regional Park 8
Lanikai Beach 10
Makaha Beach Park 17
Makapu'u Beach Park 11
Malaekahana Bay State Recreation Area 5
Pounders Beach 6
Pupukea Beach Park 2
Sandy Beach 12
Sunset Beach Park 4
Waikiki Beach 14
Waimea Beach Park 1
PACIFIC OCEAN
Hauula
Punaluu
Kahana Bay Beach Park
Kaaawa
THE WINDWARD COAST RANGE
FOREST RESERVE
Kualoa Regional Park
Mokapu Point
Kaneohe Bay
MARINE CORPS AIR STATION
HEEIA STATE PARK
Heeia
Kailua Bay
Kaneohe
Kailua
Kailua Beach Park
Waimanalo Bay
BELLOWS AIR FORCE BASE
Wilson Tunnel
Likelike Hwy.
Pali Tunnel
Pali Hwy.
Makapu'u Beach Park
Waimanalo
USS Arizona Memorail
EAST OAHU
Harbor
Tantalus
HALONA BLOW HOLE
HICKAM AFB
PUNCHBOWL NAT'L MEM. CEMETERY
Sandy Beach
Honolulu
Hawaii Kai
Hanauma Bay
Honolulu International Airport
Waikiki
Ala Moana Beach Park
Maunalua Bay
Koko Head
Waikiki Beach
Diamond Head
Mamala Bay
Kaiwi Channel

Beaches Best Bets

Ala Moana Beach Park has shady lawns, a lagoon, and picnic tables.

Best for a **Picnic**

★★ Ala Moana Beach Park, *1200 Ala Moana Blvd. (p 155)*

Best Place to **"Shoot the Tube"**

★ Banzai/Pipeline/Ehukai Beach Park, *59–337 Ka Nui Rd. (p 155)*

Best **Snorkeling**

★★★ Hanauma Bay, *7455 Koko Kalaniana'ole Hwy. (p 155)*

Best Place to **Kayak**

★★ Kahana Bay Beach Park, *52–222 Kamehameha Hwy. (p 156)*

Best **Windsurfing**

★★★ Kailua Beach, *450 Kawailoa Rd. (p 156)*

Best for **Kids**

★ Ko Olina Lagoons, *Aliinui Dr. (p 157)*

Best **Scenic Beach Park**

★★ Kualoa Regional Park, *49–600 Kamehameha Hwy. (p 157)*

Best for **Swimming**

★★ Lanikai Beach, *Mokulua Dr. (p 158)*

Best for **Expert Body Surfing**

★ Makapu'u Beach Park, *41–095 Kalaniana'ole Hwy. (p 158)*

Best **Secluded Beach**

★★★ Malaekahana Bay State Recreation Area, *Kamehameha Hwy. (p 159)*

Best **Diving**

★ Pupukea Beach Park, *59–727 Kamehameha Hwy. (p 159)*

Best Beach for **Watching Bodyboarders**

★ Sandy Beach, *8800 Kalaniana'ole Hwy. (p 160)*

Best for **People-Watching**

★★ Sunset Beach Park, *59–100 Kamehameha Hwy. (p 161)*

Best for **Sunbathing & Partying**

★★★ Waikīkī Beach, *from Ala Wai Yacht Harbor to Diamond Head Park (p 161)*

Best for **Big Waves**

★★ Waimea Bay Beach Park, *51–031 Kamehameha Hwy. (p 162)*

O'ahu Beaches A to Z

★ Ala Moana Beach Park HONOLULU The gold-sand Ala Moana ("by the sea") stretches for more than a mile along Honolulu's coast between downtown and Waikīkī. This 76-acre (31-ha) midtown beach park, with spreading lawns shaded by banyans and palms, is one of the island's most popular playgrounds, with its own lagoon, yacht harbor, tennis courts, music pavilion, picnic tables, and plenty of wide-open green spaces. The water is calm almost year-round, protected by black lava rocks set offshore. There's a large parking lot as well as metered street parking. *1200 Ala Moana Blvd. (btw. Kamakee St. & Atkinson Dr.). TheBus: 20.*

★ Banzai/Pipeline/Ehukai Beach Park NORTH SHORE There are three separate areas here, but because the sandy beach is continuous, most people think of it as one beach park. Located near Pupukea, **Ehukai Beach Park** is 1 acre (.4 ha) of grass with a parking lot, great for winter surfing and summer swimming. **Pipeline** is about 100 yards (91m) to the left of Ehukai. When the winter surf rolls in and hits the shallow coral shelf, the waves that quickly form are steep—so steep, in fact, that the crest of the wave falls forward, forming a near-perfect tube, or "pipeline." Just west of Pipeline is the area surfers call **"Banzai Beach."** The Japanese word *banzai* means "10,000 years"; it's given as a toast or as a battle charge, meaning "go for it." In the late 1950s, filmmaker Bruce Brown was shooting one of the first surf movies ever made, *Surf Safari,* when he saw a bodysurfer ride a huge wave. Brown yelled, "Banzai!" and the name stuck. In the winter, this is a very popular beach with surfers and surf fans. *Access via Ehukai Beach Park, 59–337 Ka Nui Rd. (off Kamehameha Hwy.), Pupukea. TheBus: 8, then transfer to TheBus 55.*

Hanauma Bay is popular for snorkeling and scuba-diving.

A Word of Warning

Wherever you are on O'ahu, remember that you're in an urban area. Never leave valuables in your car. Thefts do occur at O'ahu's beaches, and locked cars are not a deterrent.

★★★ Hanauma Bay KOKO HEAD This small, curved, 2,000-foot (610m) gold-sand beach is packed elbow-to-elbow with people year-round. The bay's shallow shoreline water and abundant marine life draw snorkelers, but this beach is also popular for sunbathing and people-watching. The deeper water outside the bay is

Pūpūkea Beach Park

great for scuba diving. Hanauma Bay is a conservation district; don't touch any marine life or feed the fish. Facilities include parking, restrooms, a pavilion, a grass volleyball court, lifeguards, barbecues, picnic tables, and food concessions. Alcohol is prohibited in the park; no smoking past the visitor center. Expect to pay $1 per vehicle to park and a $7.50-per-person entrance fee (children 12 and under are free). Avoid the crowds by going early on a weekday morning; once the parking lot's full, you're out of luck. *7455 Koko Kalaniana'ole Hwy. (at Hanauma Bay Rd.). www1.honolulu.gov/parks/facility/hanaumabay/hbayfees.htm. Closed Tues. Open 6am–7pm summer; 6am–6pm winter. Take TheBus to escape the parking problem: The Hanauma Bay Shuttle (TheBus: 22) runs from Waikīkī to Hanauma Bay every half-hour 8:45am–1pm; you can catch it at the Ala Moana Hotel, the Ilikai Hotel, or any city bus stop. It returns every hour noon–4:30pm.*

★★ Kahana Bay Beach Park WINDWARD This white-sand, crescent-shaped beach is backed by a huge, jungle-cloaked valley with dramatic, jagged cliffs and is protected by ironwood and kamani trees. The bay's calm water and shallow, sandy bottom make it a safe swimming area for children. The surrounding park has picnic areas, camping, and hiking trails. The wide sand-bottom channel that runs through the park and out to Kahana Bay is one of the largest on O'ahu—it's perfect for kayakers. *52–222 Kamehameha Hwy., Kahana. TheBus: 19 or 20, then transfer to TheBus 55.*

★★★ Kailua Beach WINDWARD Windward O'ahu's premier beach is a 2-mile-long (3.2km), wide golden strand with dunes, palm trees, panoramic views, and offshore islets that are home to seabirds. The swimming is excellent, and the warm, azure waters are usually decorated with bright sails; this is O'ahu's premier windsurfing beach as well. It's also a favorite spot to sail catamarans, bodysurf the gentle waves, or paddle a kayak. Water conditions are quite safe, especially at the mouth of Kaelepulu Stream, where toddlers play in the freshwater shallows at the middle of the beach park. Facilities include lifeguards, picnic tables, barbecues, restrooms, a

Staying Safe in the Water

According to the latest statistics from the Hawai'i State Department of Health, the number of drownings of nonresidents in Hawai'i, most of them in the ocean, is increasing. Below are some tips to keep in mind when swimming in Hawaii's gorgeous waters:

- Never swim alone.
- Always supervise children in the water.
- Always swim at beaches with lifeguards.
- Know your limits—don't swim out farther than you know you can swim back.
- Read the posted warning signs before you enter the water.
- Call a lifeguard or 911 if you see someone in distress.

volleyball court, a public boat ramp, and free parking. *450 Kawailoa Rd., Kailua. TheBus: 19, then transfer to TheBus 57A.*

★ Ko Olina Lagoons LEEWARD The developer of the 640-acre (259-ha) Ko Olina Resort has created four white-sand lagoons to make the rocky shoreline more attractive and accessible. The lagoons offer calm, shallow waters and a powdery white-sand beach bordered by a broad, grassy lawn. No lifeguards are present, but the generally tranquil waters are great for swimming, are perfect for kids, and offer some snorkeling opportunities around the boulders at the entrance to the lagoons. Two lagoons have restrooms, and there's plenty of public parking. *Off Aliinui Dr. (btw. Olani & Mauloa places), Ko Olina Resort. TheBus: 20, then transfer to TheBus 40 & walk 1 mile along highway to Ko Olina Resort.*

★★ Kualoa Regional Park WINDWARD This 150-acre (61-ha) coconut palm–fringed peninsula is

Windsurfing at Kailua Beach

the biggest beach park on the windward side and one of Hawaii's most scenic. The park has a broad, grassy lawn and a long, narrow, white-sand beach ideal for swimming, walking, beachcombing, kite flying, or sunbathing. The waters are shallow and safe for swimming year-round, and at low tide, you can swim or wade out to the islet of Mokolii (popularly known as Chinaman's Hat), which has a small sandy beach and is a bird preserve. Picnic and camping areas are available. ***49–600 Kamehameha Hwy., Kualoa. TheBus: 13, then transfer to TheBus 55.***

★★ Lanikai Beach WINDWARD One of Hawai'i's best spots for swimming, gold-sand Lanikai's crystal-clear lagoon is like a giant saltwater swimming pool. The beach is a mile (1.6km) long and thin in places, but the sand is soft, and onshore trade winds make this an excellent place for sailing and windsurfing. Kayakers often paddle out to the two tiny offshore Mokulua islands, which are seabird sanctuaries. Sun worshipers: Arrive in the morning; the Ko'olau Mountains block the afternoon rays. ***Mokulua Dr., Kailua. TheBus: 20, then transfer to TheBus 57.***

★★★ Makaha Beach Park LEEWARD When surf's up here, it's spectacular: Monstrous waves pound the beach from October to April. Nearly a mile (1.6km) long, this half-moon gold-sand beach is tucked between 231-foot (70m) Lahilahi Point, which locals call Black Rock, and Kepuhi Point, a toe of the Waianae mountain range. Summer is the best time for swimming. Children hug the shore on the north side of the beach, near the lifeguard stand, while surfers dodge the rocks and divers seek an offshore channel full of big fish. Facilities include restrooms, lifeguards, and parking. ***84–369 Farrington Hwy. (near Kili Dr.), Waianae. TheBus: 2, then transfer to TheBus C (Country Express–Makaha).***

★ Makapu'u Beach Park WINDWARD Hawaii's most famous bodysurfing beach is a beautiful 1,000-foot-long (305m) gold-sand beach cupped in the stark black Koolau cliffs. Summertime waters are perfect for swimming and diving but in winter, Makapu'u is hit with big, pounding waves that are ideal for expert bodysurfers. Small boards—no longer than 3 feet (.9m) and without skeg (bottom fin)—are

Calm summer waters at Makaha Beach give way to big waves in the winter.

Makapu'u Beach Park

permitted; regular board surfing is banned. Facilities include restrooms, lifeguards, barbecue grills, picnic tables, and parking. *41–095 Kalaniana'ole Hwy. (across the street from Sea Life Park), Waimānalo. TheBus: 22.*

★★ Malaekahana Bay State Recreation Area NORTH SHORE This almost mile-long white-sand crescent lives up to just about everyone's image of the perfect Hawaiian beach: It's excellent for swimming, and at low tide you can wade offshore to Goat Island, a sanctuary for seabirds and turtles. Facilities include restrooms, barbecue grills, picnic tables, outdoor showers, and parking. *Kamehameha Hwy. 83 (2 miles/3.2km north of the Polynesian Cultural Center). TheBus: 19, then transfer to TheBus 55.*

★ Pounders Beach NORTH SHORE This wide beach, extending a quarter-mile (.4km) between two points, is easily accessed from the highway and very popular on weekends. At the west end of the beach, the waters usually are calm and safe for swimming (during May–Sept). However, at the opposite end, near the limestone cliffs, there's a shore break that can be dangerous for inexperienced bodysurfers; the bottom drops off abruptly, causing strong rip currents. Go on a weekday morning to have the beach to yourself. *Kamehameha Hwy. (about a half-mile/.8km south of Polynesian Cultural Center), Laie. TheBus: 55.*

★ Pupukea Beach Park NORTH SHORE This 80-acre (32-ha) beach park, very popular for snorkeling and diving, is a Marine Life Conservation District. Locals divide the area into two: **Shark's Cove** (which is *not* named for an

The roiling waves of Sandy Beach at Koko Head are for experienced bodysurfers only.

Don't Get Burned: Smart Tanning Tips

Hawai'i's Caucasian population has the highest incidence of malignant melanoma (deadly skin cancer) in the world. And nobody is completely safe from the sun's harmful rays: All skin types and races can burn. To ensure that your vacation won't be ruined by a painful sunburn, here are some helpful tips:

- **Wear a strong sunscreen at all times.** Use a sunscreen with an SPF of 15 or higher; people with light complexions should use SPF 30. Apply it liberally and reapply every 2 hours.
- **Wear a hat and sunglasses.** The hat should have a brim all the way around to cover not only your face but also the sensitive back of your neck. Make sure your sunglasses have UV filters.
- **Protect children from the sun.** Infants under 6 months should not be in the sun at all. Older babies need zinc oxide to protect their fragile skin, and all children should be slathered with sunscreen frequently.
- **If it's too late.** The best remedy for a sunburn is to stay out of the sun until all the redness is gone. Aloe vera, cool compresses, cold baths, and anesthetic benzocaine also help with the pain of sunburn.

abundance of sharks), great for snorkeling and, outside the cove, good diving; and at the southern end, **Three Tables** (named for the three flat sections of reef visible at low tide), also great for snorkeling, where the water is about 15 feet (4.6m) deep, and diving outside the tables, where the water is 30 to 45 feet (9.1–14m) deep. It's packed May to October, when swimming, diving, and snorkeling are best; the water is usually calm, but watch out for surges. In the winter, when currents form and waves roll in, this area is very dangerous, even in the tide pools, and also much less crowded. No lifeguards. *59–727 Kamehameha Hwy. (Pupukea Rd.), Pupukea. TheBus: 55.*

★ **Sandy Beach** KOKO HEAD Sandy Beach is one of the best bodysurfing beaches on O'ahu. It's also one of the most dangerous. The 1,200-foot-long (366m) gold-sand beach is pounded by wild waves and haunted by a dangerous shore break and strong backwash; the experienced bodysurfers make

Windsurfing at Kailua Beach

Pūpūkea Beach Park, a Marine Life Conservation District

wave riding look easy, but it's best just to watch the daredevils risking their necks. Weak swimmers and children should definitely stay out of the water here—Sandy Beach's heroic lifeguards make more rescues in a year than at any other beach on O'ahu. Lifeguards post flags to alert beachgoers to the day's surf: Green means safe, yellow means caution, and red indicates very dangerous water conditions; always check the flags before you dive in. Facilities include restrooms and parking. Go weekdays to avoid the crowds and weekends to catch the bodysurfers in action. *8800 Kalaniana'ole Hwy. (about 2 miles/3.2km east of Hanauma Bay). TheBus: 22.*

★★ Sunset Beach Park NORTH SHORE Surfers around the world know this famous site for its spectacular winter surf—the huge thundering waves can reach 15 to 20 feet (4.5–6m). During the winter surf season (Sept–Apr), swimming is very dangerous here, due to the powerful rip currents. The only safe time to swim is during the calm summer months. The wide sandy beach is a great place to people-watch, but don't go too close to the water when the lifeguards have posted the red warning flags. *59–100 Kamehameha Hwy. (near Paumalu Place). TheBus: 55.*

★★★ Waikīkī Beach WAIKĪKĪ No beach anywhere is so widely known or so universally sought after as this narrow, 1½-mile-long (2.4km) crescent of imported sand (from Moloka'i) at the foot of a string of high-rise hotels. Home to the world's longest-running beach party, Waikīkī attracts nearly five million visitors a year from every corner of the planet. Waikīkī is actually a string of beaches that extends from **Sans Souci State Recreational Area,** near Diamond Head to the east, to **Duke Kahanamoku Beach,** in front of the Hilton Hawaiian Village Beach Resort & Spa to the west. Great stretches along Waikīkī include **Kuhio Beach,** next to the Moana Surfrider, which provides the quickest access to the Waikīkī shoreline; the stretch in front of the Royal Hawaiian Hotel known as **Grey's Beach,** which is canted so that it catches the rays perfectly; and **Sans Souci,** the small, popular beach in front of the New Otani Kaimana Beach Hotel that's locally known as "Dig Me"

Waikīkī Beach attracts nearly 5 million visitors each year.

Beach because of all the gorgeous bods strutting their stuff here. Waikīkī is fabulous for swimming, board and bodysurfing, outrigger canoeing, diving, sailing, snorkeling, and pole fishing. Every imaginable type of marine equipment is available for rent here. Facilities include showers, lifeguards, restrooms, grills, picnic tables, and pavilions at the **Queen's Surf** end of the beach (at Kapiolani Park, between the zoo and the aquarium). ***Stretching from Ala Wai Yacht Harbor to Diamond Head Park. TheBus: 20.***

Waimea Bay Beach Park

★★★ Waimea Bay Beach Park

NORTH SHORE This deep, sandy bowl has gentle summer waves that are excellent for swimming, snorkeling, and bodysurfing. To one side of the bay is a huge rock that local kids like to climb up and dive from. The scene is much different in winter, when waves pound the narrow bay, sometimes rising to 50 feet (15m) high. When the surf's really up, very strong currents and shore breaks sweep the bay—and it seems like everyone on O'ahu drives out to Waimea to get a look at the monster waves and those who ride them; to avoid the crowds, go on weekdays. Facilities include lifeguards, restrooms, showers, parking, and nearby restaurants and shops in Haleiwa town. ***51–031 Kamehameha Hwy., Waimea. TheBus: 55.*** ●

7 The Great Outdoors

O'ahu's Best Hiking & Camping

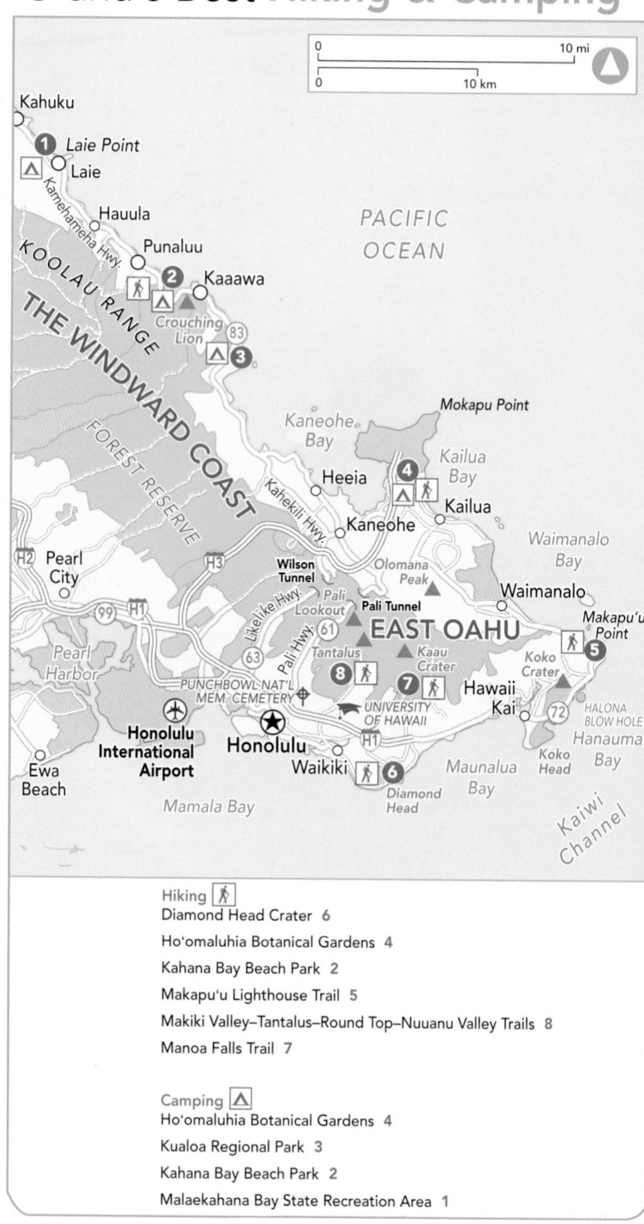

Hiking

Diamond Head Crater 6

Ho'omaluhia Botanical Gardens 4

Kahana Bay Beach Park 2

Makapu'u Lighthouse Trail 5

Makiki Valley–Tantalus–Round Top–Nuuanu Valley Trails 8

Manoa Falls Trail 7

Camping

Ho'omaluhia Botanical Gardens 4

Kualoa Regional Park 3

Kahana Bay Beach Park 2

Malaekahana Bay State Recreation Area 1

Previous page: Surfing in Oahu

On O'ahu you can camp by the ocean, hike in a tropical rainforest, and take in scenic views that will imprint themselves on your memory forever. If you plan to camp, bring your own gear or rent through Go Camp O'ahu (www.gocampoahu.com. ☎ **808/726-7469**), the only company on the island that rents camping equipment. Pick out the gear you want online, from a basic two-person tent to packages including an air mattress, pillows, linens, coolers, and beach chairs, and the owner, Chris Wysocki, will deliver it to your campsite. If you plan to go hiking, take a fully charged cellphone, in case of emergency.

★★★ **Diamond Head Crater**
Hiking This is a short but steep walk to the summit of the 750-foot (229m) volcanic cone, Hawaii's most famous landmark, with a reward of a 360-degree view of the island. The 1.4-mile (2.3km) round-trip takes about 1½ hours and the entry fee is $1. Bring water, a hat to protect yourself from the sun, and a camera. You might want to put all your gear in a pack to leave your hands free for the climb. Go early, preferably just after the 6am opening, before the midday sun starts beating down. Gates lock at 6pm; the last hiker is allowed in at 4:30pm (daily). *Monsarrat & 18th aves. www.hawaiistateparks.org/parks/oahu/diamond-head-state-monument. Daily 6am–6pm. Fee $1 per person or $5 per car. Bus: 58.*

Safety Tip

When planning sunset activities, be aware that Hawai'i, like other places close to the equator, has a very short (5–10 min.) twilight period after the sun sets. After that, it's dark. If you hike out to watch the sunset, be sure you can make it back quickly, or take a flashlight.

★ **Ho'omaluhia Botanical Gardens**
Hiking & Camping This relatively unknown windward-side camping area, outside Kāne'ohe, is a real find. *Ho'omaluhia* means "peace and tranquility," an apt description for this 400-acre (162-ha) lush botanical garden. Standing among the rare plants, with craggy cliffs in the background, it's hard to believe you're just a half-hour from downtown Honolulu. A 32-acre (13-ha) lake sits in the middle of the scenic park (no swimming or boating is allowed), and there are numerous hiking trails. The Visitor Center can suggest a host of activities, ranging from guided walks to demonstrations of ancient Hawaiian plant use. Facilities include a tent-camp area, restrooms, cold showers, picnic tables, grills, and water. Camping permits are free and issued via the City and County of Honolulu's online camping permit system (https://camping.honolulu.gov) while supplies last. You can obtain a permit up to 3 weeks in

Downtown Honolulu and Waikīkī from the rim of Diamond Head Crater

Hiking in Ho'omaluhia Botanical Gardens

advance. Stays are limited to Friday, Saturday, and Sunday nights only. *Ho'omaluhia Botanical Gardens, 45–680 Luluku Rd. (at Kamehameha Hwy.), Kāne'ohe. ☎ 808/233-7323. www1.honolulu.gov/parks/hbg/hmbg.htm. Daily 9am–4pm. Guided hikes (reserve in advance) 10am Sat & 1pm Sun. Bus: 55.*

★★ Kahana Bay Beach Park

Camping Under jungle cliffs, with a beautiful, gold-sand crescent beach framed by pine needle casuarina trees, Kahana Bay Beach Park is a place of serene beauty. You can swim, bodysurf, fish, hike, picnic or just sit and listen to the trade winds whistle through the beach pines. Both tent and vehicle camping are allowed at this oceanside oasis. Camping permits must be obtained online (see Camping Permits on p 167). There is an $18 fee per campsite per night. Facilities include restrooms, picnic tables, drinking water, public phones, and a boat-launching ramp.

Hiking Spectacular views of this verdant valley and a few swimming holes are the rewards of a 4.5-mile (7.2km) loop trail above the beach. The downsides to this 2- to 3-hour, somewhat ardent adventure are mosquitoes (clouds of them) and some thrashing about in dense forest where a bit of navigation is required along the not-always-marked trail. The trail starts behind the Visitor's Center at the Kahana Valley State Park. *52–222 Kamehameha Hwy. (Hwy. 83), btw. Ka'a'awa & Kahana. https://camping.ehawaii.gov/camping/all,details,1679.html. Open during daylight hours only. Bus: 55.*

★★ Kualoa Regional Park

Camping Located on a peninsula in Kāne'ohe Bay, this park has a spectacular setting right on a gold-sand beach, with a great view of Mokoli'i Island. Facilities include restrooms, showers, picnic tables, drinking fountains, and a public phone. *49–600 Kamehameha Hwy., across from Mokoli'i Island (btw. Waikane & Ka'a'awa). Bus: 55.*

★ Makapu'u Lighthouse Trail

Hiking This easy 45-minute (one-way) hike winds around the 646-foot-high (197m) sea bluff to the Lighthouse. The rewards are the views: the entire Windward Coast, across the azure Pacific and out to Manana (Rabbit) Island. Spot the whales in the winter. *Kalani'anaole Hwy. (half mile/.8km down the road from the Hawai'i Kai Golf Course), past Sandy Beach. Bus: 22.*

Camping Permits

You must get a permit for all camping in all parks on O'ahu. For Honolulu County Parks (such as Kualoa Regional Park), contact Honolulu Department of Parks and Recreation, 650 King St., Honolulu, HI 96713 (☎ 808/523-4525; https://camping.honolulu.gov), for information and permits. County Parks charge $32 for a 3-day permit and $52 for a 5-day permit. For state parks, there's an $18 fee for camping (per campsite per night), and you must get a permit. Permits are limited to 5 nights and can only be obtained at https://camping.ehawaii.gov/camping. County and state parks do not allow camping Wednesdays or Thursdays.

Water Safety

Water might be everywhere in Hawai'i, but it likely isn't safe to drink. Most stream water is contaminated with bacterium leptospirosis, which produces flulike symptoms and can be fatal. So boil your drinking water, or, if boiling isn't an option, use tablets with hydroperiodide; portable water filters will not screen out bacterium leptospirosis.

★★ Makīkī Valley–Tantalus–Round Top–Nu'uanu Valley Trails

Hiking This is the starting place for some of O'ahu's best hiking trails—miles of trails converge through the area. The draws here are the breathtaking views, historic remains, and incredible vegetation. Stop at the Hawai'i Nature Center, by the trail head, for information and maps. *2131 Makiki Heights Dr.* ☎ *808/955-0100. Mon–Fri 8am–4:30pm. Bus: 4.*

Hiking to Makapu'u Point Lighthouse

★★★ Malaekahana Bay State Recreation Area

Camping This beautiful beach camping site has a mile-long (1.6km) gold-sand beach. Facilities include picnic tables, restrooms, showers, sinks, drinking water, and a phone. *Kamehameha Hwy. (btw. Laie & Kahuku).* ☎ *808/293-1736. www.hawaiistateparks.org/parks/oahu/malaekahana.cfm. Bus: 55.*

★★ Mānoa Falls Trail

Hiking This easy, .75-mile (1.2km) hike (one-way) is terrific for families; it takes less than an hour to reach idyllic Mānoa Falls. The often-muddy trail follows Waihi Stream and meanders through the forest reserve past guavas, mountain apples, and wild ginger. The forest is moist and humid and is inhabited by giant bloodthirsty mosquitoes, so bring repellent. If it has rained recently, stay on the trail and step carefully, as it can be very slippery. The trail head is marked by a footbridge. *End of Mānoa Rd., past Lyon Arboretum. Bus: 5.*

O'ahu's Best Golf Courses

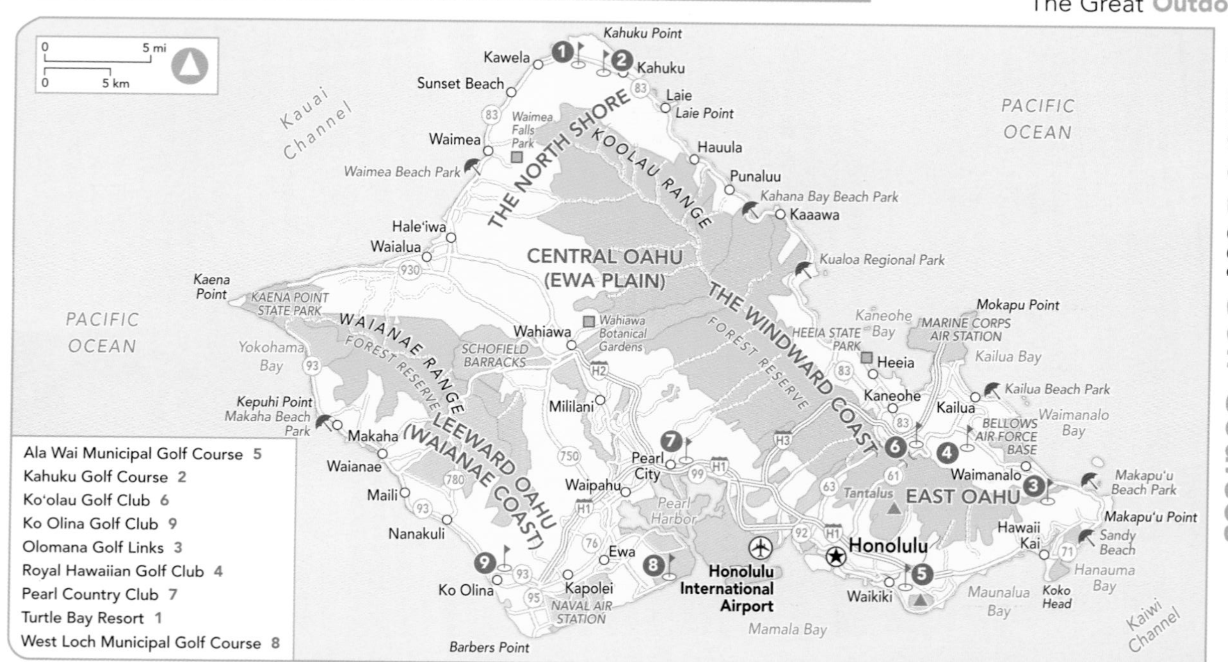

O'ahu has nearly three dozen golf courses, ranging from bare-bones municipal links to exclusive country club courses with membership fees of up to six figures a year. Below are the best of a great bunch. As you play O'ahu's courses, you'll come to know that the windward courses play much differently than the leeward courses. On the windward side, the prevailing winds blow from the ocean to shore, and the grain direction of the greens tends to run the same way—from the ocean to the mountains. Leeward golf courses have the opposite tendency: The winds usually blow from the mountains to the ocean, with the grain direction of the greens corresponding.

★ **Ala Wai Municipal Golf Course** This is O'ahu's most popular course. Duffers play some 500 rounds a day on this 18-hole municipal course, within walking distance of Waikīkī's hotels. It is a challenge to get a tee time (you can book only 3 days in advance). Ala Wai has a flat layout and is less windy than most O'ahu courses, but pay attention; some holes are not as easy as you may think. *404 Kapahulu Ave., Waikīkī. ☎ 808/733-7387 (golf course) or 808/296-2000 (tee-time reservations). www.co.honolulu.hi.us/des/golf/alawai.htm. Greens fees $55, twilight rate $28. Bus: 19, 20, or 22.*

★ **Kahuku Golf Course** This 9-hole budget golf course is a bit funky. There's only a dilapidated shack where you check in, no clubhouse, and no facilities other than a few pull carts and two porta potties. But a round at this scenic oceanside course amid the tranquillity of the North Shore is quite an experience. Duffers will love the ease of this recreational course with its gently sloping greens. No reservations are taken; tee times are first-come, first-served—and the competition is fierce for early tee times. *56–501 Kamehameha Hwy., Kahuku. ☎ 808/293-5842. www1.honolulu.gov/des/golf/kahuku.htm. Greens fees $16.50 for 9 holes. Bus: 55.*

★★ **Ko'olau Golf Club** This is a spectacularly beautiful golf course, carved out of the tropical rain forest nestled against the Ko'olau mountain range. It is also a spectacularly difficult course, narrow and winding with extreme changes in elevation. Legend has it that when Ko'olau Golf Club first opened, it was so difficult that it was given a slope rating of 162… where the maximum slope rating is 155. The official rating has dropped to a still formidable 152 from the back tees. The Windward side's wet conditions don't make it any easier (and now you know why this side is so green and lush). But when things get frustrating, just take a breath, look up at the mountains, and marvel at the beauty that surrounds you. Facilities include a pro shop, driving range, putting and chipping greens, and restaurant. *45-550 Kiona'ole Rd., Kāne'ohe. www.koolaugolfclub.com. ☎ 808/236-4653. Greens fees $145; twilight fees $110. No bus service.*

★★★ **Ko Olina Golf Club** *Golf Digest* once named this one of "America's Top 75 Resort Courses." The Ted Robinson–designed course (6,867-yard/6,279m, par 72) has rolling fairways and elevated tee and water features. The signature hole—the 12th, a par 3—has an elevated tee that sits on a rock garden with a cascading waterfall.

Olomana Golf Links

At the 18th hole, water's all around—seven pools begin on the right side of the fairway, sloping down to a lake. Book in advance; this course is crowded all the time. Facilities include a driving range, locker rooms, a Jacuzzi, steam rooms, and a restaurant and bar. Lessons are available. *92–1220 Aliinui Dr., Kapolei. ☎ 808/676-5309. www.koolinagolf.com. Greens fees (include cart) $225 ($195 for Ko Olina Resort guests), twilight rates $160. Men & women are asked to wear collared shirts. No bus service.*

★ Olomana Golf Links This par-72, 6,326-yard (5,784m) course is popular with locals and visitors alike. The course starts off a bit hilly on the front 9 but flattens out by the back 9, where there are some tricky water hazards. This course is very, very green; the rain gods bless it regularly with brief passing showers. You can spot the regular players here—they all carry umbrellas. Facilities include a driving range, practice greens, club rental, pro shop, and restaurant. *41–1801 Kalani'anaole Hwy., Waimānalo. ☎ 808/259-7926. www.olomana.golf. Greens fees $100. Bus: 57.*

★★ Royal Hawaiian Golf Club Here's another gorgeous course, often referred to as the Jurassic Park of golf courses, both for the breathtaking scenery and because it's not for the faint hearted. Designed by Perry and Pete Dye, it was recently redeveloped by hall-of-fame golfer Greg Norman. Switchback trails lead you up to wide vistas that help take the sting out of losing so many balls. Facilities include a pro shop, driving range, putting and chipping greens, and snack bar. *770 Auloa Rd., Kailua. www.royalhawaiiangc.com. ☎ 808/262-2139. Greens fees $160; twilight fees $115. Bus: 89.*

★ Pearl Country Club Looking for a challenge? Sure, the 6,230-yard (5,697m), par-72 course looks harmless enough, and the views of Pearl Harbor and the USS *Arizona* Memorial are gorgeous, but around the 5th hole, you'll start to see what you're in for: water hazards, forest, and doglegs that allow only a small margin of error between the tee and the steep out-of-bounds hillside. O'ahu residents can't get enough of it, so don't even try to get a tee time on weekends. Facilities include a driving range, practice greens, club rental, pro shop, and restaurant. *98–535 Kaonohi St., Aiea. ☎ 808/487-3802. www.pearlcc.com. Greens fees $80*

Mon–Fri, $100 Sat–Sun. Bus: 32 (stops at Pearlridge Shopping Center at Kaonohi & Moanalua sts.; you'll have to walk about a half mile/.8km from here).

★★★ Turtle Bay Resort This North Shore resort is home to two of Hawai'i's top golf courses: the 18-hole Arnold Palmer Course, designed by Arnold Palmer and Ed Seay, and the par-71, 6,200-yard (5,669m) George Fazio Course. Palmer's is the more challenging, with the front 9 playing like a British Isles course (rolling terrain, only a few trees, and lots of wind). The back 9 has narrower, tree-lined fairways and water. Fazio is a more forgiving course, without all the water hazards and bunkers. Facilities include a pro shop, driving range, putting and chipping green, and snack bar. Weekdays are best for tee times. *57–049 Kamehameha Hwy., Kahuku. ☎ 808/293-8574 or 808/293-9094. www.turtlebayresort.com. Greens fees Palmer Course $195, $120 after 1pm; Fazio Course $125 before noon, $85 after 1pm. Bus: 55.*

★ West Loch Municipal Golf Course This par-72, 6,615-yard (6,049m) course located just 30 minutes from Waikīkī, in Ewa Beach, offers golfers a challenge at bargain rates. The difficulties on this unusual municipal course, designed by Robin Nelson and Rodney Wright, are water (lots of hazards), constant trade winds, and narrow fairways. Facilities include a driving range, practice greens, a pro shop, and a restaurant. *91–1126 Okupe St., Ewa Beach. ☎ 808/675-6076. www1.honolulu.gov/des/golf/westloch.htm. Greens fees $55 for 18 holes, $28 for 9 holes. Golf cart rental $20 for 18 holes, $10 for 9 holes. Book a week in advance. Bus: 50.*

Hole 13 at Pearl Country Club, with views of Pearl Harbor

Turtle Bay Resort, home of two top golf courses

Adventures on Land

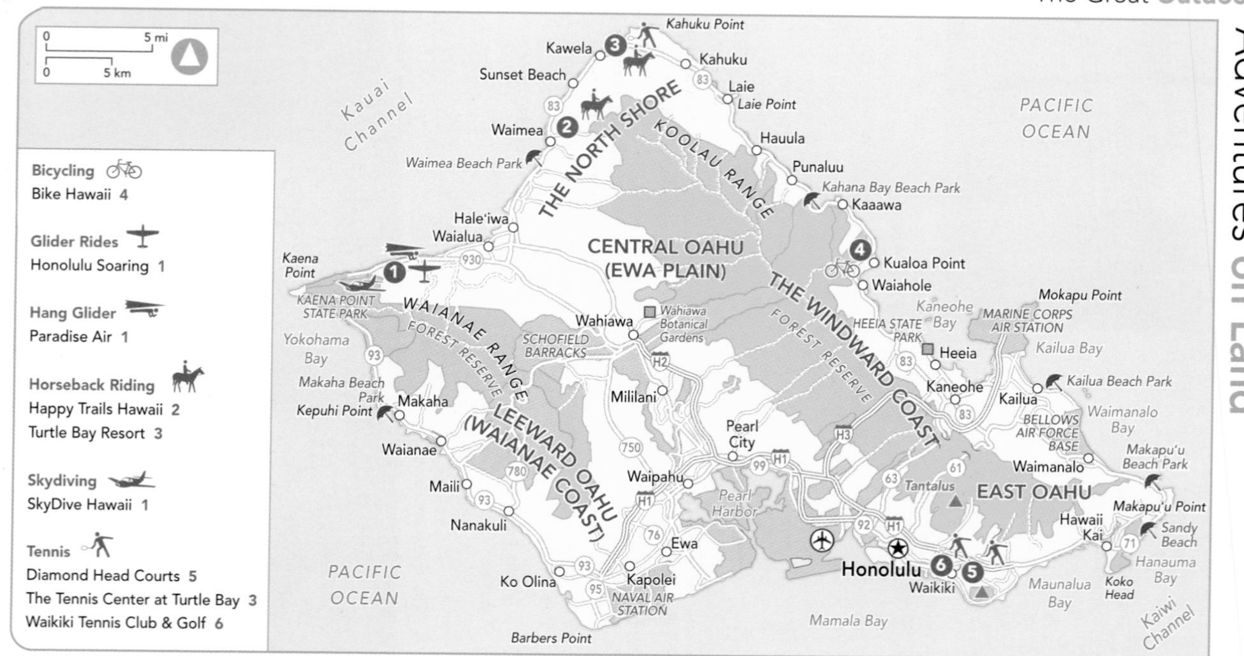

Honolulu isn't just sparkling ocean water and rainbow-colored fish; it's also the land of adventure—you can cycle back through history to an ancient, terraced taro field; soar through the air in a glider; gallop along a deserted sandy beach; or even leap from a plane and float to Earth under a parachute.

Bicycling

Get off the street and get dirty with an off-road, guided mountain bike tour from **Bike Hawaii,** through the 1,000-acre (405-ha) Ka'a'awa Valley on O'ahu's northeast shore. The tour is the same site as the annual 24 Hours of Hell in Paradise Mountain Bike Race; you'll follow dirt roads and single-track through verdant tropical landscape, dotted with mountain streams. Stops on the 6-mile (9.7km), 2-hour ride include an ancient Hawaiian house site in the midst of a terraced taro field, an old military bunker converted into a movie museum for films shot within this historical valley *(Jurassic Park, Godzilla, Mighty Joe Young, Windtalkers),* and views of sheer valley walls, panoramic ocean vistas, and lush Hawaiian vegetation. Or you can opt for the all-day bike-and-hike adventure, which starts with a 2-mile round trip hike to a private waterfall and ends with a 5-mile coast downhill a paved road through a rainforest. ☎ *877/682-7433 or 808/734-4214. www.bikehawaii.com. Adults $130, children 14 & under $77; fee includes mountain bike, van transportation, helmet, lunch, snacks, water bottle & guide.*

Glider Rides

Imagine soaring through silence on gossamer wings, a panoramic view of O'ahu below you. A glider ride is an unforgettable experience, and it's available from **Honolulu Soaring,** at Dillingham Air Field, in Mokulē'ia, on O'ahu's North Shore. The glider is towed behind a plane; at the proper altitude, the tow is dropped, and you (and the glider

Mountain biking in the Ka'a'awa Valley

Happy Trails Hawaii offers guided rides above Pūpūkea Beach and overlooking Waimea Valley.

pilot) are left to soar in the thermals. *Dillingham Air Field, Mokulē'ia. ☎ 808/677-3404. www.honolulusoaring.com. From $85 for 10 min.*

Hang Gliding

See things from a bird's-eye view as you and your instructor float high above O'ahu on a tandem hang glider with **Paradise Air.** *Dillingham Air Field, Mokulē'ia. ☎ 808/497-6033. www.paradiseairhawaii.com. Ground school plus 30 min. in the air $175.*

Horseback Riding

★ Happy Trails Hawaii NORTH SHORE This small operation welcomes families (kids as young as 6 are okay) on these guided trail rides on a hilltop above Pūpūkea Beach and overlooking Waimea Valley, on the North Shore. *59–231 Pūpūkea Rd. ☎ 808/638-RIDE (7433). www.happytrailshawaii.com. From $85 for 1½-hr. rides.*

★ Turtle Bay Resort NORTH SHORE You can trot along a deserted North Shore beach with spectacular ocean views and through a forest of ironwood trees or take a romantic evening ride at sunset with your sweetheart. *57–091 Kamehameha Hwy., Kahuku. ☎ 808/293-8811. www.turtlebayresort.com. Trail ride (45 min.) $85 ages 7 & up (children must be at least 4 ft. 4*

Bikeshare Hawai'i

O'ahu is not particularly bike-friendly—drivers still need to learn to share the road. But that may be changing by the time you read this, with the installation of new bike lanes and the launch of a city bikeshare program. This system will include 2,000 bikes scattered over 200 docking stations throughout metro Honolulu. Modeled after other systems in cities such as Paris and New York, it should make short trips, such as from your hotel to the beach, or Waikīkī to Chinatown, a breeze.

Rolling Through Waikīkī on a Segway

A fun way to tour Waikīkī is on a Segway Personal Transporter, one of those two-wheeled machines that look like an old push lawn mower (big wheels and a long handle). It takes only a few minutes to get the hang of this contraption (which works through a series of high-tech stabilization mechanisms that read the motion of your body to turn or go forward or backward), and it's a lot of fun (think back to the first time you rode your bicycle—the incredible freedom of zipping through space without walking). **Segway of Hawaii,** located at Waikīkī Beach Marriott Resort & Spa, 2552 Kalakaua Ave. (☎ **808/941-3151;** www.segwayofhawaii.com), offers instruction and several tours ranging from an introductory tour for $75 per person to a 2-hour tour of Diamond Head for $170 per person.

in./1.3m tall); sunset ride (75 min.) $115. Bus: 52 or 55.

Sky Diving

SkyDive Hawaii offers a once-in-a-lifetime experience: Leap from a plane and float to Earth in a tandem jump (you're strapped to an expert who wears a chute big enough for the both of you). *Dillingham Airfield, 68–760 Farrington Hwy., Mokulē'ia. ☎ 808/637-9700. www.skydivehawaii.com. From $175.*

Tennis

Free Tennis Courts O'ahu has 181 free public tennis courts. The courts are available on a first-come, first-served basis; playing time is limited to 45 minutes if others are waiting. The closest courts to Waikīkī are the **Diamond Head Courts.** *3908 Paki Ave. (across from Kapi'olani Park). ☎ 808/971-7150. For a list of all public tennis courts: www.honolulu.gov/rep/site/dpr/dpr_docs/tenniscourts.pdf*

★ **The Tennis Center at Turtle Bay Resort** Turtle Bay has eight Plexipave courts, two of which are lit for night play. Instruction, rental equipment, player matchup, and even a ball machine are available here. You must reserve the night courts in advance; they're very popular. *57–091 Kamehameha Hwy., Kahuku. ☎ 808/293-6024. www.turtlebayresort.com. Court time $25 (complimentary for guests); equipment rental $8; lessons from $20 for group lessons, $80 for private. Bus: 52 or 55.*

O'ahu's Best Snorkeling

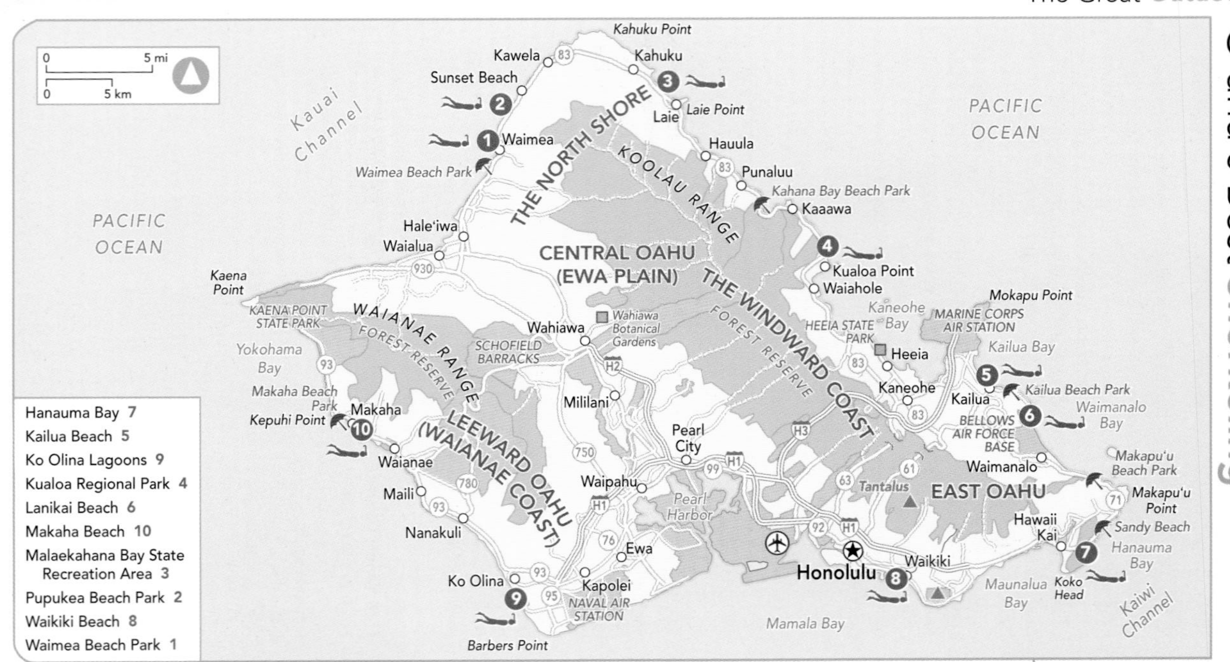

Snorkeling is a huge attraction on O'ahu—just relax as you float over underwater worlds populated with colorful clouds of tropical fish. If you've never snorkeled before, most resorts and excursion boats offer instruction, but it's plenty easy to figure it out for yourself. All you need are a mask, a snorkel, fins, and some basic swimming skills. In many places, all you have to do is wade into the water and look down. Below are O'ahu's best snorkeling beaches.

★★★ Hanauma Bay KOKO HEAD O'ahu's most popular snorkeling spot is a curved, 2,000-foot (610m) gold-sand beach packed elbow-to-elbow with people year-round. Part of an old crater that fell into the sea, the bay's shallow shoreline water and abundant marine life are the main attractions to snorkelers. A shallow reef outside the bay protects it from the surf, keeping the waters very calm. Hanauma Bay is a conservation district; you may look at but not touch or take any marine life here. Feeding the fish is also prohibited. *7455 Kalani'anaole Hwy. (at Hanauma Bay Rd.). Or take TheBus to escape the parking problem: The Hanauma Bay Shuttle runs from Waikīkī to Hanauma Bay every half-hour 8:45am–1pm.*

★★★ Kailua Beach WINDWARD Stretched out between two points, this 2-mile-long (3.2km) golden strand (with dunes, palm trees, panoramic views, and offshore islets) offers great snorkeling (along with a host of other ocean activities) with safe water conditions most of the year. *450 Kawailoa Rd., Kailua. Bus: 56 or 57, then transfer to 70.*

★ Ko Olina Lagoons LEEWARD When the developer of the 640-acre (259-ha) Ko Olina Resort blasted four white-sand lagoons out of the shoreline to make the rocky shoreline more attractive and accessible, he created a great snorkeling area around the boulders at the entrance to each lagoon. The man-made lagoons offer calm, shallow waters and a powdery white-sand beach bordered by a broad, grassy lawn. No lifeguards are present, but the generally tranquil waters are safe. *Off Aliinui Dr.*

Snorkeling in Hanauma Bay, which was formed in a volcanic crater

There are plenty of shallow beaches for novice snorkelers.

(btw. Olani & Mauloa places), Ko Olina Resort. No bus.

★★ Kualoa Regional Park WINDWARD This 150-acre (61-ha) coconut palm–fringed peninsula is the biggest beach park on the windward side and one of Hawaii's most scenic. The sandy waters offshore are safe and have snorkeling areas. Just 500 yards (457m) offshore is the tiny islet Mokoli'i Island (popularly known as Chinaman's Hat), which has a small sandy beach and is a bird preserve—so don't spook the red-footed boobies. *49–600 Kamehameha Hwy., Kualoa. Bus: 55.*

★★ Lanikai Beach WINDWARD One of Hawaii's best spots for snorkeling is off the gold-sand Lanikai's crystal-clear lagoon (there are so many fish it feels like a giant saltwater aquarium). The reef extends out for about a half mile (.8km), with snorkeling along the entire length. *Mokulua Dr., Kailua. Bus: 19, then transfer to 57.*

★ Makaha Beach LEEWARD During the summer, the waters here are clear and filled with a range of sea life (from green sea turtles to schools of tropical fish to an occasional manta ray). Plus the underwater landscape has arches and tunnels just 40 feet (12m) down, great habitats for reef fish. *84–369 Farrington Hwy., Makaha. Bus: 8, then transfer to Country Express C.*

★★★ Malaekahana Bay State Recreation Area NORTH SHORE This almost mile-long (1.6km) white-sand crescent lives up to just about everyone's image of the perfect Hawaiian beach. I head for the rocky areas around either of the two points (Makahoa Point and Kalanai Point) that define this bay. *Kamehameha Hwy. (2 miles/3.2km north of the Polynesian Cultural Center). Bus: 8, then transfer to 55.*

★ Pūpūkea Beach Park NORTH SHORE This North Shore beach is great for snorkeling (May–Oct) not only because of the lush marine life but also because it is a Marine Life Conservation District (sort of like an

Pūpūkea Beach Park

Snorkelers and sunbathers take to the waters of Hanauma Bay.

underwater park), which means that it's illegal to take anything from this park (fish, marine critters, even coral); thus the fish are not only plentiful but also very friendly. As you face the ocean, the northern end is known as Shark's Cove (don't let the name deter you); the southern end is called Three Tables (from the shore, you can see the three flat "tables" and fairly shallow water). Summer snorkeling is great in both areas. In the winter, when the big waves roll into the North Shore, this area can be very dangerous. *59–727 Kamehameha Hwy. (Pūpūkea Rd.), Pūpūkea. Bus: 8, then transfer to 55.*

★★★ **Waikīkī Beach** WAIKĪKĪ This famous 1½-mile-long (2.4km) crescent of imported sand (from Molokai) has great snorkeling spots along nearly the entire length of the beach, but my favorite is Queen's Beach or Queen's Surf Beach, between the Natatorium and the Waikīkī Aquarium. It's less crowded here, the waters are calm, and the fish are plentiful. I usually get in the water behind the Waikīkī Aquarium and snorkel up to the Natatorium and back. *Stretching from Ala Wai Yacht Harbor to Diamond Head Park. Bus: 19 or 20.*

★★ **Waimea Beach Park**
NORTH SHORE In summer, this deep, sandy bowl has gentle waves that allow access to great snorkeling around the rocks and reef. Snorkeling isn't an option in the winter, when huge waves pummel the shoreline. *51–031 Kamehameha Hwy., Waimea. Bus: 8, then transfer to 55.*

Where to Rent Beach Equipment

If you want to rent beach toys (snorkeling equipment, boogie boards, surfboards, kayaks, and more), check out the following rental shops: **Snorkel Bob's,** on the way to Hanauma Bay at 700 Kapahulu Ave. (at Date St.), Honolulu (☎ **808/735-7944;** www.snorkelbob.com); and **Aloha Beach Service,** in the Moana Surfrider, 2365 Kalakaua Ave., Waikīkī (☎ **808/922-3111,** ext. 2341; www.alohabeachservices.com). On O'ahu's windward side, try **Kailua Sailboards & Kayaks,** 130 Kailua Rd., a block from the Kailua Beach Park (☎ **808/262-2555;** www.kailuasailboards.com). On the North Shore, get equipment from **Surf-N-Sea,** 62–595 Kamehameha Hwy., Haleiwa (☎ **808/637-9887;** www.surfnsea.com).

Adventures in the Ocean

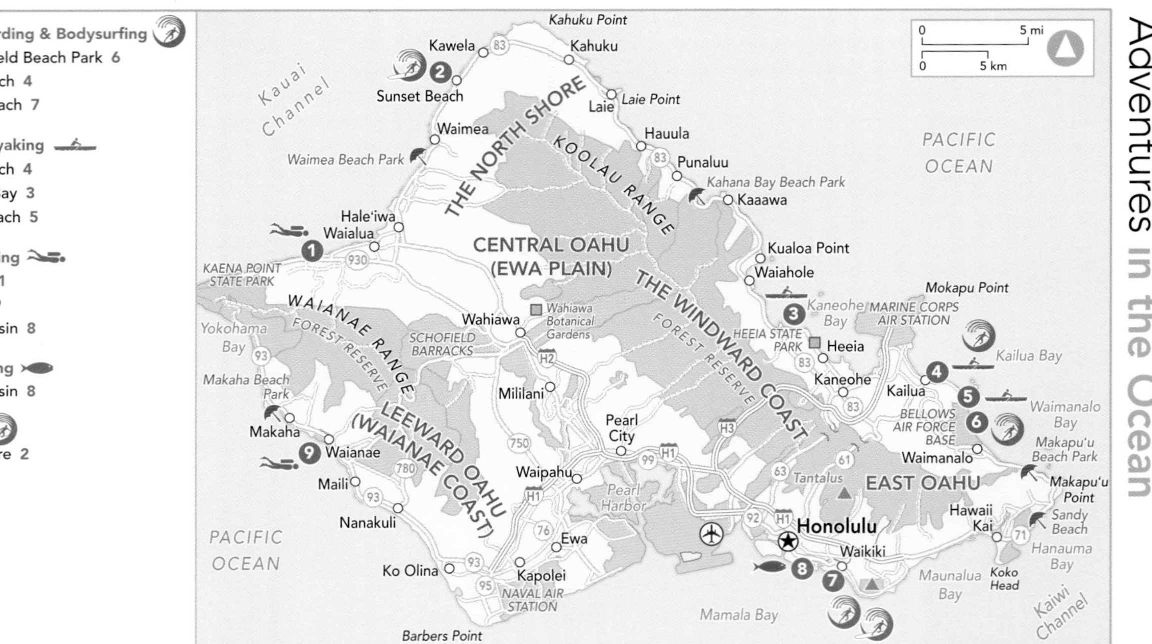
Body Boarding & Bodysurfing
Bellows Field Beach Park 6
Kailua Beach 4
Waikiki Beach 7
Ocean Kayaking
Kailua Beach 4
Kaneohe Bay 3
Lanikai Beach 5
Scuba Diving
Mokuleia 1
Waianae 9
Kewalo Basin 8
Sportfishing
Kewalo Basin 8
Surfing
North Shore 2
Waikiki 7
PACIFIC OCEAN
Kauai Channel
THE NORTH SHORE
KOOLAU RANGE
CENTRAL OAHU (EWA PLAIN)
THE WINDWARD COAST
FOREST RESERVE
WAIANAE RANGE
FOREST RESERVE
LEEWARD OAHU (WAIANAE COAST)
EAST OAHU
Honolulu
Waikiki
Kailua
Kaneohe
Pearl City
Pearl Harbor
Mamala Bay
Kaiwi Channel
PACIFIC OCEAN

To really appreciate O'ahu, you need to get off the land. Strap on some scuba gear and plunge beneath the ocean, skip across the water in a sailing charter, go sportfishing and battle a 1,000-pound (454kg) marlin, glide over the water in the kayak, or ride the waves bodysurfing, board surfing, or windsurfing. Whichever ocean adventure thrills you, you will find it here.

Bodyboarding (Boogie Boarding) & Bodysurfing

Riding the waves without a board, becoming one with the rolling water, is a way of life in Hawai'i. Some bodysurfers just rely on their hands to ride the waves; others use hand boards, a boogie board, or a bodyboard. Both bodysurfing and bodyboarding require a pair of open-heeled swim fins to help propel you through the water. Good places to learn to bodyboard are in the small waves of **Waikīkī Beach** and **Kailua Beach** (both reviewed in chapter 6), and Bellows Field Beach Park, off Kalaniana'ole Hwy. 72 (Hughs Rd.), in Waimānalo (Bus: 57), which is open to the public on weekends (noon Fri to midnight Sun and holidays).

Ocean Kayaking

Gliding silently over the water, propelled by a paddle, seeing O'ahu from the sea the way the early Hawaiians did—that's what ocean kayaking is all about. Early mornings are always best, because the wind comes up around 11am, making seas choppy and paddling difficult. For a wonderful adventure, rent a kayak (the rental places will help you strap it to your car), arrive at **Lanikai Beach** just as the sun is appearing, and paddle across the emerald lagoon to the pyramid-shaped islands called Mokulua—it's an experience you won't forget. A second favorite kayak launching area is **Kailua Beach.** Kayak equipment rental starts at $12 an hour for a single kayak and $25 an hour for a double kayak. See the box "Where to Rent Beach Equipment" on p 179.

★ Holokai Kayak and Snorkel Adventures Revel in amazing views both above and below the water on the Windward Coast by

A bodyboarder takes on some waves.

Sailing & Snorkeling Tours

One of the most fun and effortless ways to get in the water is a sail off Waikīkī. Many catamarans launch from Waikīkī, but the **Holokai Catamaran (☎ 808/922-2210;** www.sailholokai.com) is one of my favorite of the "booze cruises." It's the least crowded and rowdy, and the drink selection is the best, with multiple Maui Brewing Co. brews and a decent island cocktail. The **Sunset Sail** is the most popular and festive, with an open bar, while the **Tradewind Sail,** which pushes off in the afternoon, is mellower. The most romantic? The **Fireworks Sail,** which seemingly takes you right under the weekly Friday-night fireworks show.

Picture this: floating in the calm waters off the Waianae coast, where your 42-foot (13m) sailing catamaran has just dropped you off. You watch turtles swimming in the reef below, and in the distance, a pod of spinner dolphins appears. In the winter, you may spot humpback whales on the morning cruise, which also includes continental breakfast and other refreshments and snorkel gear, instruction, and a floatation device. Sound good? Call **Wild Side Tours (☎ 808/306-7273;** www.sailhawaii.com). Tours leave from the Waianae Boat Harbor. The morning sail/snorkel tour costs $195 (ages 7 and up; not recommended for younger children).

signing up for a 4-hour guided tour. You'll see the majestic Ko'olau Range from your kayak. Then, as you head to Coconut Island (aka Gilligan's Island), you'll stop to snorkel and admire the fish and turtles in the almost-always calm Kāne'ohe Bay. Or, you can go at your own pace with the self-guided kayak or stand-up paddleboard option—they'll point you in the direction of the disappearing sandbar Ahu o Laka, as well as the good snorkel spots. What's even better? Proceeds go to Kama'aina Kids (which runs environmental education programs for children) and improving He'eia State Park. *46-465 Kamehameha Hwy., Kāne'ohe, at He'eia State Park.* ☎ *808/781-4773. www.holokaiadventures.com. Tour $129 adults, $109 kids 5 –12, self-guided $99.*

The shallow waters at Pūpūkea Beach Park are ideal for first-time snorkelers.

Kayaking on the windward coast

★ **Kailua Sailboards & Kayaks** First-time kayakers can learn a lot on the "excursion" tour, designed for the novice. The fee covers lunch, all equipment, lessons, transportation from Waikīkī hotels, and 2 hours of kayaking in Kailua Bay. *130 Kailua Rd. ☎ 808/262-2555. www.kailuasailboards.com. Excursion tour $139 adults, $119 kids 3–12.*

Scuba Diving

O'ahu is a wonderful place to scuba dive, especially for those interested in wreck diving. One of the more famous wrecks in Hawaii is the ***Mahi,*** a 185-foot (56m) former minesweeper easily accessible just south of Waianae. Abundant marine life makes this a great place to shoot photos—schools of lemon butterfly fish and taape (blue-lined snapper) are so comfortable with divers and photographers that they practically pose. Eagle rays, green sea turtles, manta rays, and white-tipped sharks occasionally cruise by as well, and eels peer out from the wreck. For nonwreck diving, one of the best dive spots in summer is **Kahuna Canyon,** a massive amphitheater located near Mokulē'ia. Walls rising from the ocean floor create the illusion of an underwater Grand Canyon. Inside the amphitheater, crabs, octopuses, slippers, and spiny lobsters abound (be aware that taking them in summer is illegal), and giant trevally, parrotfish, and unicorn fish congregate as well. Outside the amphitheater, you're likely to see an occasional shark in the distance. Because O'ahu's greatest dives are offshore, your best bet is to book a two-tank dive from a dive boat. Hawaii's oldest and largest outfitter is **Aaron's Dive Shop,** 307 Hahani St., Kailua (☎ **808/262-2333;** www.hawaii-scuba.com). A two-tank boat dive costs $129, including transportation from the Kailua shop. **Living Ocean Scuba ★**, 1125 Ala Moana Blvd. (www. livingoceanscuba.com; ☎ **808/436-3438**), offers dives for both first-time and certified divers. Living Ocean takes divers to south shore sites such as the **Sea Tiger**, a former Chinese trading vessel that was confiscated for carrying illegal immigrants to Hawa'i, then sunk in 1999 to create a dive site. Divers can penetrate the wreck, which also teems with marine life: whitetip reef sharks, turtles, eagle rays, and plenty of fish. The two-tank boat dives start at $100 per person. While Living Ocean dives primarily from the south shore, they can also help set up dive trips on other sides of the island.

Sportfishing

Marlin (as big as 1,200 lb./544kg), tuna, ono, and mahimahi await the baited hook in Hawaii's coastal and channel waters. No license is required; just book a sportfishing vessel out of Kewalo Basin, on Ala Moana Boulevard (at Ward Ave.), the main location for charter fishing boats on O'ahu, located between the Honolulu International Airport and Waikīkī, or contact **Sportfish Hawaii.** This sportfishing booking agency helps match you with the best fishing boat; every vessel it books has been inspected and must meet rigorous criteria to guarantee that you will have a great time. ☎ *877/388-1376 or 808/396-2607. www.sportfishhawaii.com. $908–$1,200 for a full-day exclusive charter (you, plus 5 friends, get the entire boat to yourself), $650–$875 for a half-day exclusive, from $220 for a full-day share charter (you share the boat with 5 other people).*

Submarine Dives

Here's your chance to play Jules Verne and experience the underwater world from the comfort of a submarine. ***Atlantis* Submarine** will take you on an adventure below the surface in high-tech comfort, narrating your tour as you watch tropical fish and sunken ships just outside the sub; if swimming's not your thing, this is a great way to see Hawai'i's sea life. ***Warning:*** Skip this if you suffer from claustrophobia. *Shuttle boats to the sub leave from Hilton Hawaiian Village Pier.* ☎ *800/548-6262 or 808/973-9811. www.atlantisadventures.com/Waikiki. $115 for adults, $48 for kids 12 & under (children must be at least 36 in. tall). Tip: Book online for discount rates.*

Surfing

The ancient Hawaiian sport of *hee nalu* (wave sliding) is probably the sport most people picture when they think of the islands. In summer, when the water's warm and there's a soft breeze in the air, the south swell comes up. It's surf season in Waikīkī, the best place on O'ahu to learn how to surf. For lessons, find **Hans Hedemann Surf School** (www.hhsurf.com; ☎ **808/924-7778**) at the Park Shore Waikīkī (and, if you're on the North Shore, there's also an outpost at Turtle Bay Resort). Hans Hedemann, a champion surfer for some 34 years, gives private lessons—at $400 for a three-hour session. (He has taught celebrities such as Cameron Diaz and Adam Sandler.)

Atlantis Adventures submarine, for those who want to go underwater without getting wet

Sea Life Primer

You're likely to spot one or more of the following fish while underwater:

- **Angelfish** can be distinguished by the spine, located low on the gill plate. These fish are very shy; several species live in colonies close to coral.
- **Blennies** are small, elongated fish, ranging from 2 to 10 inches (5–25cm) long, with the majority in the 3- to 4-inch (7.6–10cm) range. Blennies are so small that they can live in tide pools; you might have a hard time spotting one.
- **Butterflyfish,** among the most colorful of the reef fish, are usually seen in pairs (scientists believe they mate for life) and appear to spend most of their day feeding. Most butterflyfish have a dark band through the eye and a spot near the tail resembling an eye, meant to confuse their predators (moray eels love to lunch on them).
- **Moray** and **conger eels** are the most common eels seen in Hawai'i. Morays are usually docile except when provoked or when there's food around. Although morays may look menacing, conger eels look downright happy, with big lips and pectoral fins (situated so that they look like big ears) that give them the appearance of a perpetually smiling face.
- **Parrotfish,** one of the largest and most colorful of the reef fish, can grow up to 40 inches (102cm) long. They're easy to spot—their front teeth are fused together, protruding like buck teeth that allow them to feed by scraping algae from rocks and coral. Native parrotfish species include yellowbar, regal, and spectacled.
- **Scorpion fish** are what scientists call "ambush predators." They hide under camouflaged exteriors and ambush their prey. Several kinds sport a venomous dorsal spine. These fish don't have a gas bladder, so when they stop swimming, they sink—that's why you usually find them "resting" on ledges and on the ocean bottom. They're not aggressive, but be very careful where you put your hands and feet in the water so as to avoid those venomous spines.
- **Surgeonfish,** sometimes called *tang,* get their name from the scalpel-like spines located on each side of the body near the base of the tail. Several surgeonfish, such as the brightly colored yellow tang, are boldly colored; others are adorned in more conservative shades of gray, brown, or black.
- **Wrasses** are a very diverse family of fish, ranging in length from 2 to 15 inches (5–38cm). Wrasses can change gender from female to male. Some have brilliant coloration that changes as they age.

Oahu is the perfect place to learn to hang ten.

If the expenditure is beyond your budget, go for a $75 2-hour group lesson (maximum four people) taught by other friendly instructors.

Surf's Up!

To find out where the waves are, call the **Surf News Network Surfline** (☎ 808/596-SURF [7873]) to get the latest surf conditions.

Experiencing *Jaws:* Up Close & Personal

Ocean Ramsey and her crew at **One Ocean Diving** ★★★ (www.oneoceandiving.com) are on a first-name basis with some of the sharks they swim with. That's right, *swim with,* cage free. And you can join them, with little more than a snorkel, mask, and fins on your feet (this is a snorkeling trip, not scuba diving). As you ride the boat out, about 3 miles offshore from Hale'iwa, where sharks are known to congregate, the crew educates you about shark behavior. For one, they're really not that interested in humans. Two, most of the sharks you'll see are sandbar and Galapagos sharks, which are not considered dangerous. And three, if you should see a potentially more threatening shark, such as a tiger shark, they teach you how to conjure your alpha shark: Stay at the top of the ocean, and don't turn your back on them. Your guides are always alert and nearby; only three people are allowed in the water at a time. Once I got used to the sight of the sharks around me, I began to admire their beauty and grace. One Ocean Diving hopes to change misconceptions about sharks and bring awareness to their plight as their numbers dwindle. A dive with them is as educational as it is exciting. Rates are $150 a person, and a snorkel mask and fins are provided; you must be 4 feet or taller to enter the water.

The Savvy Traveler

Before You Go

Government Tourist Offices

The **Hawai'i Visitors and Convention Bureau (HVCB)** has an office at 2270 Kalākaua Ave., Ste. 801, Honolulu, HI 96815 (☎ **800/GO-HAWAII** [464-2924] or 808/923-1811; www.gohawaii.com). The **O'ahu Visitors Bureau** is at 2270 Kalākaua Ave., Ste. 801, Honolulu, HI 96815 (☎ **877/525-OAHU** [6248] or 808/524-0722; www.gohawaii.com/oahu).

The Best Time to Go

Most visitors don't come to Honolulu when the weather's best in the islands; rather, they come when it's at its worst everywhere else. Thus, the **high season**—when prices are up and resorts are booked to capacity—generally runs from November to March or mid-April (depending on when Easter falls). The last 2 weeks of December in particular are the prime time for travel. If you're planning a holiday trip, make your reservations as early as possible, count on holiday crowds, and expect to pay top dollar for accommodations, car rentals, and airfare. Whale-watching season begins in January and continues through the rest of winter, sometimes lasting into May.

The **off seasons,** when the best bargain rates are available, are spring (mid-Apr to mid-June) and fall (Sept to October)—a paradox, because these are the best seasons in terms of reliably great weather. If you're looking to save money, or if you just want to avoid the crowds, this is the time to visit. Hotel rates tend to be significantly lower during these off seasons. Airfares also tend to be lower—again, sometimes substantially—and good packages and special deals are often available.

Note: If you plan to come to Honolulu between the last week in April and the first week in May, be sure to book your accommodations, air reservations, and car rental in advance. In Japan, the last week of April is called **Golden Week,** because three Japanese holidays take place one after the other. The islands are especially busy with Japanese tourists during this time.

Due to the large number of families traveling in **summer** (June–Aug), you won't get the fantastic bargains of spring and fall. A note for surfers: In summer (roughly June to the beginning of Sept), the surf comes from the south, Waikīkī. During this time, the other side of the island, the North Shore, is calm. During winter (roughly Nov–Feb), big waves roll into the North Shore, and Waikīkī's water is placid.

Festivals & Special Events

WINTER. At the Van's **Triple Crown of Surfing,** the world's top professional surfers compete in events for more than $1 million in prize money. Competition takes place on the North Shore whenever the surf's up, from mid-November through December. Visit www.vanstriplecrownofsurfing.com. The second Sunday in December is the **Honolulu Marathon,** one of the largest marathons in the world, with more than 30,000 competitors. Call ☎ **808/734-7200** (www.honolulumarathon.org). In late January or early February (depending on the lunar calendar), the red carpet is rolled out for **Chinese New Year** with a traditional lion dance, fireworks, food booths, and a host of activities. Call ☎ **808/533-3181 (www.chinatownhi.com).**

Previous page: The open-air Waikīkī Trolley is a fun way to see the island.

Depending on surf conditions, February or March brings the **Buffalo's Big Board Classic** at Makaha Beach. You'll see traditional Hawaiian surfing, long boarding, and canoe surfing. Call ☎ 808/951-7877 (no website).

SPRING. The **Annual Easter Sunrise Service** is celebrated with the century-old sunrise services at the National Cemetery of the Pacific, Punchbowl Crater, Honolulu. Call ☎ **808/532-3720.** May 1 means Lei Day in Hawaii (www.honolulu.gov/parks/programs/leiday). Mid-May brings the **World Fire-Knife Dance Championships and Samoan Festival,** Polynesian Cultural Center, Lā'ie, where junior and adult fire-knife dancers from around the world converge for one of the most amazing performances you'll ever see. Authentic Samoan food and cultural festivities round out the fun. Call ☎ **808/293-3333** (www.polynesianculturalcenter.com).

SUMMER. In June, the **King Kamehameha Celebration,** a state holiday, features a massive floral parade, *hoolaulea* (party), and much more. Call ☎ **808/586-0333** (ags.hawaii.gov/Kamehameha). The third weekend in June brings the **King Kamehameha Hula Competition** to the Neal Blaisdell Center; it's one of the top hula competitions in the world, with dancers from as far away as Japan. Call ☎ **808/586-0333**. In late July, head for the annual **Ukulele Festival,** Kapiolani Park Bandstand, Waikīkī, a free concert with a ukulele orchestra of some 600 students (ages 4–92). Hawai'i's top musicians all pitch in (www.ukulelefestivalhawaii.org/en). Late July is the annual **Queen Liliuokalani Keiki Hula Competition** at the Neal Blaisdell Center, Honolulu. More than 500 *keiki* (children) representing 22 *halau* (hula schools) from the islands compete in this dancefest. Call ☎ **808/521-6905;** (http://blaisdellcenter.com)**. Hawaiian Slack-Key Guitar Festival Gabby Style**, Queen Kapiolani Park Bandstand, Honolulu, features Hawaii's folk music performed by the best musicians in Hawai'i. Call ☎ 808/226-2697 (www.slackkeyfestival.com).

FALL. The statewide **Aloha Festivals,** with parades and other events

Useful Websites

- **www.gohawaii.com**: An excellent, all-around guide to activities, tours, lodging, and events by the members of the Hawaii Visitors and Convention Bureau.
- **www.gohawaii.com/oahu**: The Oahu chapter of the state visitors' bureau lists activities, dining, lodging, parks, shopping, and more.
- **www.hawaiian105.com**: Hawaiian music plays around the clock at this radio station.
- **www.staradvertiser.com**: Honolulu's daily newspaper includes a section on entertainment.
- **www.weather.com**: Up-to-the-minute worldwide weather reports are available here.

HONOLULU'S AVERAGE TEMPERATURES & RAINFALL

MONTH	HIGH (F/C)	LOW (F/C)	WATER TEMP (F/C)	RAIN (IN/CM)
Jan	80/27	66/19	75/24	3.5/9
Feb	81/27	65/18	75/24	2.5/6.5
Mar	82/28	67/19	76/24	2.5/6.5
Apr	83/28	68/20	77/25	1.5/4
May	85/29	70/21	79/26	1/2.5
June	87/31	72/22	81/27	0.5/1.5
July	88/31	74/23	81/27	0.5/1.5
Aug	89/32	75/24	81/27	0.5/1.5
Sept	89/32	74/23	81/27	1/2.5
Oct	87/31	73/23	81/27	2.5/6.5
Nov	84/29	71/22	79/26	3/7.5
Dec	82/28	68/20	76/24	4/10

celebrating Hawaiian culture and friendliness throughout the state, take place in September and October. Call ☎ **808/483-0730** (www.alohafestivals.com) for a schedule of events. The annual **Hawaii International Film Festival** takes place the first 2 weeks in November. This cinema festival with a cross-cultural spin features filmmakers from Asia, the Pacific Islands, and the United States. Call ☎ **808/792-1577** (www.hiff.org).

The Weather

Because Honolulu lies at the edge of the tropical zone, it technically has only two seasons, both of them warm. The dry season corresponds to summer, and the rainy season generally runs during the winter, from November to March. It rains every day somewhere in the islands at any time of the year, but the rainy season can cause "gray" weather and spoil your tanning opportunities. Honolulu and Waikīkī generally may have a brief rain shower, followed by bright sunshine and maybe a rainbow. The **year-round temperature** usually varies no more than about 10°, but it depends on where you are. Honolulu's **leeward** sides (the west and south, where Waikīkī and Honolulu are located) are usually hot and dry, whereas the **windward** sides (east and north) are generally cooler and moist. If you want arid, sunbaked, desertlike weather, go leeward. If you want lush, often wet, junglelike weather, go windward. If you want to know how to pack just before you go, check CNN's online 5-day forecast at www.cnn.com/weather. You can also get the local weather by calling ☎ **808/973-4380.**

Restaurant & Activity Reservations

I can't say it enough: Book well in advance if you're determined to eat at a particular spot or participate in a certain activity. For popular restaurants, if you didn't call in advance, try asking for early or late hours—often tables are available before 6:30pm and after 9pm. You could also call the day before or first thing in the morning, when you may be able to take advantage of a cancellation.

Cell (Mobile) Phones

In general, it's a good bet that your phone will work in Honolulu, although coverage may not be as good as in your hometown.

Getting There

By Plane

Fly directly to Honolulu. **United Airlines** (☎ 800/864-8331; www.ual.com) offers the most frequent service from the U.S. mainland. **Alaska Airlines** (☎ 800/252-7522; www.alaskaair.com) has flights from Seattle, Portland, Oakland, San Diego, and Anchorage. **American Airlines** (☎ 800/433-7300; www.aa.com) offers flights from Dallas, Chicago, and Los Angeles. **Delta Air Lines** (☎ 800/221-1212; www.delta.com) flies nonstop from the West Coast. **Hawaiian Airlines** (☎ 800/367-5320; www.hawaiianair.com) offers nonstop flights to Honolulu from several West Coast cities, Las Vegas, and New York City as well as Tokyo and Sydney.

Airlines serving Honolulu from places other than the U.S. mainland include **Air Canada** (☎ 800/776-3000; www.aircanada.ca); **Air New Zealand** (☎ 0800/737-000 in New Zealand, 800/262-1234 in the U.S.; www.airnewzealand.com); **Air Pacific Airways** (☎ 679-672-0888 or 800/227-4446 in the U.S.; www.airpacific.com); **Qantas** (☎ 13 13 13 in Australia, 800/227-4500 in the U.S.; www.qantas.com.au); **Japan Air Lines** (☎ 0570 025 121 worldwide, 800/525-3663 in the U.S.; www.jal.com); **Jetstar** (☎ 866/397-8170; www.jetstar.com) from Sydney; **All Nippon Airways** (**ANA;** ☎ 310 782 3011 worldwide, 800/235-9262 in the U.S.; www.ana.co.jp); **China Airlines** (☎ 886 2 2545 5700 in Taipei, 800/227-5118 in the U.S.; www.china-airlines.com); **Korean Air** (☎ 1588 2001 in Seoul, 800/438-5000 in the U.S.; www.koreanair.com); and **Philippine Airlines** (☎ 632 855 8888 in Manila, 800/435-9725 in the U.S.; www.philippineair.com).

Getting Around

Really, the only way to get around Honolulu and the entire island is to rent a car. There is bus service, but you must be able to put all your luggage under the seat (no surfboards or golf clubs), plus the bus service is set up for local residents, and many visitor attractions do not have direct routes from Waikīkī. The best way to get a good deal on a car rental is to book online. Surprisingly, Honolulu has one of the least expensive car-rental rates in the country—starting at $35 a day (including all state taxes and fees); the national average is about $56. Cars are usually plentiful, except on holiday weekends, which in Hawai'i also means King Kamehameha Day (June 10 or the closest weekend), Prince Kūhiō Day (Mar 26), and Admission Day (third weekend in Aug). All the major car-rental agencies have offices in Honolulu: **Alamo** (☎ 800/327-9633; www.goalamo.com), **Avis** (☎ 800/321-3712; www.avis.com), **Budget** (☎ 800/218-7992; www.budget.com), **Dollar** (☎ 800/800-4000; www.dollarcar.com), **Enterprise**

(☎ 800/325-8007; www.enterprise.com), **Hertz** (☎ 800/654-3011; www.hertz.com), **National** (☎ 800/227-7368; www.nationalcar.com), and **Thrifty** (☎ 800/367-2277; www.thrifty.com). It's almost always cheaper to rent a car at the airport than in Waikīkī or through your hotel (unless there's one already included in your package deal).

To rent a car in Hawai'i, you must be at least 25 years old and have a valid driver's license and a credit card. Hawai'i is a no-fault state, which means that if you don't have collision-damage insurance, you are required to pay for all damages before you leave the state, regardless of whether the accident was your fault. Your personal car insurance back home may provide rental-car coverage; read your policy or call your insurer before you leave home. Bring your insurance identification card if you decline the optional insurance, which usually costs from $20 to $42 a day, and obtain the name of your company's local claim representative before you go. Some credit card companies also provide collision-damage insurance for their customers; check with yours before you rent.

Fast Facts

ATMS Hawaii pioneered the use of **ATMs** nearly 3 decades ago, and now they're everywhere. You'll find them at most banks, in supermarkets, at Long's Drugs, and in most resorts and shopping centers. **Cirrus** (☎ **800/424-7787;** www.mastercard.com) and **PLUS** (www.visa.com) are the two most popular networks; check the back of your ATM card to see which network your bank belongs to (most banks belong to both these days).

BABYSITTING The first place to check is with your hotel. Many hotels have babysitting services or will provide you with lists of reliable sitters. If this doesn't pan out, call **People Attentive to Children** (PATCH; ☎ **808/839-1988;** www.patchhawaii.org), which will refer you to individuals who have taken its childcare training courses.

BANKING HOURS Bank hours are Monday through Thursday from 8:30am to 4pm, Friday from 8:30am to 6pm; some banks are open on Saturday.

BED & BREAKFAST, CONDOMINIUM & VACATION HOMES RENTALS You'll find plenty of listings on airbnb.com and vrbo.com. Make sure to check the reviews to know what you're getting into.

BUSINESS HOURS Most offices are open from 8am to 5pm. Most shopping centers are open Monday through Friday from 10am to 9pm, Saturday from 10am to 5:30pm, and Sunday from 10am to 5 or 6pm.

CLIMATE See "The Weather" on p 190.

CONSULATES & EMBASSIES Honolulu has the following consulates: **Australia,** 1000 Bishop St., Penthouse Ste., Honolulu, HI 96813 (☎ 808/524-5050); **Federated States of Micronesia,** 3049 Ualena St., Ste. 908, Honolulu, HI 96819 (☎ 808/836-4775); **Japan,** 1742 Nuuanu Ave., Honolulu, HI 96817 (☎ 808/543-3111); and **Republic of the Marshall Islands,**1888 Lusitana

St., Ste. 301, Honolulu, HI 96813 (☎ 808/545-7767).

CUSTOMS Depending on the city of your departure, some countries (such as Canada) clear customs at the city of departure, while other countries clear customs in Honolulu.

DENTISTS If you need dental attention on O'ahu, find a dentist near you through the website of the **Hawai'i Dental Association** (www.hawaiidentalassociation.net).

DINING With a few exceptions at the high end of the scale, dining attire is fairly casual. It's a good idea to make reservations in advance if you plan on eating between 7 and 9pm.

DOCTORS Straub Clinic & Hospital's **Doctors on Call** (www.straubhealth.org; ☎ **808/971-6000**) can dispatch a van if you need help getting to the main clinic or to its additional clinics at the Hilton Hawaiian Village and the Sheraton Waikīkī.

ELECTRICITY Like Canada, the United States uses 110–120 volts AC (60 cycles), compared to 220–240 volts AC (50 cycles) in most of Europe, Australia, and New Zealand. If your small appliances use 220 to 240 volts, you'll need a 110-volt transformer and a plug adapter with two flat parallel pins to operate them here. Downward converters that change 220–240 volts to 110–120 volts are difficult to find in the United States, so bring one with you.

EMBASSIES See "Consulates & Embassies," above.

EMERGENCIES Dial ☎ **911** for the police, an ambulance, or the fire department. For the **Poison Control Center,** call ☎ **800/222-1222.**

EVENT LISTINGS The best sources for listings are the Friday edition of the local daily newspaper, ***Honolulu Star-Advertiser*** (www.staradvertiser.com); and the weekly shopper, ***MidWeek*** (www.midweek.com). There are also several tourist publications, such as ***This Week on Oahu*** (www.thisweek.com).

INTERNET CENTERS Every major hotel and even many small B&Bs have Internet access. Many of them offer high-speed wireless; check ahead of time, because the charges can be exorbitant. The best Internet deal in Hawai'i is the service at the **public libraries** (to find the closest location near you, check www.publiclibraries.com/hawaii.htm or www.librarieshawaii.com), which offer free access if you have a library card. You can purchase a 3-month visitor card for $10.

LGBT TRAVELERS The **International Gay & Lesbian Travel Association** (IGLTA; ☎ 954/630-1637; www.iglta.org) is the trade association for the gay and lesbian travel industry and offers an online directory of gay- and lesbian-friendly travel businesses.

MAIL & POSTAGE To find the nearest post office, call ☎ **800/ASK-USPS** (275-8777) or log on to www.usps.gov. The closest post office to Waikīkī is located at 330 Saratoga Rd. **PASSPORTS** Always keep a photocopy of your passport with you when you're traveling. If your passport is lost or stolen, having a copy significantly facilitates the reissuing process at your consulate. Keep your passport and other valuables in your room's safe or in the hotel safe.

PHARMACIES Pharmacies I recommend are **Longs Drugs** (www.cvs.com for locations). There are two

24-hour pharmacies in Honolulu at 2470 S. King St. (☎ 808/947-2651), and 1330 Pali Hwy., near Vineyard Boulevard (☎ 808/536-7302).

SAFETY Although Hawai'i is generally a safe tourist destination, visitors have been crime victims, so stay alert. The most common crime against tourists is rental-car break-ins. Never leave any valuables in your car, not even in your trunk. Be especially careful in high-risk areas, such as beaches and resorts. Never carry large amounts of cash with you. Stay in well-lighted areas after dark. Don't hike on deserted trails or swim in the ocean alone. If you are a victim of crime, contact The **Visitor Aloha Society of Hawaii (VASH),** Waikīkī Shopping Plaza, 2250 Kalakaua Ave., Ste. 403–3 (☎ **808/926-8274;** www.visitoralohasocietyofhawaii.org).

SPECTATOR SPORTS Each January, you've got the Sony Open, the pro-golf tournament; **Hawaiian outrigger canoe races,** from May to September (☎ **808/383-7798;** www.y2kanu.com); and **surfing** (www.triplecrownofsurfing.com).

TAXIS Taxis are abundant at the airport; an attendant will be happy to flag one down for you. Fares are standard for all taxi firms; from the airport, expect to pay about $35 to $40 to Waikīkī and about $25 to downtown Honolulu (plus tip). Try **The Cab** (☎ **808/422-2222**) or **EcoCab** (☎ **808/979-1010**), an all-hybrid taxi fleet. **Uber,** the taxi-hailing app, has arrived in Honolulu. Use it on your phone to summon and pay for a taxi or livery (standard taxi meter rates, plus a $1 surcharge; gratuity automatically added).

TELEPHONE For directory assistance, dial ☎ **411;** for long-distance information, dial 1, then the appropriate area code and 555-1212. Pay phones cost 50¢ for local calls (all calls on the island of Oahu are local calls). The area code for all of Hawaii is 808. Calls to other islands are considered long distance, so you have to dial 1 + 808 + the seven-digit phone number.

TIPPING Tipping is ingrained in the American way of life. Here are some rules of thumb: In hotels, tip bellhops at least $1 per bag ($3–$5 if you have a lot of luggage) and tip the chamber staff $1 to $2 per person per day (more if you've left a disaster area for him or her to clean up, or if you're traveling with kids and/or pets). Tip the doorman or concierge only if he or she has provided you with some specific service (such as calling a cab). In restaurants, bars, and nightclubs, tip service staff 15 to 20 percent of the check and tip bartenders 10 to 15 percent. Tipping is not expected in cafeterias and fast-food restaurants. Tip cab drivers 15 percent of the fare and tip skycaps at airports at least $1 per bag ($3–$5 if you have a lot of luggage).

TOILETS Your best bet is Starbucks or a fast-food restaurant. You can also head to hotel lobbies and shopping centers. Parks have restrooms, but generally they are not very clean and are in need of major repairs.

TOURIST OFFICES See "Government Tourist Offices" on p 188.

TRAVELERS WITH DISABILITIES Travelers with disabilities are made to feel very welcome in Hawaii. Hotels are usually equipped with wheelchair-accessible rooms, and tour companies provide many special services. The only travel agency in Hawaii specializing in needs for travelers with disabilities is **Access**

Aloha Travel (☎ **800/480-1143;** www.accessalohatravel.com), which can book rental vans, accommodations, tours, cruises, airfare, and just about anything else you can think of.

Handi Wheelchair Transportation (☎ **808/946-6666**) is a private company offering wheelchair taxi services in air-conditioned vehicles that are specially equipped with ramps and wheelchair lockdowns. Handicabs offer a range of taxi services (airport pickup to Waikīkī hotels is $62 one-way for up to four). To rent wheelchair-accessible vans, contact **Access Aloha Travel** (☎ **800/480-1143;** www.accessalohatravel.com); for hand-controlled cars, contact **Avis** (☎ **800/331-1212;** www.avis.com) and **Hertz** (☎ **800/654-3131;** www.hertz.com). The number of hand-controlled cars in Hawaii is limited, so be sure to book well in advance. Vision-impaired travelers who use a Seeing Eye dog need to present documentation that the dog is a trained Seeing Eye dog and has had rabies shots. For more regulations and information, contact the State of Hawaii Animal Industry Division (☎ **808/483-7151;** www.hdoa.hawaii.gov).

Hawai'i: A Brief History

AROUND 250–700 Paddling outrigger canoes, the first ancestors of today's Hawaiians follow the stars and birds across the sea to Hawaii, which they call "the land of raging fire."

AROUND 1300 The transoceanic voyages stop for some reason, and Hawai'i begins to develop its own culture in earnest. The settlers build temples, fishponds, and aqueducts to irrigate taro plantations. Sailors become farmers and fishermen. Each island is a separate kingdom. The *alii* (royalty) create a caste system and establish taboos. Violators are strangled. High priests ask the gods Lono and Ku for divine guidance. Ritual human sacrifices are common.

1778 Captain James Cook, trying to find the mythical Northwest Passage to link the Pacific and Atlantic oceans, sails into Waimea Bay on Kaua'i, where he is welcomed as the god Lono. Overnight, Stone Age Hawai'i enters the age of iron. Nails are traded for fresh water, pigs, and the affections of Hawaiian women. The sailors bring syphilis, measles, and other diseases to which the Hawaiians have no natural immunity, thereby unwittingly wreaking havoc on the native population.

FEB. 14, 1779 Hawaiians kill Cook and four of his crew in Kealakekua Bay on the Big Island.

1782 Kamehameha I begins his campaign to unify the Hawaiian islands.

1804 King Kamehameha I conquers Oahu in a bloody battle fought the length of Nu'uanu Valley, and then moves his court from the island of Hawai'i to Waikīkī. Five years later, he relocates to what is now downtown

Honolulu, next to Nimitz Highway at Queen and Bethel streets.

1810 Kamehameha I unites the Hawaiian Islands under a single leader.

1819 This year brings events that change the Hawaiian Islands forever: Kamehameha I dies, his son Liholiho is proclaimed Kamehameha II, and, under the influence of Queen Kaahumanu, Kamehameha II orders the destruction of *heiau* (temples) and an end to the *kapu* (taboo) system, thus overthrowing the traditional Hawaiian religion. The first whaling ship, *Bellina,* drops anchor in Lahaina.

1823 The whalers meet their rivals for this hedonistic playground: the missionaries, who arrive from New England, bent on converting the pagans. Intent on instilling their brand of rock-ribbed Christianity in the islanders, the missionaries clothe the natives, ban them from dancing the hula, and nearly dismantle their ancient culture. They try to keep the whalers and sailors out of the bawdy houses, where a flood of whiskey quenches fleet-size thirsts and where the virtue of native women is never safe.

1845 King Kamehameha III moves the capital of Hawai'i from Lahaina to Honolulu, where more commerce can be accommodated due to the natural harbor there. Honolulu is still the capital and dominant city today.

1848 The Great Mahele is signed by King Kamehameha III, which allows commoners and foreigners to own land outright or in "fee simple," a concept that continues today.

1882 America's only royal residence, Iolani Palace, is built on O'ahu.

1885 The first contract laborers from Japan arrive to work on the sugar-cane plantations.

JAN. 17, 1893 A group of American sugar planters and missionary descendants, with the support of U.S. Marines, imprisons Queen Liliuokalani in her own palace in Honolulu and illegally overthrows the Hawaiian government.

1898 Hawai'i is annexed to the United States.

1900 Hawai'i becomes a U.S. territory. The Great Chinatown fire leaves 7,000 people homeless in Honolulu.

1922 Prince Jonah Kalanianaole Kuhio, the last powerful member of the royal Hawaiian family, dies.

1927 First nonstop air flight is made from the mainland to Honolulu.

DEC. 7, 1941 Japanese Zeros bomb American warships based at Pearl Harbor, plunging the United States into World War II.

MAR. 18, 1959 Hawai'i becomes the last star on the Stars and Stripes, the 50th state of the Union. This year also sees the arrival of the first jet airliners, which bring 250,000 tourists to the fledgling state.

1967 The state of Hawai'i hosts one million tourists this year.

1990s Hawai'i's state economy goes into a tailspin following a series of events: First, the Gulf War severely curtails air travel to the island; then Hurricane Iniki slams into Kaua'i, crippling its infrastructure; and, finally, sugarcane companies across the state begin shutting down, laying off thousands of workers.

2008–10 One of the biggest booms to Hawai'i's tourism comes from a son of Hawai'i, Barack Obama, when he becomes the 44th president of the United States.

2014 Since this year, record numbers of tourists arrive in Hawai'i, with an increasing number of visitors from China.

2017 The construction boom of high-end resorts, hotels, and condos is fueled by the increase of tourism and the in-progress rail project, which, as proposed, will link Kapolei to Ala Moana Center.

The Hawaiian Language

The official languages of Hawai'i are English and Hawaiian. From the 1830s to the 1950s, the language was in danger of extinction as the number of native speakers of Hawaiian declined. But since the late 20th century, the Hawaiian language has been experiencing a revival, fueled by an interest in preserving native Hawaiian culture.

These days, all visitors will hear the words *aloha* (hello/goodbye/love) and *mahalo* (thank you). If you've just arrived, you're a *malihini.* Someone who's been here a long time is a *kama'āina.* When you finish a job or your meal, you are *pau* (finished). On Friday it's *pau hana,* work finished. You eat *pūpū* (Hawaii's version of hors d'oeuvres) when you go *pau hana.*

The Hawaiian alphabet, created by the New England missionaries, has only 12 letters: the five regular vowels (a, e, i, o, and u) and seven consonants (h, k, l, m, n, p, and w). The vowels are pronounced in the Roman fashion, that is, *ah, ay, ee, oh,* and *oo* (as in "too")—not *ay, ee, eye, oh,* and *you,* as in English. For example, *huhu* is pronounced *who-who.* Most vowels are sounded separately, though some are pronounced together, as in Kalakaua: *Kah-lah-cow-ah.*

Useful Words & Phrases

Here are some basic Hawaiian words that you'll often hear in Hawai'i and see throughout this book. For a more complete list of Hawaiian words, point your Web browser to www.hisurf.com/hawaiian/dictionary.html.

ali'i	Hawaiian royalty
aloha	greeting or farewell
hālau	school
hale	house or building
heiau	Hawaiian temple or place of worship
kahuna	priest or expert
kama'āina	old-timer
kapa	tapa, bark cloth
kapu	taboo, forbidden
keiki	child
lanai	porch or veranda
lomilomi	massage
mahalo	thank you
makai	a direction, toward the sea
mana	spirit power
mauka	a direction, toward the mountains
mu'umu'u	loose-fitting gown or dress
ono	delicious
pali	cliff
paniolo	Hawaiian cowboy(s)
wiki	quick

Eating in **Honolulu**

In the mid-1980s, Hawai'i Regional Cuisine (HRC) ignited a culinary revolution. Waves of new Asian residents have planted the food traditions of their homelands in the fertile soil of Hawai'i, resulting in unforgettable taste treats true to their Thai, Vietnamese, Japanese, Chinese, and Indo-Pacific roots. Traditions are mixed and matched—when combined with the fresh harvests from sea and land for which Hawai'i is known, these ethnic and culinary traditions take on renewed vigor and a cross-cultural, yet uniquely Hawaiian, quality.

At the other end of the spectrum is the vast and endearing world of "local food." By that I mean plate lunches and poke, shave ice and saimin, bento lunches and *manapua*—cultural hybrids all. A **plate lunch,** usually ordered from a lunch wagon, consists of fried mahimahi (or teriyaki beef or shoyu chicken), "two scoops rice," macaroni salad, and a few leaves of green—typically julienned cabbage. Heavy gravy is often the condiment of choice, accompanied by a soft drink in a paper cup or straight out of the can. Another favorite is **saimin**—the local version of noodles in broth topped with scrambled eggs, green onions, and sometimes pork.

The **bento,** another popular quick meal available throughout Hawai'i, is a compact, boxed assortment of picnic fare usually consisting of neatly arranged sections of rice, pickled vegetables, and fried chicken, beef, or pork. From the plantations come ***manapua,*** a bready, doughy sphere filled with tasty fillings of sweetened pork or sweet beans. The daintier Chinese delicacy **dim sum** is made of translucent wrappers filled with fresh seafood, pork hash, and vegetables, served for breakfast and lunch. For dessert or a snack, the prevailing choice is **shave ice,** the island version of a snow cone.

Recommended **Reading**

Fiction

The first book people often think about is James A. Michener's *Hawaii* (Fawcett Crest, 1974). This epic novel manages to put the island's history into chronological order, but remember, it is still fiction, and very sanitized fiction at that. For a more contemporary look at life in Hawai'i today, one of the best novels is *Shark Dialogue,* by Kiana Davenport (Plume, 1995). The novel tells the story of Pono, the larger-than-life matriarch, and her four daughters of mixed races. Lois-Ann Yamanaka uses a very "local" voice and stark depictions of life in the islands in her fabulous novels *Wild Meat and the Bully Burgers* (Farrar, Straus, Giroux, 1996), *Blu's Hanging* (Avon, 1997), and *Heads by Harry* (Avon, 1999).

Nonfiction

Mark Twain's writing on Hawai'i in the 1860s offers a wonderful introduction to Hawai'i's history. One of his best books is *Mark Twain in Hawaii: Roughing It in the Sandwich Islands* (Mutual Publishing, 1990).

Another great depiction of the Hawaii of 1889 is *Travels in Hawaii* (University of Hawaii Press, 1973), by Robert Louis Stevenson. For contemporary voices on Hawaii's unique culture, one of the best books to get is *Voices of Wisdom: Hawaiian Elders Speak,* by M. J. Harden (Aka Press, 1999). Some 24 different *kahuna* (experts) in their fields were interviewed about their talents, skills, or artistic practices.

The recently rereleased *Native Planters in Old Hawaii: Their Life, Lore and Environment* (Bishop Museum Press, Honolulu, 2004) was originally published in 1972 but is still one of the most important ethnographic works on traditional Hawaiian culture, portraying the lives of the common folk and their relationship with the land before the arrival of Westerners.

History

There are many great books on Hawai'i's history, but one of the best places to start is with the formation of the Hawaiian islands, vividly described in David E. Eyre's *By Wind, By Wave: An Introduction to Hawaii's Natural History* (Bess Press, 2000). In addition to chronicling the natural history of Hawai'i, Eyre describes the complex interrelationships among the plants, animals, ocean, and people that are necessary.

For a history of "precontact" Hawai'i, David Malo's *Hawaiian Antiquities* (Bishop Museum Press, 1976) is the preeminent source. Malo was born around 1793 and wrote about Hawaii at that time as well as the beliefs and religion of his people. It's an excellent reference book, but not a fast read. For more readable books on old Hawaii, try *Stories of Old Hawaii* (Bess Press, 1997), by Roy Kakulu Alameide, on myths and legends; *Hawaiian Folk Tales* (Mutual Publishing, 1998), by Thomas G. Thrum; and *The Legends and Myths of Hawaii* (Charles E. Tuttle Company, 1992), by His Hawaiian Majesty King David Kalākaua.

The best story of the 1893 overthrow of the Hawaiian monarchy is told by Queen Lili'uokalani, in her book *Hawaii's Story by Hawaii's Queen Liliuokalani* (Mutual Publishing, 1990). When it was written, it was an international plea for justice for her people, but it is a poignant read even today. It's also a "must read" for people interested in current events and the recent rally in the 50th state for sovereignty. Two contemporary books on the question of Hawai'i's sovereignty are Tom Coffman's *Nation Within—The Story of America's Annexation of the Nation of Hawaii* (Epicenter, 1998), and *Hawaiian Sovereignty: Do the Facts Matter?* (Goodale, 2000), by Thurston Twigg-Smith, which explores the opposite view. Twigg-Smith, former publisher of the statewide newspaper the *Honolulu Advertiser,* is the grandson of Lorrin A. Thurston, one of the architects of the 1893 overthrow of the monarchy. His so-called politically incorrect views present a different look on this hotly debated topic.

For more recent history, Lawrence H. Fuchs's *Hawaii Pono* (Bess Press, 1991) is a carefully researched tome on the contributions of each of Hawai'i's main immigrant communities (Chinese, Japanese, and Filipino) between 1893 and 1959.

An insightful look at history and its effect on the Hawaiian culture is *Waikīkī, a History of Forgetting and Remembering,* by Andrea Feeser (University of Hawaii Press, 2006). A beautiful art book (designed by Gaye Chan), this is not your normal coffee-table book but a different look at the cultural and environmental history of Waikīkī. Using historical texts, photos, government documents, and interviews, this book lays out the story of how Waikīkī went from a self-sufficient agricultural area to a tourism mecca.

Another great cultural book is Davianna Pomaikai McGreggor's *Na Kua'aina, Living Hawaiian Culture* (University of Hawaii Press, 2007). McGregor, a professor of ethnic studies at UH, examines how people lived in rural lands and how they kept the Hawaiian traditions alive.

Index

See also Accommodations and Restaurant indexes, below.

E

F

G

H

I

J

K

L

M

Photo Credits

tomas del amo; p ii, top, aines; p ii, second, Eddy Galeotti / Shutterstock.com; p ii, third, Theodore Trimmer / Shutterstock.com; p ii, fourth, Expert Infantry; p ii, bottom, © Hawaii Tourism Authority (HTA) / Tor Johnson; p iii, top, © Hawaii Tourism Authority (HTA) / Tor Johnson; p iii, second, Theodore Trimmer / Shutterstock.com; p iii, third, jarvis gray / Shutterstock.com; p iii, fourth, © Ryan Siphers; p iii, bottom, Allen.G; p viii, aines; p 3, pinggr / Shutterstock.com; p 4, © Sanchai Kumar/ Shutterstock.com; p 5, © Ryan Siphers; p 6, Brock Roseberry; p 7, Eddy Galeotti / Shutterstock.com; p 9, top, © Mikeledray/ Shutterstock.com; p 9, bottom, © Lee Prince/ Shutterstock.com; p 10, photoskate; p 11, Theodore Trimmer / Shutterstock.com; p 13, © Vacclav/ Shutterstock.com; p 14, Michael Gordon / Shutterstock.com; p 15, Ritu Manoj Jethani; p 16, top Robert Cravens / Shutterstock.com; p 16, bottom, Michael Gordon / Shutterstock.com; p 17, top, Courtesy of the Polynesian Cultural Center; p 17, bottom, Andre Nantel; p 19, Kimberly Vardeman; p 20, Pung; p 21, Jeff Whyte / Shutterstock.com; p 22, top, Courtesy of the Bishop Museum; p 22, bottom, Jeff Whyte; p 23, ja-images / Shutterstock.com; p 24, © Ami Parikh/ Shutterstock.com; p 25, Theodore Trimmer / Shutterstock.com; p 28, Stephanie A Sellers / Shutterstock.com; p 29, top right, Mana Photo / Shutterstock.com; p 29, bottom, Ppictures; p 30, top, segawa7; p 30, bottom, © Ryan Siphers; p 31, Expert Infantry; p 33, © Ryan Siphers; p 34, top, © Ryan Siphers; p 34, bottom, Benny Marty / Shutterstock.com; p 35, randychiu; p 36, top right, © Ryan Siphers; p 36, bottom, Courtesy of the Polynesian Cultural Center; p 39, top, Smart Destinations; p 39, bottom, Jeff Whyte / Shutterstock.com; p 41, Courtesy of the Bishop Museum; p 42, © Andre Nantel/ Shutterstock.com; p 43, top left, vasen; p 43, bottom right, okimo; p 44, © Andre Nantel/ Shutterstock.com; p 45, Daniel Ramirez; p 47, DVIDSHUB; p 48, Luke H. Gordon; p 49, © Paul B. Moore/ Shutterstock.com; p 51, © Jeff Whyte/ Shutterstock.com; p 52, top, Benny Marty / Shutterstock.com; p 52, bottom, © Shuhei Fujita/ OVB; p 53, IK's World Trip; p 54, © Starwood Resorts; p 55, © Loren Jaiver; p 56, © Mana Photo/ Shutterstock.com; p 57, top, Wendy Cutler; p 57, bottom, © Walley Gobetz; p 59, © Endless Traveller/ Shutterstock.com; p 60, top left, © Drew Avery; p 60, bottom right, © Joel Abroad; p 61, Wendy Cutler; p 62, Bethany; p 65, © Hawaii Tourism Authority (HTA) / Tor Johnson; p 66, top right, © Hawaii Tourism Authority (HTA) / Tor Johnson; p 66, bottom left, © Hawaii Tourism Authority (HTA) / Tor Johnson; p 67, Courtesy of Halekulani Hotel; p 68, top left, © Hawaii Tourism Authority (HTA) / Tor Johnson; p 68, bottom right, © Hawaii Tourism Authority (HTA) / Tor Johnson; p 69, © Hawaii Tourism Authority (HTA) / Tor Johnson; p 70, © Hawaii Tourism Authority (HTA) / Tor Johnson; p 71, © Hawaii Tourism Authority (HTA) / Tor Johnson; p 73, top left, © Hawaii Tourism Authority (HTA) / Tor Johnson; p 73, bottom right, © Hawaii Tourism Authority (HTA) / Tor Johnson; p 74, © Hawaii Tourism Authority (HTA) / Tor Johnson; p 75, © Hawaii Tourism Authority (HTA) / Tor Johnson; p 77, ©Marco Garcia; 9 78, ©Marco Garcia; p 79, top left, ©Marco Garcia; p 79, bottom right, ©Marco Garcia; p 80, Krystal Tubbs; p 81, © Hawaii Tourism Authority (HTA) / Tor Johnson; p 83, top, Nagel Photography/ Shutterstock.com; p 83, bottom, © Walley Gobetz; p 84, top left, Nagel Photography/ Shutterstock.com; p 84, bottom right, © Hawaii Tourism Authority (HTA) / Tor Johnson; p 85, top, © Jeff Whyte/ Shutterstock.com; p 85, bottom, © Hawaii Tourism Authority (HTA) / Joe Solem; p 87, © Hawaii Tourism Authority (HTA) / Tor Johnson; p 88, top, © Jennifer/neatlysliced; p 88, bottom, © Hawaii Tourism Authority (HTA) / Tor Johnson; p 89, © Hawaii Tourism Authority (HTA)/ Dana

Edmunds; p 94, Courtesy of Royal Hawaiian; p 95, © Hawaii Tourism Authority (HTA) / Tor Johnson; p 96, Courtesy of Duke's; p 97, top, toooooool; p 97, bottom, Wendy Cutler; p 98, top, Arnold Gatilao; p 98, bottom, Bevis Chin; p 99, top, Jenny Salita; p 99, bottom, Courtesy Halekulani; p 100, top right, Kyle Nishioka; p 100, bottom left, Prayitno; p 101, Janine; p 104, Courtesy of Halekulani; p 105, Bernard Spragg. NZ; p 107, Courtesy of Starwood; p 108, Courtesy of The Modern Honolulu; p 109, top, Courtesy of Hyatt; p 109, bottom, Courtesy of Prince Hotel Waikiki; p 110, top, Courtesy of Starwood; p 110, bottom, Courtesy of Royal Hawaiian; p 111, Courtesy of Starwood; p 116, IK's World Trip; p 117, Courtesy of Pegge Hopper Gallery; p 118, top left, www.bluewaikiki.com; p 118, bottom right, © Ryan Siphers; p 119, top left, Kyle Nishioka; p 119, bottom right, Janine; p 120, Courtesy of People's Open Market; p 121, top left, _e.t; p 121, bottom right, © Hawaii Tourism Authority (HTA) / Tor Johnson; p 122, top right, Kanu Hawaii; p 122, bottom left, Aaron Warren; p 124, top left, © Ryan Siphers; p 124, bottom right, © Ryan Siphers; p 125, top, © Ryan Siphers; p 125, bottom, Courtesy of Hans Schlupp/ DFS Galleria; p 126, © Ryan Siphers; p 129, Kyle Nishioka; p 130, Courtesy of Starwood; p 131, Courtesy Halekulani; p 132, Courtesy of Starwood; p 133, Eric Broder Van Dyke / Shutterstock.com; p 134, © Ryan Siphers; p 135, © Hawaii Tourism Authority (HTA) / Tor Johnson; p 137, Nagel Photography / Shutterstock.com; p 138, © Hawaii Tourism Authority (HTA) / Tor Johnson; p 139, © Hawaii Tourism Authority (HTA) / Tor Johnson; p 140, © Hawaii Tourism Authority (HTA) / Tor Johnson; p 141, © Ryan Siphers; p 143, © Hawaii Tourism Authority (HTA) / Heather Titus; p 144, © Hawaii Tourism Authority (HTA) / Tor Johnson; p 145, © Hawaii Tourism Authority (HTA) / Tor Johnson; p 145, bottom, © guynamedjames / Shutterstock.com; p 146, Shane Myers Photography; p 147, E.J.Johnson Photography; p 148, © Hawaii Tourism Authority (HTA) / Daeja Faris; p 149, Courtesy of Lanikai Beach Rentals; p 150, top right, © Ryan Siphers; p 150, bottom left, © Ryan Siphers; p 151, Theodore Trimmer / Shutterstock.com; p 154, HIROSHI H; p 155, © Andrew Zarivny/ Shutterstock.com; p 156, © Hawaii Tourism Authority (HTA) / Tor Johnson; p 157, © Ryan Siphers; p 158, Allen.G; p 159, top, Leigh Anne Meeks; p 159, bottom, © Hawaii Tourism Authority (HTA) / Tor Johnson; p 160, © Ryan Siphers; p 161, © Hawaii Tourism Authority (HTA) / Tor Johnson; p 162, top, Benny Marty / Shutterstock.com; p 162, bottom, Jay Bo; p 163, jarvis gray / Shutterstock.com; p 165, © Stephen B. Goodwin/ Shutterstock.com; p 166, Leonard S Jacobs; p 167, Leonard S Jacobs; p 170, Courtesy of Visit Oahu; p 171, top right, Courtest of Pearl Country Club; p 171, bottom, Courtesy of Turtle Bay; p 173, Courtesy of Bike Hawaii; p 174, Courtesy of Happy Trails; p 177, © TanArt/ Shutterstock.com; p 178, top, © Hawaii Tourism Authority (HTA) / Tor Johnson; p 178, bottom, © Hawaii Tourism Authority (HTA) / Tor Johnson; p 179, © Jeff Whyte/ Shutterstock.com; p 181, © Jarvis Gray/ Shutterstock.com; p 182, © Ryan Siphers; p 183, © tomas del amo/ Shutterstock.com; p 184, Courtesy of Atlantis Adventures; p 186, © Mana Photo/ Shutterstock.com; p 187, © Ryan Siphers.